Mikhail Tal: The Street-Fighting Years

Alexander Koblenz

Mikhail Tal: The Street-Fighting Years
Author: Alexander Koblenz
Editor: Valeri Bronznik

Translated from the Russian by Alexei Zakharov
Typesetting by Andrei Elkov (www.elkov.ru)

Published in Russian and Latvian in the Soviet Union in 1963 by Latvian State Publishing House Riga
Analysis of games has been computer-updated by International Master Valeri Bronznik for this 2021 edition

Follow us on Twitter: @ilan_ruby
www.elkandruby.com
ISBN 978-5-6041770-5-1

Contents

Index of Games

Game	White	Black	Opening	Year
39	M. Tal	S. Furman	Fragment	1958
40	B. Spassky	M. Tal	Fragment	1958
41	I. Zilber	M. Tal	Fragment	1958
42	L. Szabo	M. Tal	Fragment	1958
43	A. Matanovic	M. Tal	Fragment	1958
44	M. Tal	M. Filip	Fragment	1958
45	M. Tal	G. Fuster	Fragment	1958
46	H. Rossetto	M. Tal	King's Indian Defense	1958
47	M. Tal	O. Panno	Ruy Lopez	1958
48	M. Tal	H. Golombek	Caro-Kann Defense	1958
49	A. Beni	M. Tal	Fragment	1958
50	A. Nikitin	M. Tal	Sicilian Defense	1959
51	E. Geller	M. Tal	Modern Benoni	1959
52	M. Tal	D. Keller	Queen's Gambit Declined	1959
53	P. Keres	M. Tal	Fragment	1959
54	M. Tal	V. Smyslov	Caro-Kann Defense	1959
55	V. Smyslov	M. Tal	Fragment	1959
56	P. Keres	M. Tal	Fragment	1959
57	M. Tal	B. Fischer	Fragment	1959
58	M. Tal	S. Gligoric	Fragment	1959
59	S. Gligoric	M. Tal	Fragment	1959
60	F. Olafsson	M. Tal	Fragment	1959
61	B. Spassky	M. Tal	Ruy Lopez	1959
62	I. Niemela	M. Tal	Modern Benoni	1959
63	M. Tal	S. Johannessen	Fragment	1959
64	M. Tal	M. Botvinnik	French Defense	1960 (1)
65	M. Botvinnik	M. Tal	Fragment	1960 (6)
66	M. Botvinnik	M. Tal	Fragment	1960 (8)
67	M. Tal	M. Botvinnik	Grunfeld Defense	1960 (11)
68	M. Tal	M. Botvinnik	Fragment	1960 (17)
69	M. Tal	L. Szabo	Fragment	1960
70	M. Tal	M. Najdorf	Sicilian Defense	1960
71	M. Botvinnik	M. Tal	Fragment	1961 (1)
72	M. Tal	M. Botvinnik	Fragment	1961 (2)
73	M. Botvinnik	M. Tal	Fragment	1961 (7)
74	M. Tal	M. Botvinnik	Caro-Kann Defense	1961 (8)
75	M. Botvinnik	M. Tal	King's Indian Defense	1961 (13)
76	M. Botvinnik	M. Tal	Fragment	1961 (15)
77	M. Tal	M. Botvinnik	Fragment	1961 (20)

Foreword to the English Edition

When I started playing chess in March 1979 in Riga, everything about the game was associated with Mikhail Tal in my city. Especially a few months later, after Tal's victories in Montreal and the Riga Interzonal.

However, when you start you're not necessarily connected to the top yet. You play in your family, go to chess school and learn simple things about the game.

Being passionate about reading I tried not to miss any book or chess magazine from my father's library. For some reason, Tal and Damsky's book *Attack with Mikhail Tal* was not there but... the small book on Tal by Alexander Koblenz that you now hold in your hands turned out to be the perfect substitute!

A special memory from the book is those lines that might easily go unnoticed:

After playing a tournament game, he would stay in the Riga chess club until late evening, giving improvised simultaneous displays and playing innumerable casual games.

Leaving the club late, Misha was full of excitement. With his cap askew and his coat fluttering in the wind, he would walk about the Riga streets with his friends, who were chess lovers as passionate as him.

"Of course, you should have played knight f3 to e5; if he captured that knight, a sacrifice on f7 would decide things..." The words, intelligible only to other chess players, rang in the air. The occasional passers-by would stop, look at those oddballs, and shake their heads in confusion...

I vividly recall my own post-mortems. Did I stay in the chess school until everyone had finished? Of course I did! Would I also walk back with friends? Yes! But something was different. More than 30 years after Tal's teenage years Riga had grown into a pretty big city and the young players mainly lived in different districts. So we only managed a short exchange of words with an ice-cream and... tram number 6 or bus number 16 and so on. Until the next day. No deep analysis, everyone was just relying on their knowledge.

The most important part of Koblenz's book for me was my impatient desire to repeat Tal's path to the top, which reading the book sounded simple: even the game annotations looked easy. OK, today we see with the computer that those sometimes brief comments are not always accurate, but I believe that's of minor importance.

It was another 2-3 years before I got to know Koblenz, and a little later (still being extremely shy) Mikhail Tal himself. However, my path had been marked out much earlier and it was thanks to this book on Tal's street fights.

Thinking about the past, I realize that the biggest treasure that chess players possessed (and I was one of the last players to get the grandmaster title without computer preparation) was chess emotions. When searching for the truth, you knew that it might not be the ultimate truth, so emotions were the direct bridge from your knowledge to intuition.

The union of Alexander Koblenz and Mikhail Tal was a very emotional one, and reading the book you barely notice how hard their work together on chess was. You read short notes on Tal's almost irrational chess and only between the lines realize how accurately Koblenz and Tal analyzed positions of adjourned games (for example, against Spassky or Botvinnik), and how serious their opening preparation was. Koblenz didn't provide any concrete insights on how to become a grandmaster, he only wrote a sincere story which highly inspired me.

I am very happy that this old but highly instructive book is finally out in English. The old Russian edition has always been a special treasure for me and I truly enjoyed reading it through again (yes, the original version without editor's notes, though I have seen those as well) before writing these few lines.

Alexei Shirov, Riga,
17 February 2021

Introduction

The name of the ex-world champion Mikhail Tal is famous in the chess world. His games, rapid ascension and world championship win, and then the return match loss, have been widely discussed. The interest in the Riga grandmaster is understandable – no chess player before him has managed to climb to the very top of chess Olympus so soon.

Tal's successes were explained in various ways. Some talked about his special playing style and exceptional luck that accompanied him in tournaments. Others pointed out his "Mozart-like" lightness and even "demonic strength", which supposedly allowed him to achieve great success without much effort. I must immediately disappoint those who opened this book in search for sensations: no "Tal enigma" has ever existed. The talented player's way to the top was difficult and full of trials and tribulations. This book will tell you about the stages along this way, the wins and losses, the fulfilled hopes and disappointments.

Twelve Years Ago

Assembly hall of Riga Middle School number 22. A thin boy with a shy smile approaches the demonstration board. He quickly moves a piece. Black's reply, another move – the solution is correct!

I remember that it wasn't the quickness of the solution that most impressed me, but a drastic change I saw in the boy as soon as he approached the board. He transformed completely. The smile on his face immediately disappeared, he became incredibly serious.

Later, I learned that Misha was a goalkeeper in his class football team, school checkers champion and one of the most active members of the Young Pioneers' Palace chess circle. He was also an avid piano player, his favorite composers being Tchaikovsky and Chopin.

The young Tal studied well, but his mathematics teacher was unhappy: Misha preferred to solve everything in his mind, without writing anything in the exercise book. However, he would make exceptions for the boys from senior classes who'd approach him during the break.

"Misha, quick, help me solve this!"

And, even though it was much more interesting to play football in the courtyard, he would pick up a pencil and quickly write down columns of numbers.

Tal's memory has been exceptional since childhood. During the 24th Soviet chess championship, master Aivars Gipslis and I jokingly asked Misha, "Do you remember which line Keres played in the Queen's Gambit against Boleslavsky in the third round of the 20th Soviet championship?"

"Stop pulling my leg," the grandmaster answered. "Boleslavsky played Keres in round 19, not round 3. It was Boleslavsky who had white, and he played the Ruy Lopez."

The passionate, selfless enthusiasm for chess struggle has never left Tal ever since he learned chess. After playing a tournament game, he would stay in the Riga chess club until late evening, giving improvised simultaneous displays and playing innumerable casual games.

Leaving the club late, Misha was full of excitement. With his cap askew and his coat fluttering in the wind, he would walk about the Riga streets with his friends, who were chess lovers as passionate as him.

"Of course, you should have played knight f3 to e5; if he captured that knight, a sacrifice on f7 would decide things..." The words, intelligible only to other chess players, rang in the air. The occasional passers-by would stop, look at those oddballs, and shake their heads in confusion...

And his mother would call the club yet again: "Do you know if Misha has finished his game? He hasn't eaten his lunch yet..."

In one such evening, Misha managed to win a truly brilliant game. Here's the finale of the game played at the 1949 youth tournament in Riga.

No. 1
M. Tal – A. Leonov
1949, Riga, Junior Tournament, round 7

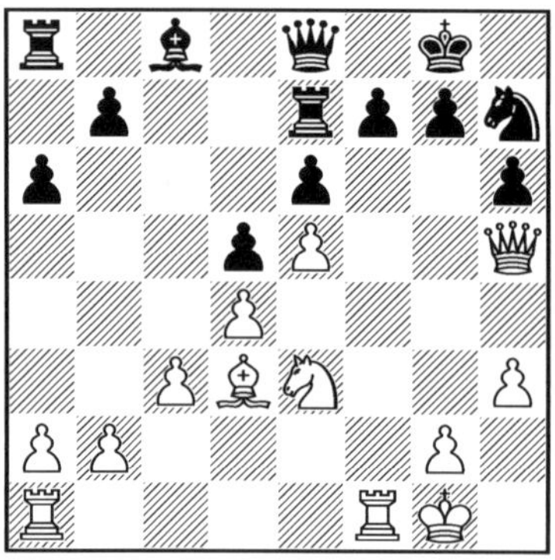

19.♖f6!

A great blockading move. White parries the threat f7-f5 and, in his turn, threatens 20.♖xh6.

19...♕f8

19...♘xf6 didn't help, because after 20.exf6 gxf6 21.♕xh6 f5, white wins with 22.♘g4!. After 19...gxf6, there's 20.exf6 ♘xf6 21.♕xh6 ♕f8 22.♕xf6 ♖d7 23.♘g4 ♕g7 24.♕h4, with an unstoppable attack.

Editor's note: According to the computer, in the line shown by Koblenz black's play can be radically improved with 21...♘e4!! (instead of 21...♕f8, which is actually a mistake) 22.♗xe4 f5, and after 23.♗xf5 exf5 24.♘xd5♖e6 25.♕g5+♖g6 26.♘e7+ ♔g7 27.♘xg6 ♕xg6 28.♕e7+ ♕f7 black can hold. However, instead of 20.exf6, white should play 20.♗xh7+, which is winning – 20...♔xh7 21.♘g4 ♕f8 22.♖f1 f5 23.♘f6+ ♔h8 24.♖f3 (threatening ♖f3-g3-g8+) 24...♕g7 25.♖g3!+–.

20.♖f4! ♗d7 21.♘g4 ♗e8 22.♘f6+! ♘xf6 23.exf6 ♖c7 24.fxg7 ♔xg7 25.♕e5+ Black resigned.

The passion for chess didn't stop Tal from graduating from high school ahead of time (he absorbed the whole elementary school program in just one year), and then from Latvian State University, where he majored in literature.

Tal already realized in his youth that to be successful in chess, it's necessary to work very hard. This means studying theory, analyzing games of masters and grandmasters, playing through your own games, and learning from your mistakes.

But he had no time for that. School during the days, tournaments in the evenings, so he could only study theory at night.

"Come to our home," Misha's father would invite me, "perhaps you can reason with him? He read chess books until morning again."

Once, during a walk, I seized the moment and tried to prove the importance of a correct daily regimen to Misha. He listened intently, keeping a polite silence.

"I'm sure you'll become a master," I said in the end, "but to achieve real success in chess, you need health."

We said our goodbyes, and I sighed with relief: I had seemingly managed to convince him.

However, Misha's father called me again the next morning...

The worries of his father, an old, respected doctor, were understandable. We had to influence the young enthusiast in some way. However, the circle of the talented teenager's interests was very wide, and the desire to understand the mysteries of chess art became a real passion. Later, I came to the conclusion that this full mental burden gave Tal what he wanted the most – a feeling of deep internal satisfaction.

Even now, Tal loathes any kind of "quiet" rest. In all the years I've known him, I've never seen him at rest. Tal is busy at any time of day: he writes an article, or discusses the new issue of *Sahs*, or analyzes some game, or prepares for a lecture...

Before the 25th Soviet chess championship, Tal went to Kemeri to rest a bit. However, he only managed to stay at the resort for three days and then "fled" back to Riga.

This mental overexertion, this inability to spare himself, was always Tal's Achilles heel. Perhaps this was one of the main reasons for his collapse which left both specialists and casual fans of the young grandmaster mystified.

Years of Trials

After Tal defeated Botvinnik and became world champion, many were sure that his brilliant chess abilities must have manifested themselves when he was a small child. However, Misha's first steps in chess were no different from anyone else's. He would constantly lose to his cousin, a regular chess opponent of his, and get very frustrated afterwards.

Misha achieved fourth category at the age of 11, and second category two years later. Soon, Mikhail was called up to the Latvian youth team. He played on last board, and the result – one win, two draws, and one loss – showed that he didn't deserve a higher place in the team.

In 1950, the young player earned first category. The next year, he took part in his first adult tournaments – the championships of Latvia and Riga – and only shared 11th and 14th places.

Tal was especially "unlucky" in the openings. He would often get a difficult, hard-to-defend position right from the outset.

However, even back then the young chess player showed his ability to quickly and precisely calculate lines, attack ingeniously and search for hidden tactical resources in a difficult position.

The finale of the game played in the 1951 Latvian championship was very characteristic.

No. 2
A. Strautmanis – M. Tal
1951, Riga, Latvian Championship

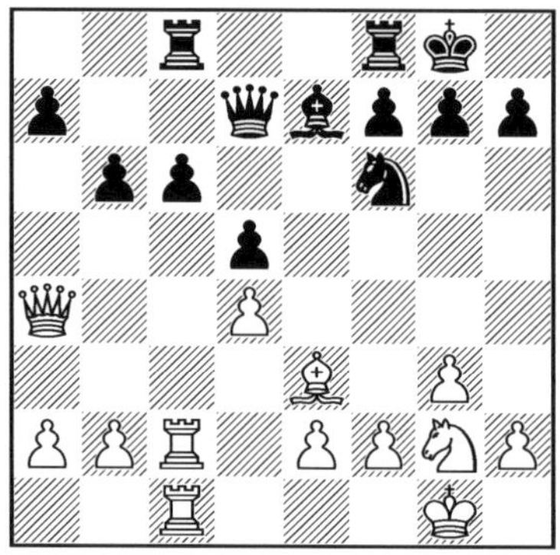

White has put a lot of pressure on the c6 pawn. It looks like black will have a hard time avoiding defeat, however, he finds a way to save the game.

17...♘e4! 18.f3 (18.♖xc6 is of course bad due to 18...♘c5!) **18...♘d6 19.♖xc6 ♘c4**

Looks like a blunder...

20.♖6xc4 b5! 21.♖xc8 bxa4 22.♖8c7 ♕e8 23.♖xa7 ♗d8

It was better to put the bishop on d6.

Editor's note: Koblenz's recommended move 23...♗d6 is better because it prevents white from invading the eighth rank with his rooks.

24.♖a8

Editor's note: 24.♖c8 was worth considering, to split the duties of the two rooks: one of them would seize the eighth rank, while the other attacked the a4 pawn.

24...♕b5 25.♖cc8 ♗e7 26.♖xf8+ ♗xf8 27.♔f2, and the game ended in a **draw**.

In the autumn of the same year, Misha played in an All-Union youth tournament and scored just 3.5 points out of 9. He performed better in the 1952 Latvian SSR Championship: he took 7th place, and became the republic's champion the following year.

"You shouldn't make so many sacrifices," the team captain advised Tal before he headed to Kharkov for a youth tournament. Tal knew that his penchant for daring attacks and risky combinations would cause concern.

"At first, I tried not to take risks," Tal recalled, "and played quietly. But then I just couldn't help it. I got an inviting opportunity in a game against an Uzbekistan player..."

International master Rashid Nezhmetdinov told me what happened in that game.

"During that tournament, I acted as the Russian SFSR team coach. Then master V. Tarasov ran up to me and said, 'Look what the little Tal is doing! He sacrificed a queen. Incredible!' We rushed up to the table."

No. 3
I. Birbrager – M. Tal
1953, Kharkov, 20th Soviet Team Championship, round 5

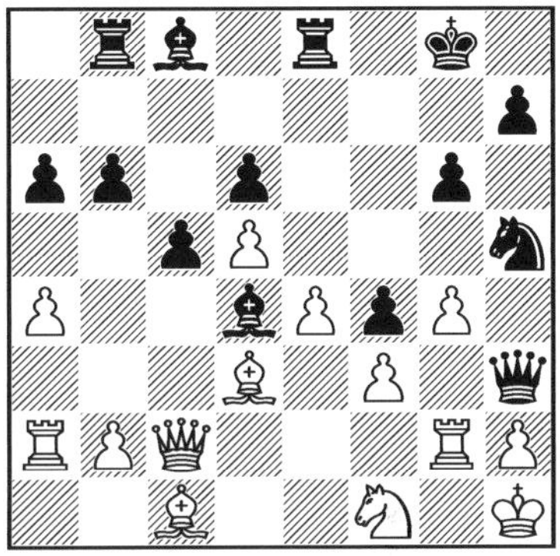

25...♕xf3

Editor's note: Analysis shows that after 25...♗xg4!! 26.♖xg4 ♕xf3+ 27.♖g2 ♕h3, threatening f4-f3, black gets a decisive attack.

26.♘d2 ♗xg4!

Editor's note: According to MegaDatabase, this capture followed only after the players repeated the position once (26... ♕e3 27.♘f1 ♕f3 28.♘d2, and only then 28...♗xg4), but we'll go along with Koblenz's version. Concerning his exclamation mark for black's last move, we can say that it was awarded for the pure playing value of Tal's move, because it poses his opponent serious practical problems. However, from the objective point of view, the queen sacrifice is incorrect.

Black only gets a knight for the queen. However, the white king feels uncomfortable.

27.♘xf3 ♗xf3 28.h4 (defending against the threat 28...♖e5, 29...♘g3+ and 30...♖h5#) **28...♖f8 29.♗e2** (white could resist more tenaciously with 29.b3).

Editor's note: The wording suggests that Koblenz thought that even after the strongest move 29.b3 white's position would still be difficult. However, computer analysis shows that, with this move, white could get his a2 rook involved in defense and, with precise play, even convert his material advantage to a win. Nevertheless, the game move was the decisive mistake.

29...♘g3+ 30.♔h2 ♗xg2 31.♔xg2 ♘xe2 32.♕xe2 f3+ 33.♕xf3 ♖xf3 34.♔xf3 ♖f8+ 35.♔g3 ♗e5+ 36.♔g2 ♗f4 White resigned.

The young player's sharp combinational vision and his ability to find the most unexpected attacking resources started to garner respect. Even back then, Tal hated passive defense. And when he had to defend, he would use any opportunity to counterattack immediately.

If a young player has good defensive skills, this shows a true chess talent. Tal's play confirms this rule of thumb.

No. 4
K. Klasups – M. Tal
1952, Riga, Latvian Championship

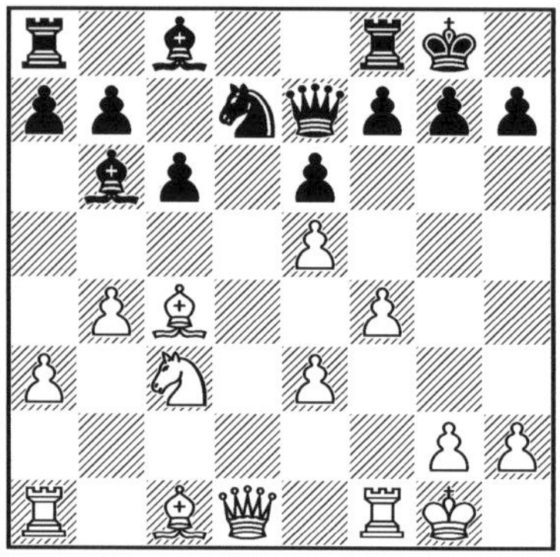

The young Tal's tenacity and persistence in defense can be illustrated with numerous examples. Here's a game from the 1952 Latvian Championship. Trying to prevent the freeing move f7-f6, white played **14.♕b3**

There followed

14...f6!

Nevertheless! Black is trying to disrupt the blockade with any means possible. The idea of this counter-attack will become clearer several moves later.

15.♗xe6+ ♔h8 16.♘e4

Editor's note: 16.♘a4, with the idea to drive the b6 bishop away or trade it, could give white an advantage. The game move, however, leads to a position where white has to struggle for equality.

16...fxe5 17.♔h1

Editor's note: The correct move was 17.f5, for instance, 17...♘f6 18.♘xf6 ♗xe6 19.♕xe6 ♕xe6 20.fxe6 ♖xf6 21.♖xf6 gxf6 22.a4 ♖e8 23.a5 ♗c7 24.e4 ♖xe6 25.♗e3 a6 26.♗c5 ♗d6 27.♖d1 ♗xc5+ 28.bxc5 ♖e7 29.♔f2, and, despite black's extra pawn, the ending is drawn.

17...exf4 18.exf4 ♘f6 19.♘g5 ♘e4!

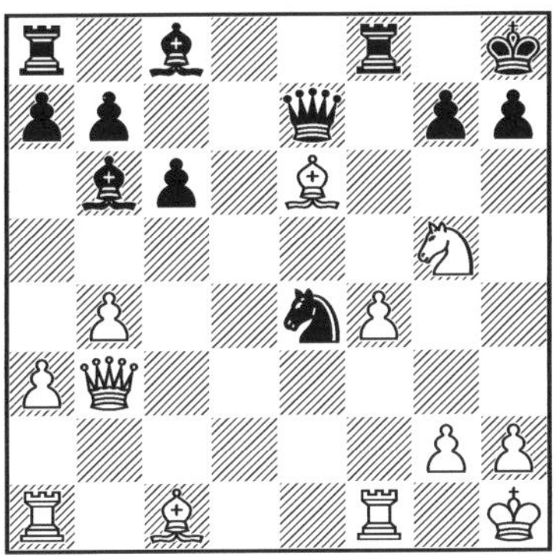

20.♘f7+

White accepts the challenge. After 20.♘xe4 ♗xe6, the black bishops will seriously harass his opponent.

Editor's note: However, the capture on e4 was a much lesser evil than the game move, which simply loses.

20...♖xf7 21.♗xf7 ♘f2+ 22.♔g1 ♘d3+ 23.♔h1 ♕e2 24.♗b2 ♗h3!

How quickly the position has changed! Black's counter-attack crushes his opponent.

25.♗xg7+

Desperation. After 25.gxh3, there was 25...♕e4+, winning.

25...♔xg7 26.♗d5 cxd5 27.♕xd5 ♔h8 28.♕g5

28.gxh3 still didn't work due to 28...♖g8.

28...♗d4 29.gxh3 ♖g8 30.♖ae1 ♘xe1 White resigned.

And here's what happened in the 1953 Latvian SSR championship semi-final:

No. 5
J. Mileika – M. Tal
1953, Riga, Latvian Championship

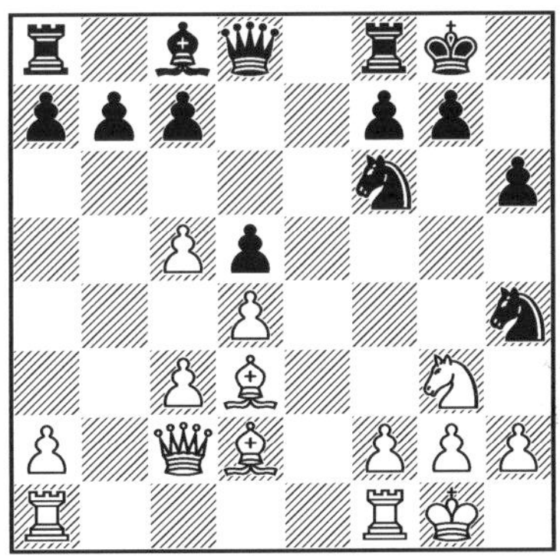

14...♕d7!

This move begins a well thought-out defensive plan. Black takes control over the f5 square. The natural 15.♖fe1 is met by 15...♘xg2 with a dangerous attack.

Editor's note: It seems that Koblenz was too optimistic here. Analysis shows that after 15.♖fe1 ♘xg2? 16.♔xg2, black can't create a real attack – for instance, 16...

♕h3+ 17.♔g1 ♘g4 18.♘f1 ♕f3 19.♗e3, and white repels all the threats and keeps the material. Perhaps Tal wouldn't actually have sacrificed the knight and would have chosen some other move instead, accepting that his position is worse and needs protection. In any case, the immediate 14...b6 (Tal only played that on the next move) looks better – it attacks the c5 pawn that cramps black's position and also intends a7-a5 and ♗c8-a6, trading the opponent's active bishop.

15.f3 b6! 16.cxb6

Editor's note: With this move, white loses all the advantage. The correct continuation was 16.♕c1! bxc5 (*16...♘g6 17.♗xh6!*, and if *17...gxh6 18.♕xh6 ♕c6,* then white has a pleasant choice between two winning moves: *19.♖ae1* with the idea ♖e1-e5-g5, and *19.♗xg6 fxg6 20.♕xg6+ ♔h8 21.♘h5*) 17.♗xh6! with a big advantage (black can't capture the bishop: 17...gxh6? 18.♕xh6 ♘g6 19.♘f5! ♘e8 20.♖fe1!+−).

16...axb6 17.♖fe1

Editor's note: Now the idea ♕c2-c1 and ♗d2xh6 doesn't work: 17.♕c1 ♘g6! 18.♗xh6 gxh6 19.♕xh6 ♕d6!, and black holds (20.♖ae1?? ♕f4!−+; 20.♗xg6 fxg6 21.♕xg6+ ♔h8, and white has nothing decisive, because the f6 knight isn't pinned).

17...c5 18.♖e5 c4 19.♗f5 ♕a4 20.♕c1 ♘xf5 21.♘xf5 ♗xf5 22.♖xf5 ♕d7!

Tal provokes his opponent to sacrifice an exchange. A bold decision, because this weakens the black king's position.

Even back then, despite his youth, Tal was completely sure: to win, you should be ready to take risks.

23.♖xf6 gxf6 24.♗xh6 ♖fe8 25.♕f4 ♔h7 26.♕h4

26.♕xf6 was met with 26...♖g8 27.♕h4 ♖g6! with counterplay. We should note that white could still draw with 26.♗f8! ♖xf8 27.♕h4+ ♔g6 28.♕g3+ etc.

26...♔g6!

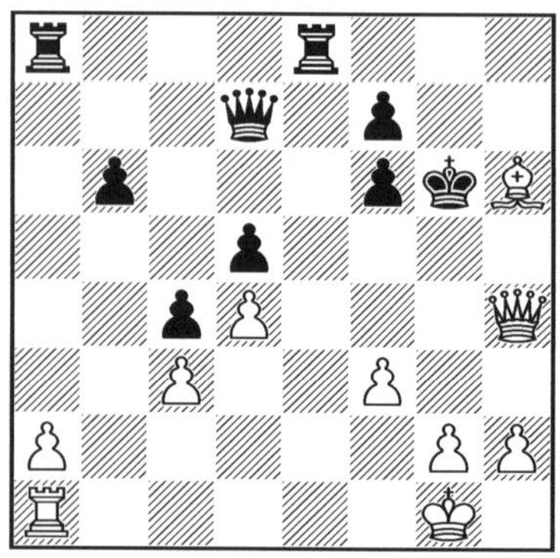

We shouldn't forget that the king can play an active role in defense as well!

27.g4

Editor's note: A mistake. White could still force a draw with the same idea of 27.♗f8 (there are also other equivalent resources) 27...♖xf8 28.♕g3+.

27...♖h8 28.♕h5+ ♔h7 29.♔h1 ♔g8 30.♖g1 ♕e6

Editor's note: This decision could have cost Tal half a point. The correct move was 30...♖e8!, and after 31.g5 f5 32.g6 f6 33.♕h4 ♖e6, black's position is won.

31.g5 f5

A natural reaction. The attacking side is trying to open lines. Black, however, is trying to keep the position closed as much as possible.

32.g6 f6 33.g7

Editor's note: The immediate transfer of the queen to the h2-b8 diagonal could save white – 33.♕h4! ♖xa2 34.♕f4! (threatening 35.♕b8+; *34.g7? ♖h7* is a mistake that transposes into the actual game) 34...♖e2 (after *34...♖a8? 35.h4*, only black is at risk) 35.g7 ♖h7 36.♕b8+ ♕e8 37.♕d6! ♖xh6 38.♕xd5+ ♕e6 *(38...♖e6? 39.♖e1)* 39.♕a8+ ♕e8 40.♕d5+ with perpetual check.

33...♖h7 (white's attack fizzles out) **34.♕h4 ♖xa2 35.♕g3 ♖e2 36.♖a1 ♕e8 37.♕h4 ♖e6,** and **white resigned** after a few more moves.

The game below is a great example of the young Tal's dynamic style.

No. 6, Sicilian Defense
M. Tal – M. Pasman
1953, Riga, Latvian Championship

1.e4 c5 2.♘f3 d6 3.d4 cxd4 4.♘xd4 ♘f6 5.♘c3 a6 6.f4

This active move was fashionable back then, but is now quite rare.

6...e5 7.♘f3 ♘bd7 8.♗d3 ♗e7 9.0-0 0-0 10.♔h1 b5 11.a3 ♕c7 12.fxe5 dxe5 13.♘h4

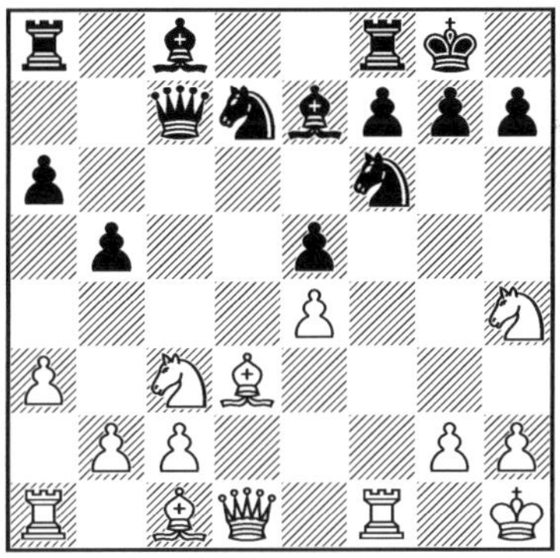

13...♘c5

Editor's note: In a modern grandmaster game J. Geller – B. Savchenko, Moscow 2011, black preferred 13...♘b6!?, covering the d5 square and intending to put the knight on c4 at some point.

14.♗g5

Until now, the game had followed theory. Tal played his first moves quickly – the opening studies paid off. White has an open f-file, his pieces are concentrated on the kingside, and the strategic plan is clear: attack the king's position.

14...♕d8 15.♘f5 ♗xf5 16.♖xf5 ♘fd7 17.♗xe7 ♕xe7 18.♘d5 ♕d6 19.♕g4

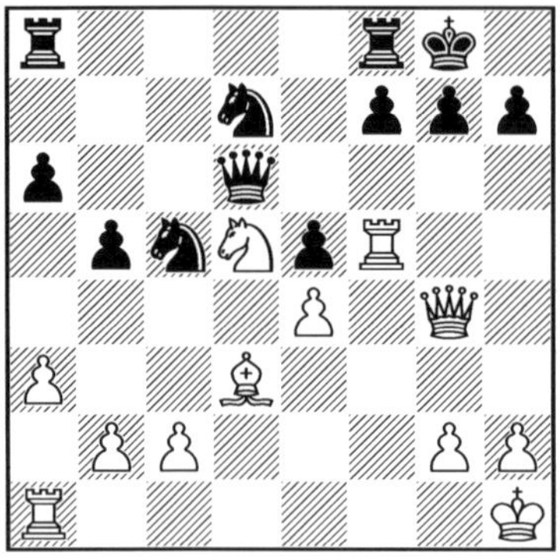

Starting a multi-move combination with a sacrifice of two pieces. This game brilliantly shows the young player's exceptional ability to create incredible combination complications. The difficulty of the combination lies in the fact that the following play isn't forced: white methodically attacks while being two pieces down. One of Tal's greatest strengths first manifested itself in this game. Even if his opponent gets counterplay, he rarely loses the initiative, finding more and more targets for attack. He attacks incessantly, creating one threat after the other.

19...g6

Editor's note: Black could defer this committal move for a while, choosing, for instance, 19...♖ac8 instead, activating the rook.

20.♖af1 f6 21.h4

Editor's note: As we shall see, had black played correctly, such a sharp continuation could have come back to hit white like a boomerang. 21.♖5f3 was a good move, with the idea of ♕g4-h4.

21...♔h8 22.♖5f3

Editor's note: The computer insists on 22.♖5f2 f5 23.♕e2, going into passive defense, but Tal obviously didn't play 21.h4 for that.

22...f5

White, of course, saw this counter-strike.

23.exf5! ♕xd5

After 23...gxf5, white had 24.♗xf5 ♕xd5 25.♗xh7!

Editor's note: The computer continues this line with a hard-to-find move 25...♕c4, and since 26.♕h5 loses to 26...♕xf1+ 27.♖xf1 ♖xf1+ 28.♔h2 ♘f6, white has to trade queens and go into an endgame materially down.

24.fxg6 ♖xf3 25.g7+ ♔g8 26.♗xh7+

The d3 bishop has been "revived" after great effort from white. However, to destroy the opposing king's position, this bishop needs to be sacrificed.

26...♔xh7 27.♖xf3 ♘e4!

Editor's note: 27...♕e6! is even stronger, preventing white from pushing the h-pawn.

28.h5 ♘df6 29.♕g6+ ♔g8 30.h6

White's combination ends here. To save the game, black needs to play just one correct move

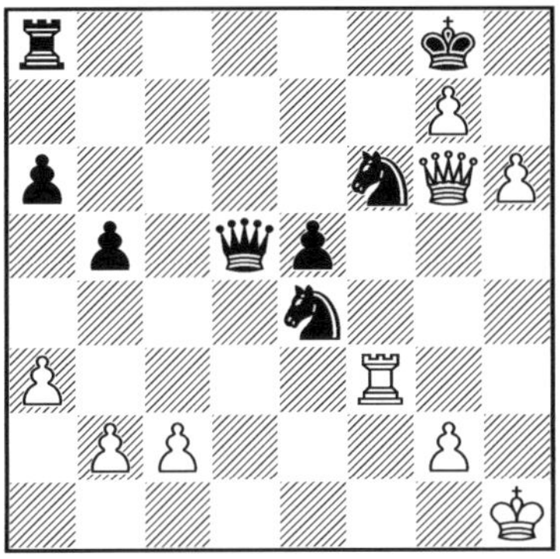

30...♖a7

The decisive mistake; it was hard for black to foresee all the consequences. He could have drawn with 30...♘h7! 31.♖f8+ ♘xf8 32.gf=♕+ ♔xf8 33.♕g7+ ♔e8 34.h7 ♕d1+ 35.♔h2 ♕h5+ etc.

Editor's note: Actually, black's position is won after 30...♖a7, and he had other good resources as well, such as 30...♖d8–+ or 30...♖c8–+.

31.♔h2!

This quiet move begins a hidden maneuver.

31...♖e7

Editor's note: Only this move is the losing mistake. After 31...♕d2! black repelled the attack and won, because 32.♖h3 is refuted by 32...♕f4+ 33.g3 *(33.♔g1 ♘g5–+)* 33...♕f2+ 34.♔h1 ♘g5! 35.♕xg5 ♖d7 36.♕c1 ♖d2 with a mating counter-attack, while after 32.h7+ ♘xh7 33.♕xe4 ♕d6, black simply gets a decisive material advantage.

32.♖h3! ♘h7 33.♖d3 ♕a8 34.♕xe4!

That's it! After the check on d8, white promotes a new queen and pushes the black king to the center of the board.

34...♕xe4 35.♖d8+ ♔f7 36.g8=♕+ ♔f6 37.♖d6+ ♔f5 38.♕g6+ ♔f4 39.g3+ ♔e3 40.♖d3+ ♕xd3 41.♕xd3+ Black resigned.

Leningrad, autumn 1953. The strongest of the strongest arrived for the national team championship. Once the Latvian team had sat down at their tables, the Lithuanian master I. Vistaneckis approached me.

"Listen, Koblenz, did you bring the republic's first team or a schoolboy team? In the autumn, the boys should be studying, not traveling!"

Indeed, with the exception of I. Zhdanov and myself, all the players from Latvia were younger than 20!

And still, the decision of the Latvian Chess Federation to send young players to an important competition was correct. To become a strong chess player, you should face serious tests. The 1953 Soviet team championship turned out to be just such a test for many currently well-known players.

The dangerous-looking experiment turned out alright.

The young Latvian players – Janis Klavins, Mark Pasman, Israel Zilber, Aivars Gipslis and Mikhail Tal (the latter two still looked like kids) – were at the center of attention. The "schoolboys" got ahead of many experienced opponents and qualified for the final.

The match against the Russian SFSR was the most exciting. The result of the 5-hour battle was sensational: Latvia won 5-4. There were some chances to take third place. The result of the adjourned game between candidate master Tal and international master G. Ilivitsky was very important (see diagram).

No. 7
M. Tal – G. Ilivitsky
1953, Leningrad, 3rd Soviet Team Championship

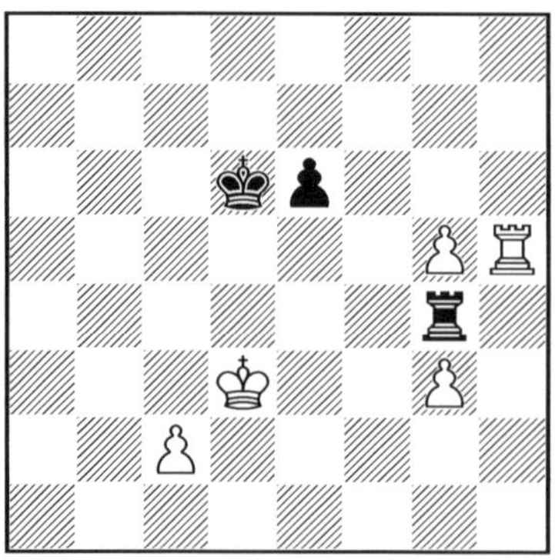

Here's how the game ended.

46.♔e3! ♖xg3+ 47.♔f4 ♖g2 48.c4 ♖c2

48...♔c5 was of course bad due to 49.g6+ and 50.♖g5.

Editor's note: Black could have drawn, for instance, with 48...e5+ 49.♔f5 *(49.♔e4 ♖g4+ 50.♔f5 ♖xc4 51.g6 ♖f4+ 52.♔g5 ♔e7; 49.♔e3 ♖g4)* 49...♖f2+ 50.♔g6 e4; 48...♖g1 or 48...♖f2+ 49.♔g3 ♖f1 was also enough.

49.g6 ♔e7 50.c5 ♔f6 51.♖g5!

The winning move.

51...e5+ 52.♔e4 ♔g7 (52...♔xg5 53.g7) **53.♔d5 Black resigned**.

Tal played second board in the competition and scored 4.5/7. For this success, the Highest Qualifying Commission decided to allow candidate master M. Tal to play a match for the master's title.

The Leningrad competition made Tal more confident in his abilities. He prepared for that match very seriously. The first stage of preparation was the 1954 Latvian SSR championship. During the draw, Janis Klovans asked the other participants to uphold an old tradition. The fact of the matter was, that in the last three years the championship had been won each time by a first-year student of the Latvian University, and Klovans had just enrolled...

The tradition wasn't broken. Klovans played brilliantly and won the Latvian championship. Tal had to settle for 2nd–3rd place.

In the summer, Tal played a qualifying match against the multiple champion of the Belorussian SSR, experienced master V. Saigin. There were 14 games in the match, and the Riga player won 8-6. For this victory, the young player was awarded the honored title “USSR Master of Sports”.

Game 8 was Tal’s best creative achievement in the match.

No. 8, Catalan Opening
V. Saigin – M. Tal
1954, Riga, Master Title Match, game 8

1.d4 ♘f6 2.c4 c5 3.♘f3 e6 4.g3 cxd4 5.♘xd4 d5 6.♗g2 e5 7.♘f3 d4!

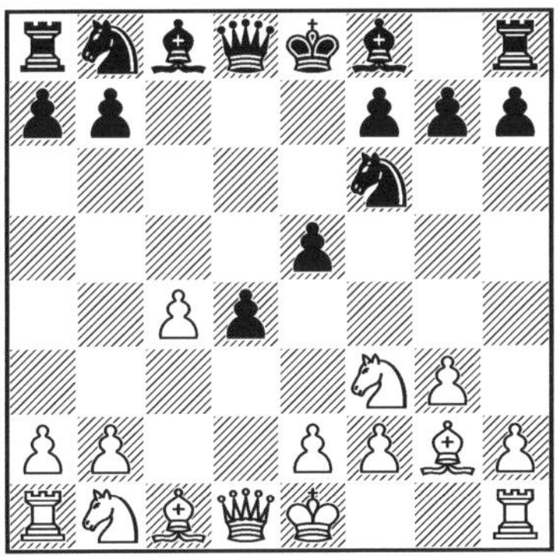

White can’t capture on e5 due to 8...♕a5+, and the advanced pawn disrupts communication lines between the flanks.

8.0-0 ♘c6 9.e3 ♗e7 10.exd4 exd4 11.♘bd2

Editor’s note: In modern times, the main line is 11.♗f4.

11...♗e6 12.♖e1 0-0 13.b3 ♕d7 14.♗b2 ♖ad8 15.a3 a5 16.♘e5 ♘xe5 17.♖xe5 b6 18.♘f3 ♗c5

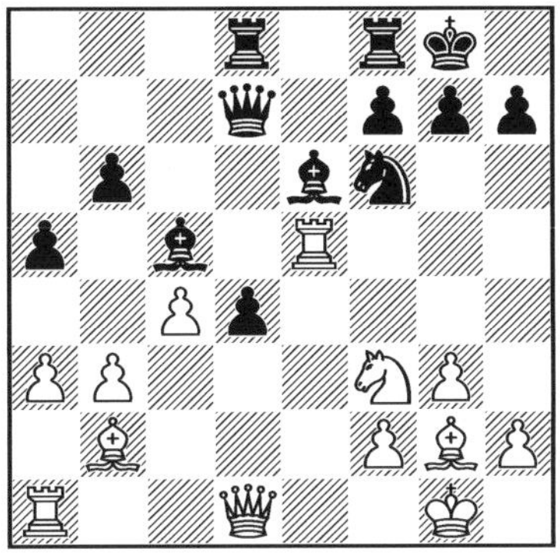

19.♕d2

After 19.b4, Tal intended to play 19...axb4 20.axb4 ♗d6!, and the white rook has no good squares: 21.♖e2 is met with 21...♗xc4, while after 21.♖e1, there’s 21...♗xb4.

19...♘g4

After bolstering the center, black goes on the offensive.

20.♖ee1 d3! (opening the diagonal for the c5 bishop) **21.♖f1**

After 21.♘e5, black intended to play 21...♘xe5 22.♖xe5 ♗d4! After exchanging the bishops, his passed pawn will become dangerous.

21...♕d6!

This move should have been anticipated beforehand. Black parries two threats at the same time – 22.b3-b4 and 22.h2-h3. If now 22.h3, then 22...♘xf2! 23.♖xf2 ♕xg3.

Editor’s note: Koblenz’s line leads to unclear play after 24.♗e5 ♕g6 25.♔h2 ♗xf2 26.♕xf2, so white should have gone for this position.

22.♕c3

Editor's note: This move is a serious mistake, because it allows black to create a strong initiative. 22.♗c3 keeps the position equal.

22...f6 23.♖ad1

White couldn't play 23.♘g5 due to 23...♘xf2! 24.♖xf2 ♗xf2+ 25.♔xf2 fxg5+

Editor's note: White still had some defending chances after 23.♗c1!, intending ♗d2 or ♗f4.

23...♖fe8 24.♖d2 ♗f5 25.♘g5

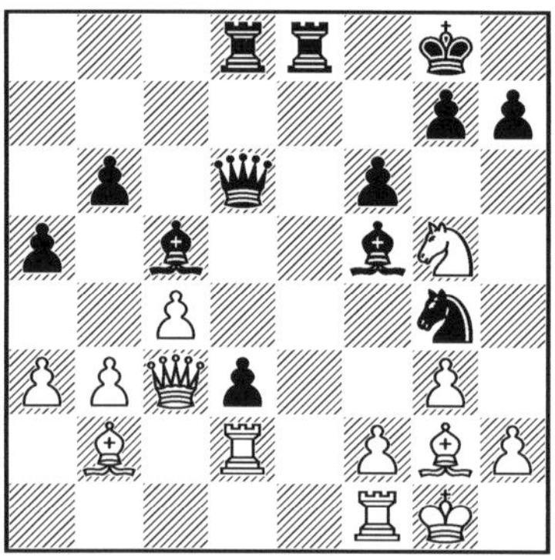

25...♘e3! (the decisive blow) **26.fxe3**

If the rook retreated, black traded the g2 bishop – an important kingside defender.

26...♗xe3+ 27.♔h1 ♗xd2 28.♕xd2 ♖e2 29.♕c3 ♖xg2! White resigned. If the rook is captured, black wins by pushing the d-pawn – 30.♔xg2 d2 31.♖d1 ♗g4 32.♘f3 ♕d3!

However, Tal's play wasn't always so consistent. The desire to complicate the position and create conditions for some kind of combination once cost him an important point.

No. 9
M. Tal – V. Saigin
1954, Riga, Master Title Match, game 11

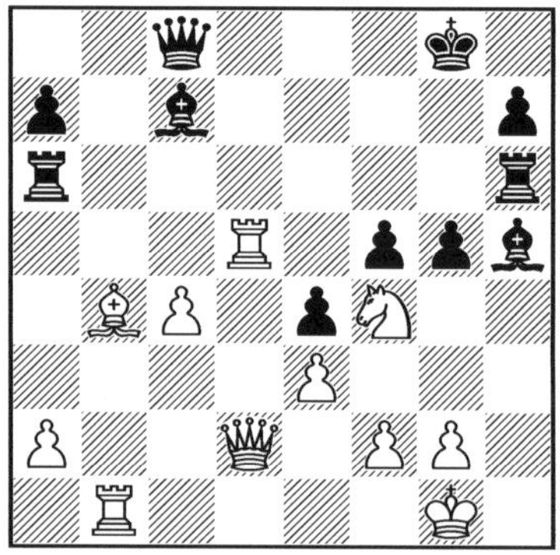

White had a simple win: 40.♘xh5 ♖xh5 41.♗d6! Because of the h5 rook's poor position and the decisive weakening of the kingside, black would just have to resign. Instead, Tal went for a complicated combination, but the spectacular finishing move turned out to be impossible!

40.♖d7 gxf4 41.♕d5+ ♖ae6 42.♕c5 ♖eg6 43.♖xc7

Editor's note: White could have forced a draw by repetition with 43.♕d5+ ♖e6 44.♕c5.

43...♖xg2+ 44.♔f1 ♕d8!

Black threatens to turn the game around with 45...♗e2+ 46.♔xe2 ♖xf2+. Tal thought that after 45.♕f8+

♕xf8 46.♗xf8 ♖hg6, he would force his opponent's resignation with the elegant 47.♗g5! When he started the combination, he simply forgot that the bishop couldn't move to g5 from f8!

The ending was miserable: **45.♕d5+ ♕xd5 46.♖c8+ ♔f7 47.♖c7+ ♔e8**, and **white resigned**.

Tal remembered this loss for a long while.

In this period, Tal's number-one enemy was hasty decision-making, so characteristic of young players.

No. 10
M. Tal – J. Klovans
1954, Riga

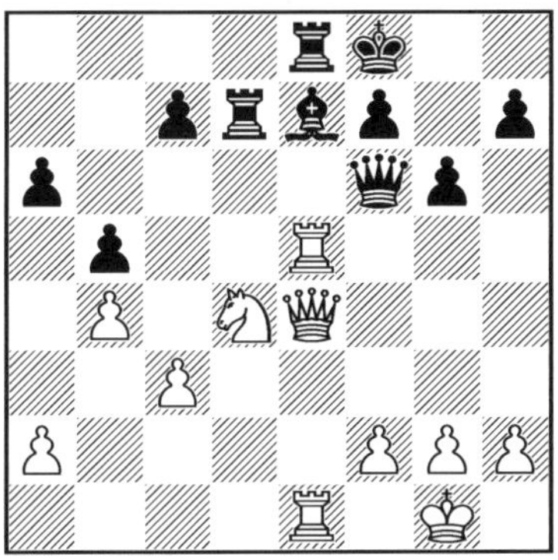

Black is in zugzwang. After 22.g3 or 22.♖e3 and ♖f3 he should lose.

Editor's note: Actually, black is not in zugzwang just yet (right now, only the e7 bishop cannot move), but after the strongest 22.♘c6! (now all black pieces are tied down with the bishop's defense), he gets very close to it and loses quickly: 22... h5 (after *22...♕d6 23.g4 ♕f6 24.g5 ♕d6 25.♖e3* it is indeed zugzwang) 23.h4 ♕d6 24.g3 ♕f6 25.♖e3 ♕d6 26.♔g2 ♕f6 27.♖f3 ♕g7 28.♖e6 f6 29.♘e5+−.

However, Tal, almost without thinking, played **22.♕c6?** After **22... ♖ed8 23.♕e4 ♗d6 (Editor's note:** 23...♗xb4, winning a pawn, is even stronger – it's now white who should struggle for a draw) **24.♖e8+ ♔g7 25.♖xd8 ♖xd8 26.♘c6**, white still has an advantage, but he needed a much bigger effort to convert it than in the original position.

Editor's note: Koblenz's evaluation looks too optimistic. The game continued **26...♖d7 27.c4** (best) **27...bxc4** (the immediate 27... ♗f8! is even better) **28.♕xc4**, and instead of **28...♕f4** (after which white doesn't have any advantage either, by the way), black could play 28...♗f8! with the idea of ♖d7-d2, seizing the initiative as a result. The game ended in a **draw** after 50 moves.

Back then, Tal often played in blitz tournaments, which, of course, affected his game. Endless blitz games are one of the reasons for "automatic" rashness in important games. Tal occasionally couldn't stand the intense struggle and tried to force events.

"Automatic play" is especially dangerous in better and won

positions. Emanuel Lasker, the ex-world champion, would say, "A won position is the hardest to win." The fact that Tal managed to overcome his impatience and nervousness in a relatively short time raised my hopes.

Filled with battle fervor, Tal, as the leader of the republic's youth team, travelled to Leningrad for the USSR youth championship. He came second in individual scores (after B. Spassky).

No. 11
M. Tal – J. Visockis
1954, Leningrad, Soviet Junior Team Championship, Latvia-Lithuania Match

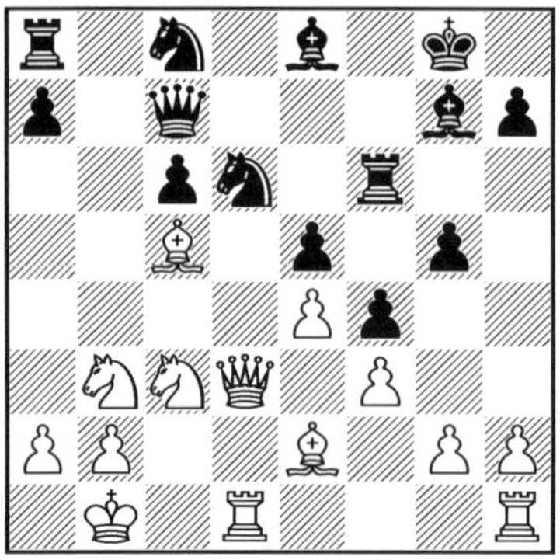

21.♘d5

Editor's note: This move is actually bad and could have led to a worse position for white.

21...cxd5 22.♕xd5+ ♘f7 23.♕xa8 ♗c6 24.♗b6!

The point of the combination. Tal left his queen deep behind enemy lines for a purpose!

24...axb6 25.♖c1 ♗xa8 (black could resist better with 25...♗f8**)**

Editor's note: Actually, after Koblenz's move 25...♗f8, black is simply better. For instance: 26.♗b5 ♗xa8 27.♖xc7 ♘cd6 28.♗d3 g4!, seizing the initiative.

26.♖xc7 ♖c6

Editor's note: Black shouldn't have gone for the rook exchange, because after it, his counterplay chances are close to zero. 26...♘cd6 was much better, planning kingside activity after g5-g4 at some point.

27.♖c1 ♖xc7 28.♖xc7 ♘cd6 29.♘d2! ♗f8 30.♗c4, and **white won**, converting his advantage.

In autumn 1954, the Soviet team championship was held in Riga. In this competition, Tal played against a grandmaster for the very first time. He was pitted against Yuri Averbakh, the current Soviet champion, in the match Daugava – Zenit.

The game was very tense. Tal played white and sacrificed a pawn in the opening. His opponent found the correct defensive plan and seized the initiative. It seemed that Tal would definitely lose. However, Averbakh made a blunder in time trouble, and the position changed drastically. The grandmaster couldn't make his 40th time-control move and lost on time in a roughly equal position.

Tal was, of course, glad that he had brought a valuable point to his team, but on the way home, he was downcast. This didn't feel like a true victory. Trying to seize the initiative out of the opening with dubious gambit lines was an unreliable method, especially against grandmasters.

How should he play against grandmasters? This question bothered him a lot. And so, against Taimanov, Tal decided to play differently, "the grandmaster way" – quietly and methodically. This ended badly – Taimanov scored an easy win. It turned out that tactical inventiveness alone wasn't enough, and in a positional game Tal was still much weaker than the top players.

His sporting results in this competition weren't brilliant: 4/10, sharing next-to-last place on first board. However, his opponents were also much stronger than those he had faced before.

The game against international master Lev Aronin especially attracted my attention. Even though Tal lost, I think that the exceptional talent of the future grandmaster really shone through in this game.

No. 12, Caro-Kann Defense
M. Tal – L. Aronin
1954, Riga, 2nd Soviet Team Cup, round 6

1.e4 c6 2.♘c3 d5 3.♘f3 dxe4 4.♘xe4 ♘f6 5.♘xf6+ gxf6 (a double-edged continuation. After 5...exf6, the game simplified considerably) **6.♗c4**

Editor's note: These days, 6.d4 is by far the most popular move.

6...♕c7

Editor's note: This move occurs rarely in current practice. Black plays 6...♗f5 more often.

7.0-0 ♗g4 8.d4 e6 9.♖e1 ♘d7 10.h3 ♗h5

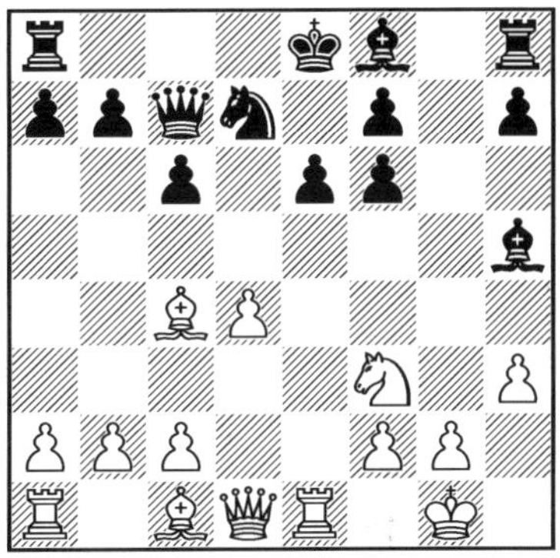

11.♗xe6!

Launching a combination with a rook and knight sacrifice.

Editor's note: This sacrifice is objectively dubious.

11...fxe6 12.♖xe6+ ♔f7

If 12...♔d8, then 13.♘g5! ♗g6 (13...♗xd1 is met with 14.♘f7+ ♔c8 15.♖e8+) 14.♖xf6!

Editor's note: The correct move is 12...♗e7 – after 13.♕e1 ♘f8 14.♖xf6

♗xf3 (but not *14...0-0-0? 15.♗f4*) 15.♖xf3 ♘g6 16.♕e6 ♖f8 17.♖xf8+ ♘xf8 18.♕g4 ♗f6 (there are other good moves as well), black is out of danger and at the very least no worse.

13.♘g5+ fxg5 14.♕xh5+ ♔xe6 15.♗xg5 ♘e5! 16.♖e1 ♕g7

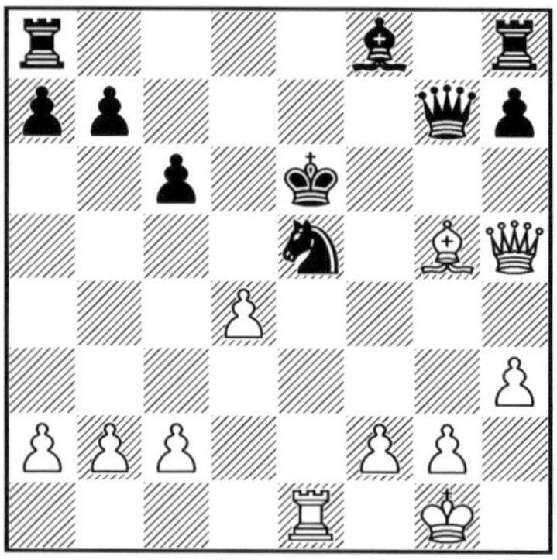

17.♕g4+?

A pity! After the game, Tal showed that white could maintain the attack with 17.dxe5! For instance, 17...♖g8 (best) 18.♕g4+ ♔f7 19.♕d7+ ♔g6 20.♕e6+ ♔xg5 21.♖e4 with the threat 22.♖g4. If 21...♔h5, then 22.♕f5+ ♕g5 23.♕xh7+ ♗h6 24.♕f7+ and ♕f3+.

Tal decided against the move because he thought it wasn't enough to win. However, black now repels the attack.

Editor's note: After 17.dxe5, instead of Koblenz's move 17...♖g8?!, black could have put up much stiffer resistance with 17...♗e7 – even though the position after 18.♗f6! ♕g6 19.♕f3 ♖hd8 20.♕b3+ ♖d5 21.♕xb7 ♕e8 22.♗xe7 ♖b8 23.♕xa7 ♖a8 24.♕b7 ♖b8 25.♕a6 ♔xe7 26.e6, where white has five pawns for the rook, a dangerous passed e-pawn and an attack, is evaluated as lost for black by the computer, it's still unclear for a human. However, instead of 17.dxe5, white had a good alternative 17.♖xe5+, and after 17...♔d7 *(or 17...♔d6 18.♗f4 ♔d7 19.♖g5 ♕xd4 20.♕g4+ ♔e8 21.♖e5+ ♗e7 22.♕g7+−)* 18.♕g4+ ♔c7 19.♕g3 ♔d7 *(19...♔b6 20.♕b3+ ♔c7 21.♖f5!+−)* 20.♕b3 b5 *(20...♔c7 21.♖f5!+−)* 21.♕e6+ ♔c7 22.♗f4 ♕d7 *(22...♔b7 23.d5!+−; 22...♔b6 23.c4! bxc4 24.a4+−)* 23.♖d5+ ♗d6 24.♕xd7+ ♔xd7 25.♖xd6+ ♔c7 26.♗e5 ♖he8 27.♖h6+ ♔b6 28.♖xh7 white obviously wins.

17...♔d6!

Aronin defends precisely. After 17...♔f7 18.♖xe5 ♔g8 19.♕h4 white maintained dangerous threats.

Editor's note: Actually, black's move is a mistake. 17...♔f7 was the correct move, even though after 18.dxe5!? (Koblenz's line *18.♖xe5 ♔g8 19.♕h4* leads to threefold repetition after *19...♕g6 20.♗f6 h6 21.♖e3 ♔h7 22.♖g3 ♕f5 23.♖f3 ♕g6*) 18...♗e7 19.♕f3+ ♔e8 20.♗f6 ♕f8 21.♗xh8 ♕xh8 22.♕g4, white has the initiative, and his next plan involves activitating the rook along the third rank.

18.dxe5+

Editor's note: After 18.♖xe5! with threats 19.♕e6+/19.♕f4/19.♕g3/19.♖f5 white won. For instance: 18...♕g6 19.c4 (intending 20.♖e7 ♗xe7 21.♗f4#) 19...♔c7 20.♖e6 ♕f7 21.♗f6 ♖g8 22.♕f5 ♕d7 23.♗e5+ ♔d8 24.c5 (threatening 25.♗f6+) 24...♗e7 25.♗f6! ♗xf6 26.♖d6 ♕xd6 27.cxd6 ♖f8 28.g4 h6 29.h4 ♖c8 30.g5 hxg5 31.hxg5 ♗g7 32.♕h7+–.

18...♔c7 19.e6 ♖g8! 20.♗f4+ ♗d6 21.♗xd6+ ♔xd6 22.♖d1+ ♔c7 23.♕f4+ ♔c8 24.g4 ♖d8! 25.♖e1 ♕c7

Editor's note: The correct move was 25...♕e7. After the game move, however, white should have played 26.♕f6! with the subsequent e6-e7, f2-f4 and, according to the computer, he has enough compensation for a draw.

26.♕f5 ♕e7

The attack has fizzled out, and **black won**, converting his material advantage.

Tal's next tournament was the 1955 Latvian SSR championship.

"A tradition is a tradition" – a Latvian University freshman should win. That year, it was Aivars Gipslis. Tal finished second...

In the same year of 1955, Tal achieved his first serious success in All-Union competitions. In the Soviet championship quarter-final in Vilnius (the Baltic zone tournament), he shared 3rd–4th place and qualified for the semi-final.

No. 13
A. Gipslis – M. Tal
1955, Vilnius, Soviet Championship Quarter-Final

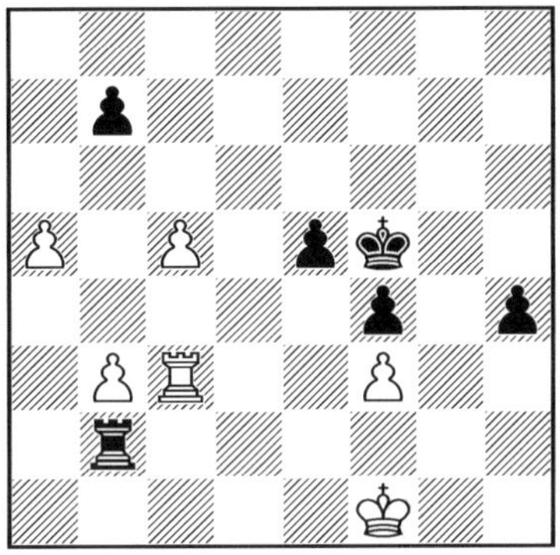

Tal played his first games without much effort, and the results showed. By the middle of the tournament, his chances of qualifying for the semi-final were minimal. However, at this critical moment, the young master suddenly transformed. He treated every game with the utmost importance. Showing great composure and tenacity, he defeated some serious opponents and finished among the prize winners.

44...h3 45.♔g1 e4 46.a6!

White's best counter-chance is to create a passed pawn. 46.fxe4+ ♔g4 47.a6 was worse due to 47...f3 48.axb7 f2+ 49.♔f1 h2 50.♖g3+ ♔h4!, and the h-pawn is unstoppable.

46...e3 47.axb7

The strongest reply was 47.♖c1, which black intended to meet with 47...♖xb3 48.axb7 ♖xb7 49.c6 ♖c7, winning.

47...♖b1+ 48.♔h2 e2 49.♖e3

(49.b8=♕ is bad due to 49...♖h1+) **49...fxe3 50.b8=♕ ♖h1+!**

With this tactical blow, black wins the game.

51.♔xh1 e1=♕+ 52.♔h2 ♕f2+ 53.♔xh3 ♕xf3+ 54.♔h2 e2 55.♕f8+ ♔e4 56.♕e8+ ♔d3 57.♕b5+ ♔e3 White resigned.

A complicated position occurred in Tal's game against Karlis Klasups, who also competed for a top place in the tournament.

No. 14
K. Klasups – M. Tal
1955, Vilnius, Soviet Championship Quarter-Final

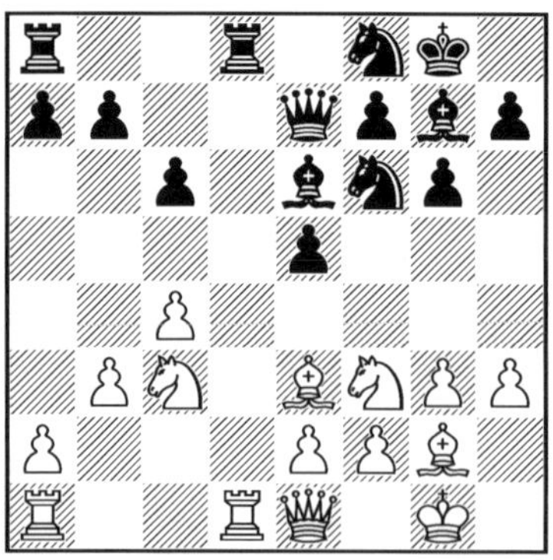

15...♗d7! (avoiding the rook exchange) **16.♖ac1 ♘h5 17.♘e4 ♘e6 18.♘d6**

It was hard to predict that after winning a pawn on the queenside, white would have to withstand an attacking storm on the opposite flank. It was better to double rooks on the d-file.

Editor's note: Actually, an attempt to double the rooks leads to a difficult position for white: 18.♖c2? (the moves with the other rook lose immediately: *18.♖d2?? f5 19.♘c3 e4 20.♘d4 f4 21.gxf4 ♘exf4–+, 18.♖d3?? f5 19.♘eg5 ♘f8!–+, 18.♖d6?? f5–+*) 18...f5 19.♘c3 (*19.♘d6? e4 20.♘h2 f4* with a strong and probably decisive attack) 19...♗e8 (threatening 20...e4) 20.♖cd2 ♖xd2 21.♗xd2 *(21.♖xd2?? f4–+)* 21...e4 22.♘h2 ♖d8 with a great positional advantage.

18...b6 19.c5 ♖ab8 20.cxb6 axb6 21.♘c4 e4 22.♘fd2

Editor's note: 22.♘d4 (threatening 23.♘xe6 ♗xe6 24.♘xb6) was safer: after the trades on d4, the position is equal, and if 22...♘c7?!, then after 23.g4! c5 (*23...♘f6 24.♗f4* with the initiative) 24.gxh5 cxd4 25.♗xd4 ♗xd4 26.♖xd4 white is better.

22...b5 23.♘a5 f5! 24.♘xc6 ♗xc6 25.♖xc6 f4! 26.gxf4 ♘exf4 27.♘f1 ♕g5 28.♖xd8+ ♖xd8

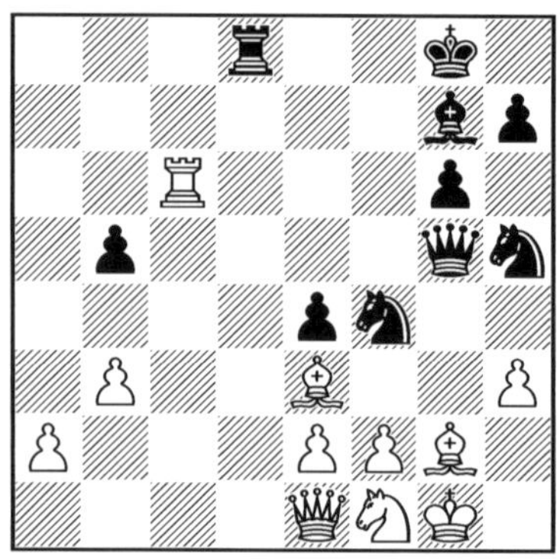

29.♗xf4

Editor's note: 29.♘g3 could have saved the game — after the subsequent 29...♘xg3 30.♗xf4 (*30.fxg3 ♘xh3+ 31.♗xh3 ♕xe3+ 32.♔g2* doesn't lose either) 30...♘xe2+ 31.♕xe2 ♕xf4 32.♕g4 ♕xg4 33.hxg4, there's a drawn endgame on the board.

29...♘xf4 30.♘g3 e3! 31.♖c2 (31.fxe3 would've been met with 31...♘xg2 32.♔xg2 ♕d5+) **31...exf2+ 32.♔xf2**

32.♕xf2 doesn't help due to 32...♗d4 33.e3 ♗xe3 34.♕xe3 ♘xh3+.

32...♗d4+ 33.♔f1 ♘h5! 34.♗f3 (after 34.♘xh5, black wins with 34...♖f8+) **34...♘xg3+ 35.♔g2 ♘e4+ 36.♗g4 h5 37.e3 ♗xe3 38.♕b4 ♕e5 39.♕e1 ♗d2 40.♕h4 g5**

The time trouble ended, and further resistance was futile. **White resigned**.

At the Soviet team championship in Lugansk I worked as Latvia's coach. I arrived in the city at 3 in the morning, but Misha wasn't in his room. I found him in the room where the Ukrainian players lived. A blitz tournament had just ended. It was easy to see by my facial expression that the coach wasn't exactly thrilled by the exhausting night competition.

Tal was very lively. Holding a sheet of paper and a pencil in his hand, he asked with a smile, "Maestro, can I enroll you in the next blitz tournament?"

However, his opponents were already out of energy.

"Maybe it's time to stop, Misha? The games are tomorrow, we should catch some sleep."

I shared a room with Tal in Lugansk. Each day in the morning, and sometimes in the evening as well, other players from the team gathered in our room. The game analyses were endless.

Tal obviously looked tired, and I asked the hotel administrator to move him to a single room. But the young master didn't even want to hear about that. He wanted to take part in the team work and help his friends. When team interests were at stake, he didn't think about himself.

No. 15
I. Lipnitsky – M. Tal
1955, Lugansk, 4th Soviet Team Championship Semi-Final

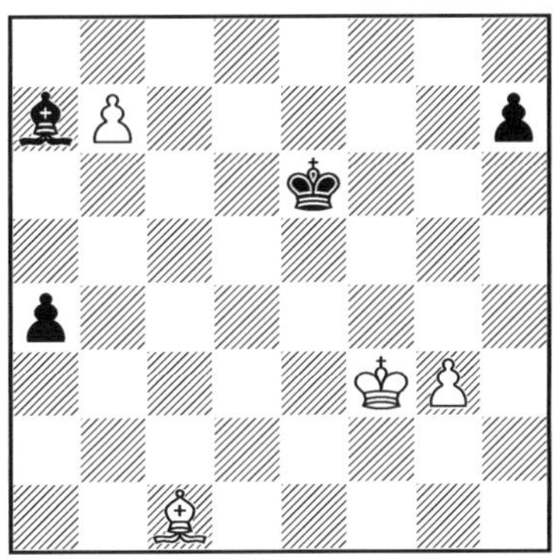

Tal played on the second board and shared 1st–3rd place in the semi-final.

He saved the game against Isaak Lipnitsky with an exceptionally tenacious defense.

In his annotations to the game, Lipnitsky wrote, "The entire Ukrainian team analyzed the adjourned position. To win, we decided to send the white king to the kingside, towards the h-pawn, or prevent the black king from reaching the g6 square. For instance, 45...♔d5 46.♗e3 ♗b8 47.♗f4 ♗a7 48.b8=♕ ♗xb8 49.♗xb8. If now 49...♔e6, then 50.♔f4 ♔f6 51.♗e5+ ♔g6 52.♗b2, and the game is won. (**Editor's note:** Instead of 49...♔e6, black should play 49...a3, and after 50.♔f4 ♔c4 51.♗e5 ♔d3! 52.g4 ♔e2 53.g5 a2 54.♔g4 ♔e3 55.♔h5 ♔f3 56.♔h6 ♔g4 57.♗f6 ♔f5, it's a draw.)

45...♔d7!

The Latvian players also did great work! Now white can't win a tempo with 46.♗e3 ♗b8 47.♗f4, because after 47...♗xf4 48.gxf4, the b7 pawn can't be defended.

46.♗f4 a3 47.b8=♕ ♗xb8 48.♗xb8 ♔e6 49.♔f4 ♔f6

That's the point behind the subtle move 45...♔d7! If the black pawn were on a4, white would win easily after 50.♗d6.

50.♗e5+ ♔g6 51.♗a1 a2 52.♗b2 h5 53.♗a1 ♔h6

If 54.♔f5, then 54...h4! 55.gxh4 ♔h5, with a draw. So, a **draw was agreed**."

Tal's best achievement in Lugansk was his win against the young Moscow champion, Evgeny Vasiukov.

In this game, white's play was very precise and determined.

No. 16, Sicilian Defense
M. Tal – E. Vasiukov
1955, Lugansk, 4th Soviet Team Championship Final, round 9

1.e4 c5 2.♘f3 ♘c6 3.d4 cxd4 4.♘xd4 g6 5.c4 ♘f6 6.♘c3 ♘xd4 7.♕xd4 d6 8.♗e2 ♗g7

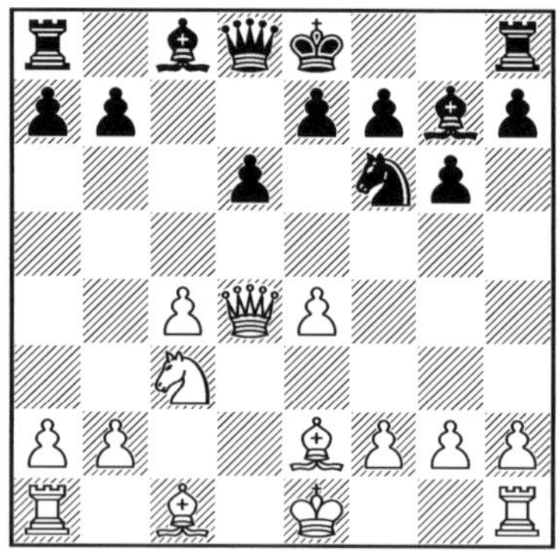

9.0-0

Editor's note: In modern top-level games, white usually doesn't hurry with castling: the current main line is 9.♗e3 0-0 10.♕d2 ♗e6 11.♖c1 ♕a5 12.f3 ♖fc8 13.b3 a6 14.♘a4 ♕xd2+ 15.♔xd2.

9...0-0 10.♕d1

Editor's note: This decision to return the queen to the starting square didn't find many followers among strong players. The most popular moves in subsequent grandmaster practice were 10.♕e3, 10.♕d3, and 10.♗g5.

10...♗e6 11.♗e3 ♕a5

Both sides have completed their development. White controls the central squares and has some positional advantage. Black's goal is to prepare a queenside attack.

12.♖c1 ♖fc8 13.b3 a6 14.f4!

White needs to be energetic, otherwise black will be the first to launch an attack with b7-b5.

14...♘g4

Inventive, but leads to white's advantage. It was better not to deviate from the marked out plan and play 14...b5.

Editor's note: Koblenz's move 14...b5 is also a suboptimal decision because of the reply 15.f5!. After 15...♗d7 (perhaps *15...gxf5 16.exf5 ♗d7* is the lesser evil, even though black's position is still very suspect) 16.fxg6 hxg6 17.e5! dxe5 18.♖xf6 and 19.♕xd7 (which has happened several times in practice), white has a big advantage. However, 14...♗g4!? is worth considering, as played in the game Haznedaroglu – Malakhov, Tripoli 2004. There followed 15.♗xg4 ♘xg4 16.♕xg4 ♗xc3 with approximate equality.

15.♗d4 ♘e3

Editor's note: Perhaps it was better to go for passive defense with 15...♘h6!?, intending to trade on d4 and then play f7-f6 and ♘h6-f7.

16.♗xe3 ♗xc3 17.f5 ♗d7 18.c5 ♖xc5

The exchange sacrifice was evidently forced. Black is assuming that the pawn and bishop pair are adequate compensation for the small material deficit. Actually, this is not true.

Editor's note: Black could play 18...♗b5, holding onto the material for a while, but after 19.♗xb5 axb5 20.♕d5, black's position is difficult.

19.♗xc5 ♕xc5+ 20.♔h1 ♕a5 21.♗c4 ♖f8 22.fxg6 hxg6 23.♕d5! b5

Editor's note: 23...♗c6 still gave some chances to save the game.

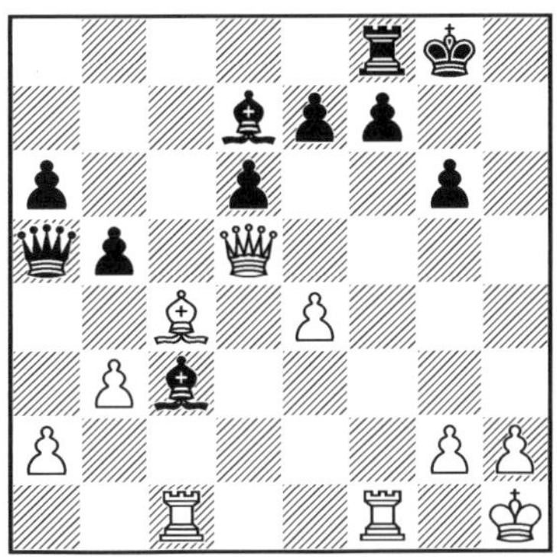

24.♖xf7 bxc4 25.♖cf1! ♖c8 26.♖f8+ ♔h7 27.♕g8+ ♔h6 28.♖xc8 ♗xc8 29.♕xc8 cxb3 30.axb3 ♗f6 31.♕f8+ ♔h7 32.♕f7+ ♔h6 33.♕d5! ♕a2 34.♕d3 a5 35.♕c4

White improves his queen's position and goes for the adjournment, hoping to find a precise path to the win during home analysis.

35...♔g7 36.g3 ♕b2 37.♕d3 ♕a2 38.♖c1 ♕f2 39.♖f1 ♕a2 40.♕f3 ♕c2 41.♖f2

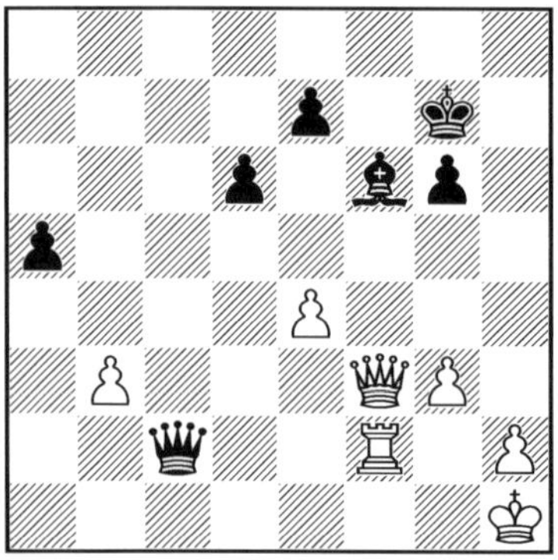

The game was adjourned here. In the resumption, there followed **41...♕b1+ 42.♔g2 ♔f7 43.h4! ♔e8 44.h5! g5 45.h6 ♔f8 46.♕f5 ♕xb3** (desperation) **47.♕c8+ ♔f7 48.h7**, and **black resigned**.

The semi-final of the 23rd Soviet championship was approaching. It was a very difficult exam. Playing in the final is every master's dream, so the semi-finals are true battles to the death. After the draw, Tal thought about the tournament table for a long time: there were very experienced players with deep theoretical knowledge among the Riga semi-final participants. These included grandmaster Viktor Korchnoi, the winner of the Bucharest international tournament, grandmaster Isaak Boleslavsky, and international master Semyon Furman, one of our best theoreticians.

Tal achieved a good start – 4.5/7. Then he won 4 games in a row and joined the leaders' group. Like in the Vilnius quarter-final, his play in the second half of the tournament was most inspired, and he finished first.

He had reached the final!

Here's one of the games from the Riga semi-final.

No. 17, Sicilian Defense
M. Tal – S. Furman
1955, Riga, 23rd Soviet Championship Semi-Final

1.e4 c5 2.♘f3 ♘c6 3.d4 cxd4 4.♘xd4 ♘f6 5.♘c3 d6 6.♗g5 e6 7.♕d2 a6 8.0-0-0 ♗d7 9.f4 ♖c8

Editor's note: This seems to be a bad move. In modern grandmaster practice, black usually plays 9...b5, 9...h6 or 9...♗e7.

10.♘f3 ♕a5

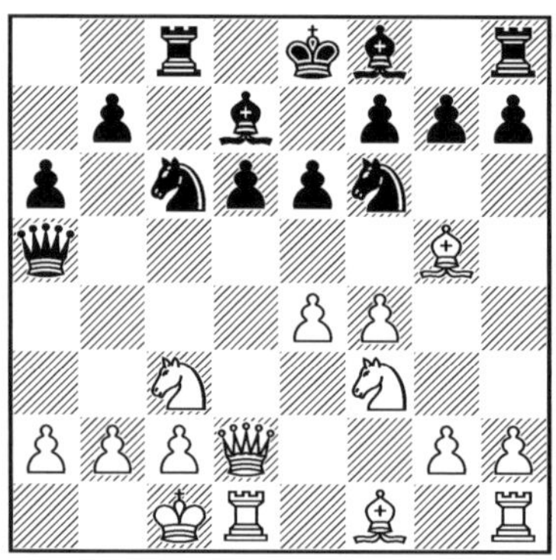

By leaving the king in the center, black hopes to organize a kingside attack. White prepares a central breakthrough.

11.♔b1!

Before the attack, white makes a necessary prophylactic move. Had he played 11.e5 immediately, black would have counterattacked with 11...♘b4 12.exf6 ♖xc3 13.♘d4 ♖a3!.

11...b5 12.♗xf6

Editor's note: As a number of subsequent games showed, the move 12.e5 poses a lot of problems for the opponent. Play usually continued 12...b4 (perhaps *12...♘d5 13.♘xd5 ♕xd2 14.♖xd2 exd5* is the lesser evil, even though after *15.a4*, black's position is quite unpleasant) 13.exf6 bxc3 14.fxg7 ♗xg7 15.♕xd6 with a big advantage.

12...gxf6 13.f5 ♘b4 14.a3 ♘c6 15.♘d4 ♘xd4

An inaccuracy. Black should have played 15...b4. For instance, 16.♘xc6 ♗xc6 17.axb4 ♕xb4 18.♕d4 ♖b8! 19.b3 a5 (**Editor's note:** this move loses to 20.♕xf6, so the correct continuation is 19...♕xd4 20.♖xd4 a5=).

16.♕xd4 ♗e7 17.♗e2 ♔d8

White threatened 18.♗h5. Perhaps 17...0-0 was better, which could be met with 18.♖d3 ♔h8 19.♖h3, with dangerous threats.

Furman hopes to find a shelter for his king in the center, but his position quickly deteriorates.

18.♖hf1 ♖b8?

Tal intended to meet 18...♖g8 with 19.fxe6 fxe6 20.♖xf6 ♖xg2 21.♖f7 ♖xc3 22.♖xe7 ♖c6 23.♖xh7 ♖xe2 24.♖h8+! ♗e8 25.♕a7 (**Editor's note:** 25.♕f6+ wins immediately) 25...♕c7 26.♕a8+ ♕c8 27.♖xd6+! ♔e7 28.♖xe8+ ♕xe8 29.♕xc6 ♕xc6 30.♖xc6, and the rook ending is hopeless for black.

Tal demonstrated this difficult line right after the game.

19.fxe6 fxe6 20.♖xf6 b4

After 20...♗xf6, white had 21.♕xf6+ ♔c7 22.e5! d5 23.♘xd5+ exd5 24.♕d6+ ♔c8 25.♖xd5 ♖b7 26.♖c5+ ♖c7 27.b4!, winning easily.

21.♖f5 e5

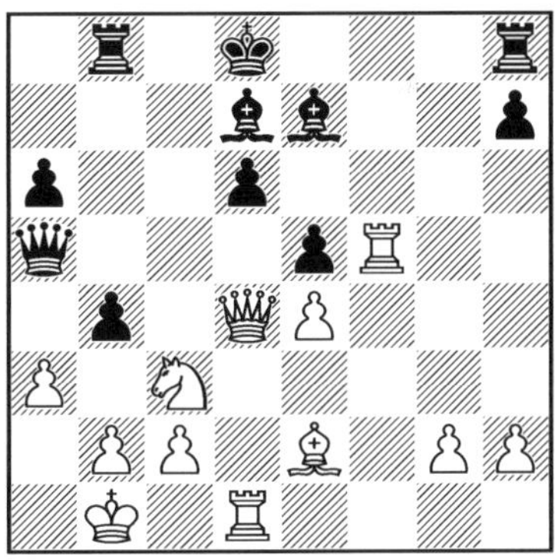

An exceptionally complicated position. Three white pieces are en prise, but he still manages to obtain a decisive advantage.

22.♕a7 ♕b6

After 22...♖c8, black could've been checkmated: 23.♘d5! bxa3

24.b4 ♕a4 25.♕b6+ ♔e8 26.♗h5#.

23.♕xb6+ ♖xb6 24.♘d5 ♗xf5 25.exf5!

The rest is simple: **25...♖b8 26.f6 ♗f8 27.axb4 ♔d7 28.g4 ♖g8 29.h4 h6 30.♖g1 e4 31.g5 hxg5 32.hxg5 ♔e6 33.♗c4 ♔e5 34.g6 ♗h6 35.♘e7 ♖gd8 36.g7**, and **black resigned**.

The years of hard work paid off.

Now it was time to think about preparing for games against the strongest grandmasters, coming up with the right strategy for a competition which would attract the attention of millions of chess fans.

The First Final

And so, we're in Leningrad. The debutant of the 23rd Soviet chess championship is all excited. He can't wait until the moment he's finally able to play against the renowned grandmasters and masters.

Tal played at ease and quickly in this important competition. He never got into time trouble. While his opponents were calculating complicated lines, he walked around the stage, looking at the unfolding events in other games with interest.

Meanwhile, there was a lot of drama in his own games. Tal crossed the safety barrier far too often, and was close to losing on many occasions. For instance, Byvshev won two pawns against him, but overlooked his opponent's disguised maneuver in time trouble, and the Riga player forced a perpetual check. In the first-round game against the Moscow master Vladimir Antoshin, Tal got into a difficult position. The young master even got a lot of flak over his wins against Vyacheslav Ragozin and Anatoly Bannik.

"An accidental success," some pundits quickly said of Tal's results.

However, we shouldn't forget that, unlike pure analysis, chess struggle has many factors – psychological considerations, time trouble, a loss of concentration because of nervous strain, etc. The fact that Tal managed to use the smallest chances and maintain his composure in difficult and sometimes even hopeless positions only speaks in his favor.

Let's remember that the young Botvinnik heard the same kind of criticism. For instance, *Shakhmaty v SSSR* wrote in 1936: "It's hard to find a master who'd managed to save as many lost and even hopeless positions as Botvinnik."

Tal's game against Vladimir Simagin was very intense. White sacrificed a knight, then a rook. Simagin had to make thirteen moves with his king, with danger lurking everywhere.

At the end of the game, the Leningrad chess fans met Tal with an ovation. With their applause, they thanked the Riga master for the true aesthetic pleasure brought by this work of chess art.

No. 18, Pirc Defence
M. Tal – V. Simagin
1956, Leningrad, 23rd Soviet Championship, round 3

1.e4 c6 2.d4 d6

Entering the players' room, the international master joked: "I lacked enough strength to push the pawn one square further."

The move 2...d6 is, of course, entirely playable and was made by black to avoid the trodden paths.

3.♘c3 ♘f6 4.f4! ♕b6

Editor's note: Today, the most popular move by far is 4...♕a5.

5.♘f3 ♗g4 6.♗e2 ♘bd7

Editor's note: In modern times, top players as a rule prefer 6...♗xf3 7.♗xf3 e5.

7.e5! ♘d5 8.0-0 ♘xc3 9.bxc3

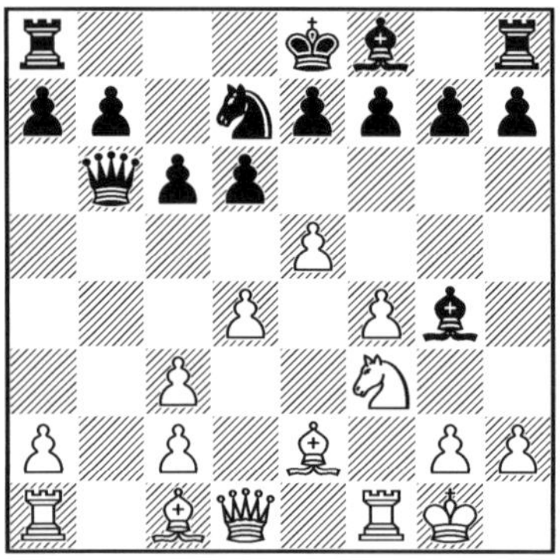

9...e6

An error. It was necessary to eliminate the dangerous knight with 9...♗xf3.

10.♘g5! ♗xe2 11.♕xe2 h6 (black provokes his opponent to sacrifice a knight) **12.♘xf7! ♔xf7 13.f5 dxe5** (**Editor's note:** 13...♘xe5 is met with 14.♗e3!+−) **14.fxe6+**

Editor's note: There was a more convincing line — 14.♕h5+ ♔e7 15.fxe6 ♔xe6 16.♗e3 ♕a5 17.dxe5 ♘xe5 18.♕f5+ ♔d6 19.♗f4+−.

14...♔xe6

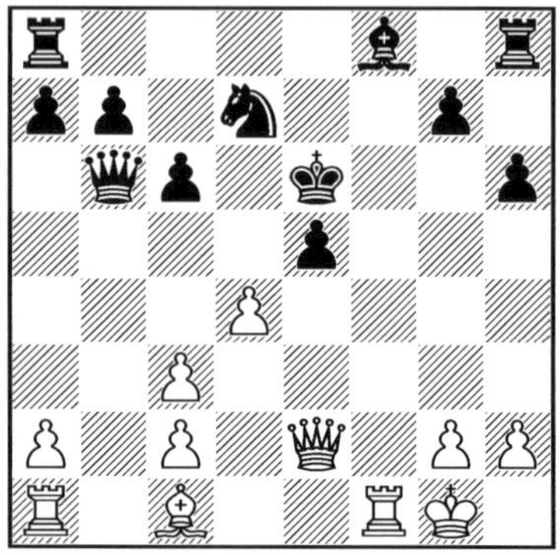

15.♖b1!

Simagin didn't expect this move. He calculated the line 15.♕g4+ ♔d6, thinking he would be able to put up stiff resistance.

15...♕xb1 16.♕c4+ ♔d6 (**Editor's note:** 16...♔e7 17.♗a3+ ♔d8 18.♖xb1 ♗xa3 19.♖xb7 ♖c8 20.♖xa7 ♗d6 was more tenacious) **17.♗a3+ ♔c7 18.♖xb1 ♗xa3 19.♕b3! ♗e7**

Black has enough material compensation for the queen, but his king is under attack.

20.♕xb7+ ♔d6 21.dxe5+?

Tal thought for a long time back on his twelfth move, but then started playing very rapidly. The consequences of this dangerous approached showed quickly. Had Tal been more careful (or rather calmer), he would've noticed the simple line 21.♖d1! e4 22.d5! ♘e5 23.dxc6+ ♔e6 24.♕b3+ ♔f5 25.♖f1+. After this mistake, white had to put a lot more effort into this attack.

21...♘xe5 22.♖d1+ ♔e6 23.♕b3+ ♔f5 24.♖f1+ ♔e4

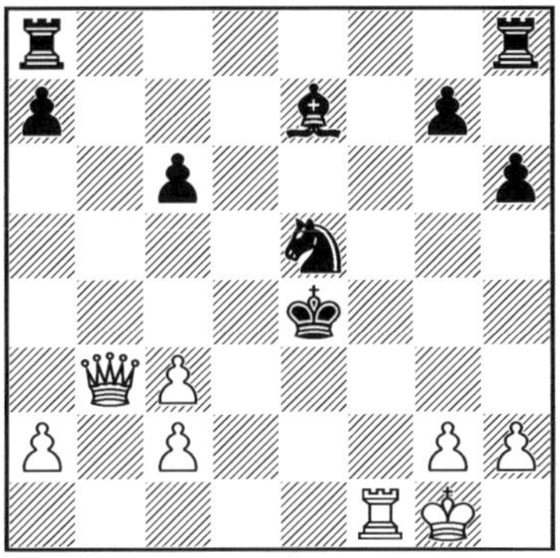

25.♖e1+

Editor's note: The simplest way to victory was 25.♕e6!, threatening ♖e1+, for instance: 25...♗c5+ 26.♔h1 ♖ae8 27.♖e1+ ♗e3 28.♕h3 ♘c4 29.♕d7! ♘e5 30.♕d4+ ♔f5 31.♖xe3 h5 32.♕e4+ ♔f6 33.♕f4+ and curtains.

25...♔f5 26.g4+ ♔f6 27.♖f1+ ♔g6 28.♕e6+ ♔h7 29.♕xe5 ♖he8 30.♖f7 ♗f8 31.♕f5+

Editor's note: 31.♕d4 is much stronger (the queen stays in the center, maintaining the pressure on both flanks), intending h2-h4 and g4-g5. The point is that black won't be able to either activate his bishop with ♗f8-c5 or double rooks on the e-file (31...♖e1+ 32.♔f2 ♖ae8?? 33.♖xf8+−).

31...♔g8 32.♔f2

An original idea! The king goes to help its major pieces. The simpler move was 32.♕g6 ♖e1+ 33.♔g2 ♖ae8 34.♖f1. (**Editor's note:** After the subsequent 34...♖1e2+ 35.♖f2 ♖2e5 36.♕xc6 ♗c5, it would be quite difficult for white to win. However, 32.♕g6 was indeed preferable to the game move.)

32...♗c5+ 33.♔g3 ♖e3+ 34.♔h4

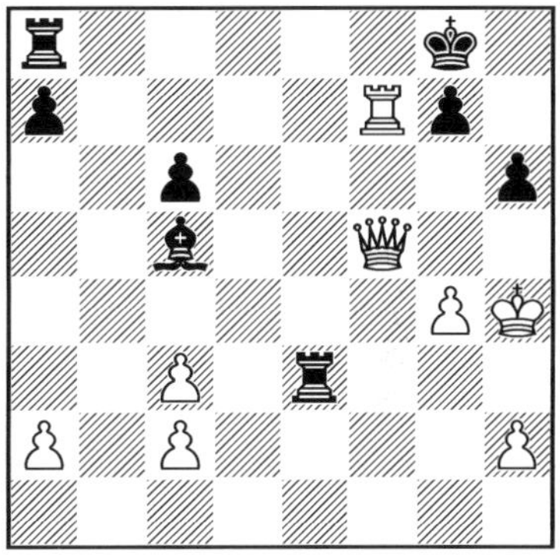

34...♖ae8

After 34...♗e7+, there was 35.g5! At first, instead of 35.g5, Tal wanted to play 35.♔h5 ♖d8 36.♖xg7+, sacrificing the second rook. However, he then noticed that after 36...♔xg7 37.♕g6+ black could avoid defeat by putting his king on f8: 37...♔f8! 38.♕xh6+ ♔f7 39.♕xe3 ♖h8+

35.♖xg7+ ♔xg7 36.♕xc5 ♖8e6

The last, decisive mistake. Later, grandmaster V. Ragozin showed that after 36...♖8e7 37.♕xc6 ♖f7, threatening 38...♖ff3, black could still draw.

37.♕xa7+ ♔g6 38.♕a8 ♔f6 39.a4 (the passed pawn assures white's victory) **39...♔e5 40.a5 ♔d5 41.♕d8+ ♔e4 42.a6 ♔f3 43.a7 ♖e2 44.♕d3+ ♖6e3 45.♕xe3+** and **black resigned**.

After a month of battles, Tal shared 5th–7th place, just one point behind the winners.

In summer 1956, Tal travelled to Sweden with the USSR team to take part in the students world team championship. In his first competition abroad, he scored 4/5.

Tal's game against the Yugoslav grandmaster Borislav Ivkov made the rounds in the world chess press. "Tal! Remember the name!" wrote the *Jugoslovensik Sahovski Glasnik* magazine back then.

Soviet Champion

In late November 1956, the semi-final of the next, 24th Soviet championship, was played in Tbilisi. Tal played there again. Grandmasters Petrosian and Korchnoi, and masters Polugaevsky, Furman, Antoshin and others, competed for the right to take part in the main competition.

Tal's start was disappointing. The first setback happened in the very first round. Analyzing his adjourned game against Kotkov, Tal found a subtle maneuver that should've won the game for him. However, during the play-off, he made a rash move that threw away all the hard-earned advantage, and the game ended in a draw.

Three more draws followed, and in the fifth round, Tal blundered and lost to master Vladlen Zurakhov. And then another three draws.

In round 9, Tal managed to outplay the "king of endgame studies", international master Genrikh Kasparyan, in a difficult endgame. It looked like a turning point. However, he then suffered a new blow. In the game against Alexander Buslaev, Tal went for a spectacular mate in an overwhelming position, blundered and lost.

Indeed, Tal's play was far from perfect at the start. Miscalculations in the middlegame and bad advantage conversion technique were the main causes for concern. His physical form was also far from perfect.

But all these failures didn't break Tal, and in the second half of the tournament, he started to win one game after another. The turning point was round 13, when Tal played Yakov Yukhtman.

Yukhtman, who usually plays rather quickly, spent more than an hour on his 17th move. Indeed, there was a lot to think about!

No. 19
M. Tal – Y. Yukhtman
1956, Tbilisi, 24th Soviet Championship Semi-Final, round 13

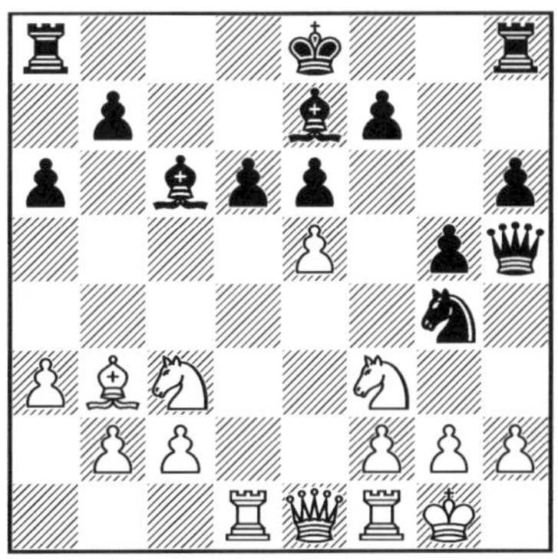

Black is hoping to get things going on the kingside, but Tal's unexpected tactical blow showed that he had other trouble coming.

17.♗d5!

Editor's note: Perhaps 17.♘d5! was even stronger.

17...♘xe5

After 17...exd5, white, of course, would have played 18.exd6

18.♘xe5 exd5

It was necessary to eliminate the bishop, but now new weaknesses emerge in black's position.

Editor's note: 18...dxe5 19.♕xe5 0-0 20.♗xc6 bxc6 21.♖d7 ♖fe8 was the lesser evil.

19.♘xd5 ♗xd5 20.♖xd5 dxe5

If 20...0-0, then 21.♘d7 ♖fe8 22.♕xe7! (22...♖xe7 23.♘f6+)

21.♖xe5 0-0 22.♖xe7

The rest is simple.

Editor's note: If we study the final part of the game more closely, it turns out that black still had good chances of saving the game.

22...♖ac8 23.♕e4 b5 24.♖e1 ♖cd8 25.c4! bxc4 26.♕xc4 ♕g6 27.♖a7 ♖fe8 28.♖xe8+ ♖xe8 29.g3 ♖e6 30.♔g2 ♖f6 31.♖a8+ ♔h7 32.♖d8!

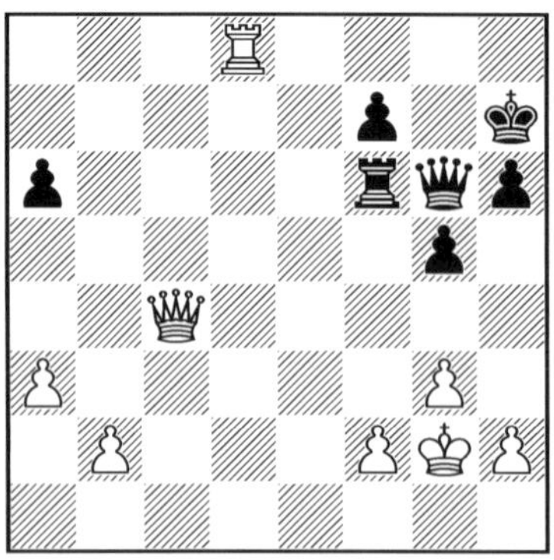

32...♖xf2+

Walking straight into a trap. After widescale simplifications, white gets a won pawn endgame.

33.♔xf2 ♕f6+ 34.♔e3 ♕xd8 35.♕d3+! ♕xd3+ 36.♔xd3 ♔g6 37.♔e4 ♔f6 38.g4 ♔e6 39.b4 h5 40.gxh5 f5+ 41.♔d4 ♔f6 42.a4 g4 43.b5 Black resigned.

Losing just half a point in the last four rounds, Tal shared 5th–6th place and again earned the right to play among the strongest in the 24th Soviet championship final.

Before I start the story about the 24th Soviet championship, I'd like to say a few words about the so-called psychological method of struggle.

It's no secret that the individual approach to opponents – i.e. studying the particular features of their playing style, creative tastes and inclinations, and using that knowledge in games – has brought Tal many valuable points. The main feature of this method, which is not exactly new in chess, is the ability to impose unfamiliar, unpleasant playing conditions on the opponent. For instance, an opening they don't like to play or a position that doesn't meet their tastes and chess temperament.

"War is war!" Let the opponent struggle against the unfamiliar conditions!

In the first round of the 24th

Soviet championship, Tal was due to play the Leningrad master Lev Aronson. After studying his games, we figured out that the Leningrad player preferred quiet maneuvering and tended to simplify the position. And so we decided to play for complications.

No. 20, Dutch Defense
L. Aronson – M. Tal
1957, Moscow, 24th Soviet Championship Final, round 1

1.d4 e6 2.c4 f5 3.♘f3 ♘f6 4.♘c3 ♗e7 5.g3 0-0 6.♗g2 d6 7.0-0 ♕e8

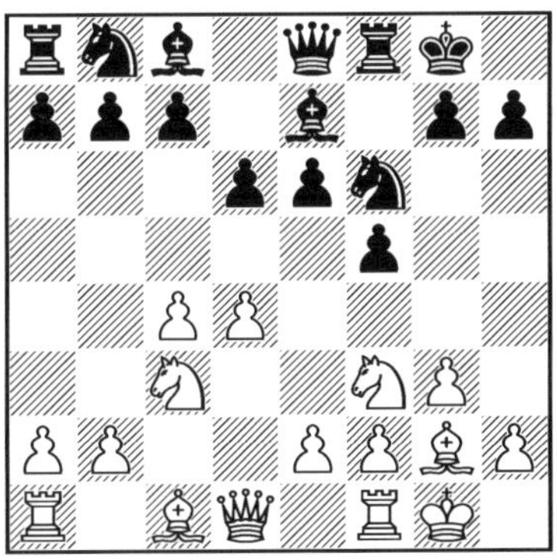

8.♖e1

Editor's note: An important alternative is 8.b3, intending to develop the bishop to a3 after ♕e8-g6 or ♕e8-h5, seriously hindering the standard pawn push e6-e5.

8...♕g6 9.e4 fxe4 10.♘xe4 ♘xe4 11.♖xe4 ♘c6

Avoiding the trap 11...♕xe4? 12.♘h4!

12.♕e2 ♗f6 13.♗d2 e5 14.dxe5 dxe5

Of course, Tal could just capture on e5 with his knight. That was more solid, but after 14...♘xe5 15.♗c3, the game would have quickly ended in a draw.

Editor's note: 14...♘xe5 is now usually met with 15.♘xe5 (instead of Koblenz's 15.♗c3) 15...♗xe5 16.♗c3!? ♗xc3 17.bxc3 – practice shows that, despite his compromised pawn structure, white has a small advantage because of his more active pieces and pressure along the long light-squared diagonal.

Black's last move is risky – the e5 pawn can become weak. However, black's 14th move was the turning point of the game. The weakness of the e5 pawn is rather relative. The main factor is that Tal managed to complicate the game, which probably didn't feature in his opponent's plans.

Now Aronson thinks he's obliged to play for a win.

15.♗c3 ♗f5 16.♘h4 ♗xh4 17.♖xh4 ♖ae8 18.♕e3 h6 19.b4 ♕f6 20.b5 ♘d8 21.♗d5+

The beginning of an erroneous plan. Had Aronson kept his cool, he would have no doubt found the prosaic move 21.c5 with the subsequent 22.♖a4.

21...♔h8

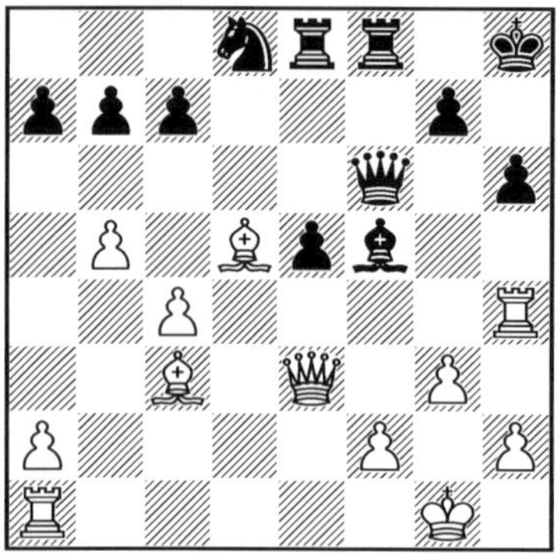

This is stronger than 21...♔h7 22.♗e4, with simplifications that are advantageous for white.

Editor's note: Instead of the simplifying 22.♗e4, white had a more unpleasant move 22.♖e1, increasing the pressure on the e5 pawn. If now 22...g5, then 23.♖e4! ♗xe4 24.♕xe4+ ♔g7 (after *24...♕g6 25.♕e3* black's position is even harder) 25.♗xe5 ♖xe5 26.♕xe5, with an extra pawn in the endgame.

22.f4?

White thinks that the position is already ripe to play for a win. 22.c5 was best. After 22...c6, there was a complicated position with mutual chances.

Editor's note: After a long think, the computer prefers the move 22.♖e1 with the main line 22...g5 23.♖e4 ♗xe4 24.♗xe4 b6 25.♗g2 ♘f7 26.♗d5 — it thinks that white's compensation (the bishop pair and pressure on the e5 pawn) is more than adequate. Another good alternative is 22.♖d1 – for instance, 22...c6 23.♗g2 g5 24.♖hd4! exd4 25.♗xd4 ♖xe3 26.♗xf6+ ♖xf6 27.♖xd8+ ♔g7 28.fxe3 with an extra pawn in the endgame. But even after Koblenz's 22.c5 c6, white is still somewhat better after the subsequent 23.bxc6 ♘xc6 (or *23...bxc6 24.♗g2*) 24.f4 because of the two bishops.

22...exf4 23.♕d2

Editor's note: After 23.♗xf6 fxe3 24.♖xh6+ ♗h7 25.♗c3 c6 26.bxc6 bxc6 27.♗g2 the position is dynamically equal – white's bishop pair is compensated by black's active rooks and the passed e3 pawn.

23...♕b6+

With this unexpected check, Tal makes the white bishop lose control over the e1 square, which will be important later. The initiative is in black's hands already!

24.♗d4

Editor's note: 24.♕d4 is more solid, with a roughly equal position – for instance, after 24...♕g6 25.♕xf4 (threatening to capture on h6) 25...♔h7 26.♗b4 ♖f6 27.♗c3 ♖ff8 28.♗b4 ♖f6, the game ends in a threefold repetition.

24...♕g6 25.♕xf4 ♔h7 26.♕xc7

Editor's note: This is an error – the queen gets too far away from the king. 26.♕d2 was the correct move.

26...♗b1! (isolating the opponent's rook) **27.♗e5**

Editor's note: White still had some chances after 27.♖f4 ♖e1+ 28.♔f2 ♖fe8 29.♕xg7+ ♕xg7 30.♗xg7 ♔xg7 31.♗f3 – black has a piece for two pawns, but it's not easy to get out of the pin along the first rank.

27...♘e6! 28.♕d6 ♕f5 29.♗f4 ♘g5

29...g5 was also possible, but Tal decided not to weaken his king's position in time trouble.

30.♕b4 ♗e4 31.♗xe4 ♖xe4 32.♖f1 ♖e2 33.♕d6

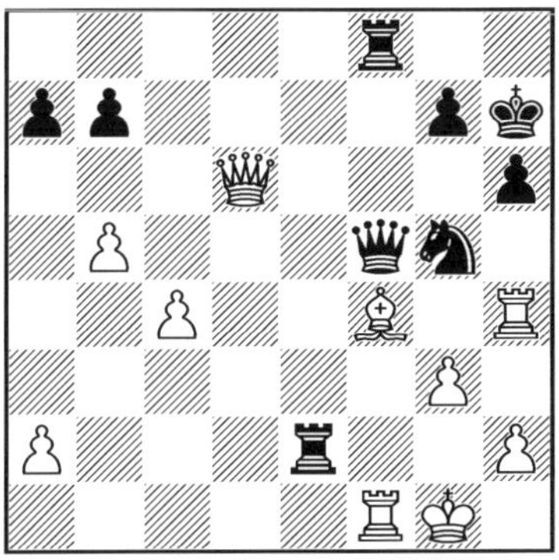

33...♖xa2!

Of course, 33...♘h3+? was bad due to 34.♖xh3 ♕xh3 35.♕d3+.

34.♕d5 ♕c2 35.c5 ♖d8! 36.♗d6 ♖e8 White resigned, as the threat 37...♖e1 cannot be stopped.

Tal's victory over Taimanov in the second round wasn't convincing. The Leningrad grandmaster got an undeniable advantage in the opening. Tal only won because of a simple tactical blow overlooked by his opponent.

In the next round, Tal faced David Bronstein, whose games he'd always admired. He couldn't wait for the game to begin.

No. 21, Grunfeld Defense
M. Tal – D. Bronstein
1957, Moscow, 24th Soviet Championship Final, round 3

1.d4 c6 2.c4 ♘f6 3.♘c3 d5 4.♘f3 g6 5.cxd5

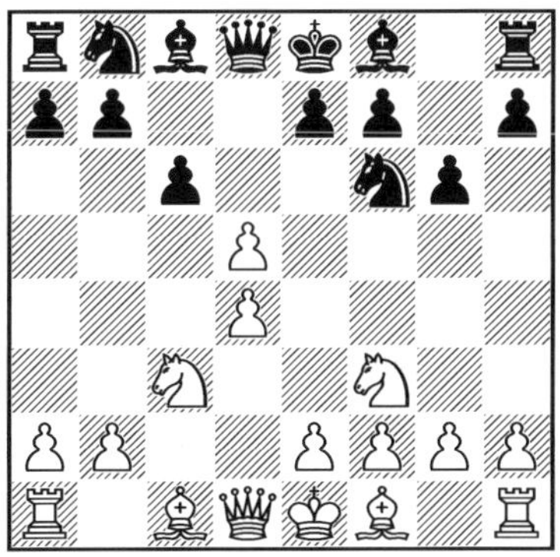

The strongest move; after 5... cxd5, black has no c-pawn anymore and so can't bring his dark-squared bishop to life with c6-c5. Bronstein, of course, knew that white would be better, and acted out of psychological considerations: the game would be simplified, and his opponent would lose the opportunity to go for tactical complications which he normally pursued.

So, Bronstein thought that the

subsequent position would not be to Tal's taste.

5...cxd5 6.♗f4 ♘c6 7.e3 ♗g7 8.♗e2 0-0 9.0-0

9.h3, preventing the trade of the dark-squared bishop, was worth considering.

Editor's note: Koblenz's proposed move 9.h3, which provides the h2 square for the dark-squared bishop and prevents ♗g4, leads to one of the main positions in this line. Even more often, white plays h2-h3 a move earlier and then develops the f1 bishop to e2 (like in this game) or d3 (which leads to another main position).

9...♘h5 10.♗e5

Editor's note: 10.♗g5 h6 11.♗h4 g5 12.♘d2!?, as played in Ruzele – Mozeris (Plateliai 2001) and Ernst – Appel (Germany BL 2014), was perhaps even more promising.

10...f6 11.♗g3 ♘xg3 12.hxg3 ♗e6 13.♕b3!

White has to play actively, otherwise black will seize the initiative with ♗f7 and e7-e5.

13...♘a5 14.♕b4 ♗f7 15.♖fd1

This prophylactic move is necessary. Black can't play 15...e5 now due to 16.dxe5 fxe5 17.♘xd5! ♗xd5 18.e4.

15...e6 16.e4! ♖b8 17.♕a3 b5

The grandmaster spent 40 minutes thinking on this move!

18.b4 ♘c4 19.♕xa7

When white grabbed the a7 pawn, Bronstein shook his head in surprise: if a grandmaster offers a sacrifice after a long think, he has obviously calculated everything very well. But Tal wasn't inclined to believe anybody at face value!

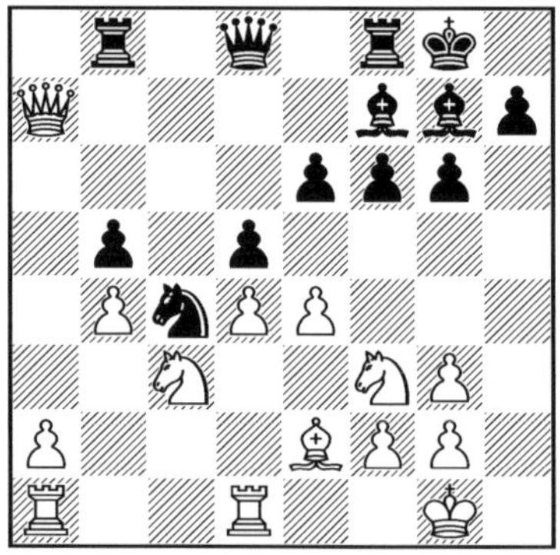

19...♗e8

Editor's note: The game move doesn't give black enough compensation for the pawn; meanwhile, after 19...♖a8 20.♕c5 *(20.♕b7?? ♘d6 21.♕c6 ♖c8–+)* 20...♖c8 21.♕xb5 ♘b2 22.♖dc1 ♗h6 23.exd5 ♗xc1 24.♖xc1 exd5, there was a complicated position evaluated as equal by the computer. 19...♖e8!? was also interesting, with the ideas of ♖e8-e7 and ♗g7-f8.

20.♗xc4 ♖f7

Following the game, Tal said that after 20...♖a8 21.♕c5 ♖c8, he was going to sacrifice the queen with 22.♗b3!? (**Editor's note:** 22.♗xd5! ♖xc5 23.♗xe6+ ♔h8 24.dxc5+– is much stronger), while if 21...♖f7, he intended to play 22.exd5!

21.♕a3

Tal breathed a sigh of relief: the white queen has come back home.

21...bxc4 22.exd5 exd5 23.♕b2 g5!

There are new unexpected threats: black is getting ready to launch a kingside attack with 24...g4 and f6-f5-f4.

24.♕d2! ♖xb4

Now the above plan would not work, because after 24...g4 25.♘e1 f5, white would play 26.♘e2. (**Editor's note:** Black has an unpleasant reply 26...♗a4, and the bishop makes itself useful, blocking the a2 passed pawn. 26.♘c2 was stronger, intending a2-a4 – the move 26...♕d6 with the ideas f5-f4 and ♗g7-h6 is not dangerous for white because of 27.♕f4.)

25.♘xd5 ♖b8 26.♘e3 ♖c8 27.♖ac1 ♖fc7 28.♖c3 ♗g6 29.♖dc1 ♗f7 30.d5 ♗f8 31.a3 ♗c5 32.♖xc4

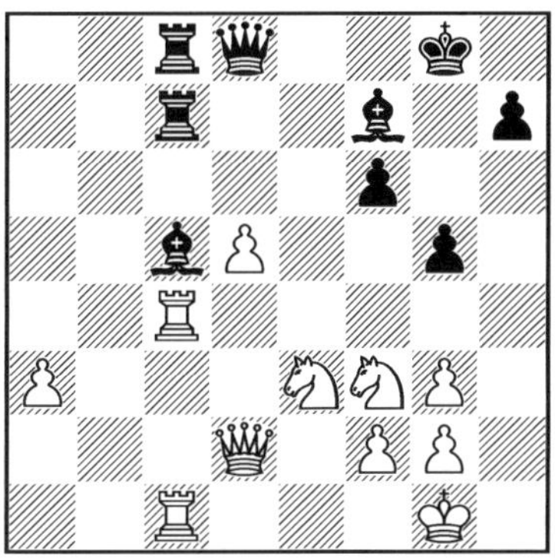

The technical stage of the game begins – white converts his material advantage.

32...♗xa3

If 32...♗xe3, then, of course, 33.♖xc7

33.♖xc7 ♖xc7 34.♖xc7 ♕xc7 35.♕d4 ♕c1+ 36.♔h2 ♕b2 37.♕e4 ♗f8 38.♘d4 h5 39.♘dc2 ♕b7 40.♘d4 ♕b2

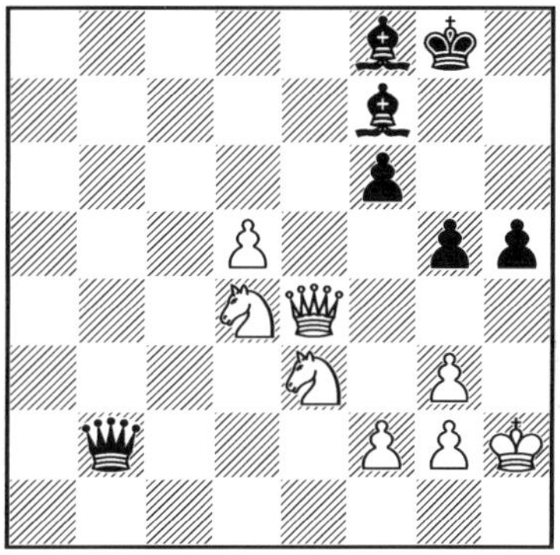

41.♘e6! (the sealed move) **41...♕xf2.**

If 41...♕e5, then 42.♕c4! or 41...♕b4 42.♕f3!

42.♘f5 h4 43.♘xf8 hxg3+ 44.♔h3 ♕g1 45.♔xg3 ♔xf8 46.♕e7+ Black resigned.

The games against Keres and Petrosian were played in an impeccable positional style by Tal – he beat the grandmasters with their own weapon.

The game Keres – Tal was played in round 16, when the tournament atmosphere was very heated. Keres led the tournament with 10 points. Tal, Bronstein and Tolush were half a point behind.

No. 22, Anti-Nimzo-Indian
P. Keres – M. Tal
1957, Moscow, 24th Soviet Championship Final, round 16

1.d4 ♘f6 2.c4 e6 3.♘f3 c5 4.e3

Keres avoids the double-edged 4.d5 and chooses a quiet development plan.

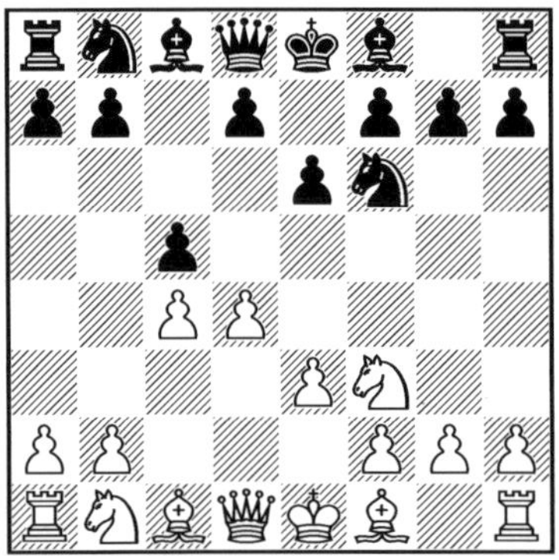

4...d5 5.a3 cxd4 6.exd4 ♗e7 7.♘c3 0-0 8.♗f4

Editor's note: A rare continuation. The main line is 8.♗d3.

8...♘c6

Editor's note: In the game Mamedyarov – Adams (Bilbao 2013), black instead played 8... b6 9.♗d3 dxc4 10.♗xc4 ♗a6 11.♗xa6 ♘xa6 12.♖c1 ♘c7 13.0-0 ♘cd5 14.♘xd5 ♘xd5 15.♗g3 ♕d7 16.♘e5 ♕b7, and the game soon ended in a draw without any problems for black.

9.♖c1

Editor's note: After 9.c5?! ♘e4 10.♕c2 g5 11.♗e3 f5 12.h3 ♗f6, black had the initiative (Grigoryan – Fridman, Kallithea 2008).

9...♘e4 10.♗d3 ♘xc3 11.♖xc3 dxc4 12.♖xc4

After 12.♗xc4 ♗f6 13.♖d3 ♕b6 black is in no trouble.

12...♕a5+ 13.♗d2

Keres is still playing quite quietly. However, this does not mean that he's playing for a draw. In that case, he would've played 13.♕d2, offering to exchange queens.

13...♕d5 14.♕c2 f5!

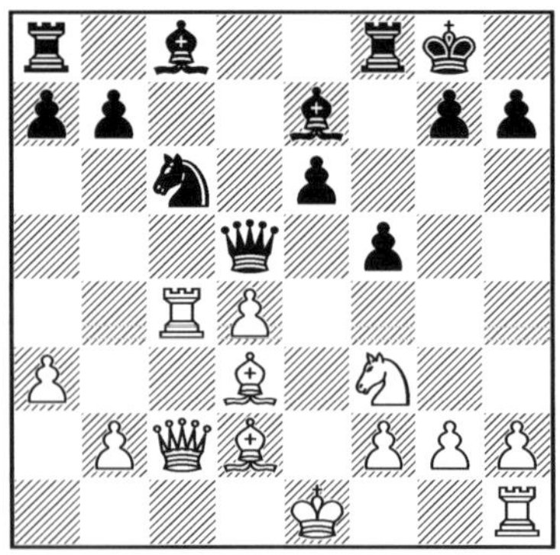

Black bolsters his queen's position in the center, not fearing potentially weakening the e-pawn.

15.0-0 ♗d7 16.♖d1

Editor's note: In the game Mishuchkov – Sakaev (St. Petersburg 1997) there followed 16.♖c1 ♖ac8=.

16...♖ac8

Winning the d4 pawn would have cost black too much: 16...b5 17.Rc3 Nxd4 18.Nxd4 Qxd4 19.Be3 Qf6 20.Bxf5!

Editor's note: Actually, Koblenz's line is not dangerous for black: after the subsequent 20...Qxf5 21.Rxd7 Rad8 22.Qxf5 exf5 23.Rcc7 Bf6, there's a drawn endgame on the board. However, instead of 19.Be3?, white has a much stronger move 19.Be2! – despite the lack of a pawn, white has a big advantage because of the great positioning of his major pieces and active bishops.

17.Be3 Na5! 18.Rxc8 Rxc8 19.Qe2 Bd6 20.Ne5

A pointless sacrifice. (**Editor's note:** Koblenz probably meant that Keres was already intending to transition to an opposite-colored bishop endgame, giving up a pawn in the process.) After 20.Rc1 Rxc1+ 21.Bxc1, white was not under any threat.

20...Ba4 21.Re1 Bxe5 22.dxe5 Rd8 23.b4

Editor's note: The resulting endgame turned out to be very difficult for white. He had to play 23.Bc2 Bxc2 24.Qxc2

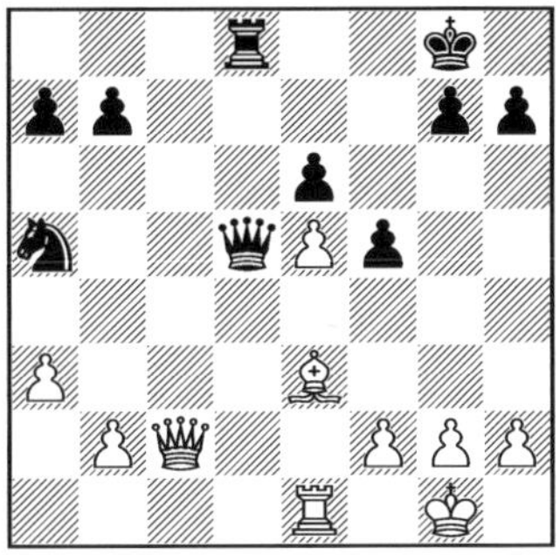

After 24...Qxe5 25.f4 Qb8 26.Bd2 Nc6 27.Qc4 Nd4 28.Be3 Qd6 29.Bxd4 Qxd4+ 30.Qxd4 Rxd4 31.Rxe6, there's a rook ending that he can easily hold – 31...Kf7 *(31...Rxf4 32.Re7=)* 32.Re5 Kf6 *(32...Rxf4 33.Rc5=)* 33.g3 with a draw.

Instead of 24...Qxe5, black had a stronger continuation 24...Nc6 25.f4 a6 with a positional advantage, but white still had more chances to hold than in the actual game.

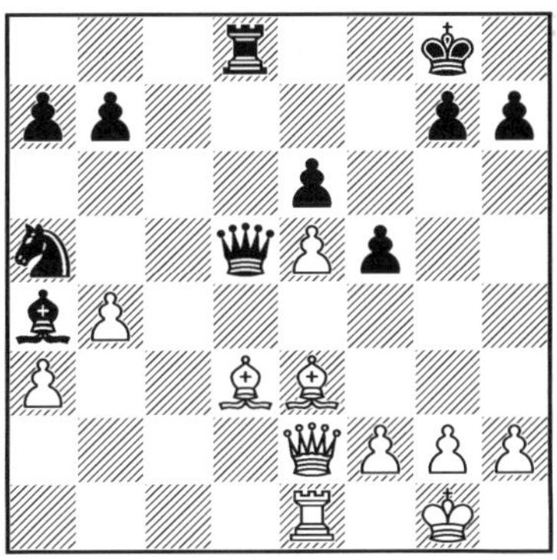

23...Bc6! 24.f3 Qxd3 25.Qxd3 Rxd3 26.bxa5 Rxa3 27.Bxa7 Rxa5

Black is a pawn up, but this advantage is quite difficult to convert because of the opposite-colored bishops.

28.♗d4 ♖a2 29.♖b1 ♖d2 30.♗c3 ♖c2 31.♗d4 ♔f7 32.h4

A new weakness. However, 32.h3 wasn't much better.

32...♔g6 33.♖b4 h6!

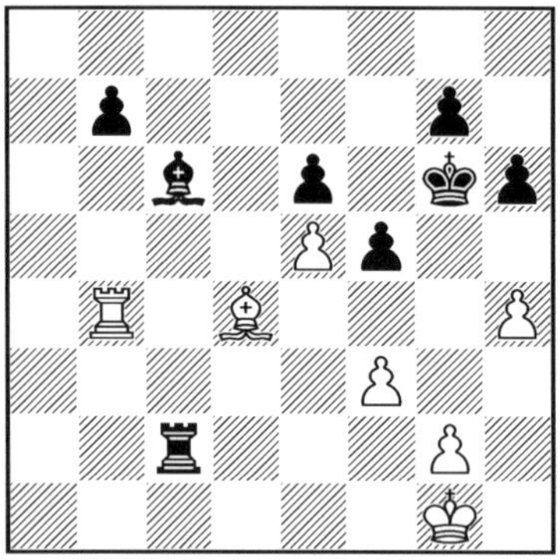

White is in time trouble, and Tal provokes his opponent's next moves, so that after 37.♗f8 the black pawns are vulnerable.

34.♖b2 ♖xb2 35.♗xb2 ♔h5 36.♗a3 ♔xh4! 37.♗f8 ♔g3 38.♗xg7 h5 39.♗h6 ♗xf3!

An elegant bishop sacrifice that quickly decides the game.

40.gxf3 ♔xf3 41.♔f1 b5 42.♗d2 h4 43.♗b4 h3 44.♔g1 ♔e2 White resigned.

No. 23, French Defense
M. Tal – T. Petrosian
1957, Moscow, 24th Soviet Championship Final, round 13

1.e4 e6 2.d4 d5 3.♘c3 ♗b4 4.e5 c5 5.a3 ♗xc3+ 6.bxc3 ♘e7 7.♕g4

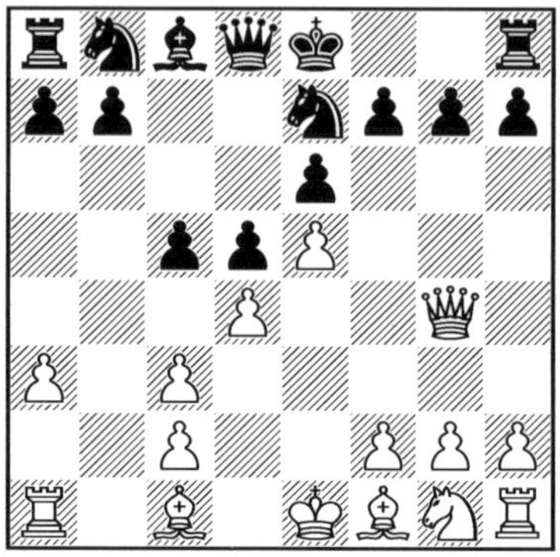

7...♘f5

Editor's note: From the point of view of modern theory, the main moves here are 7...0-0 and 7...♕c7.

8.♗d3 h5 9.♕h3

Editor's note: In subsequent tournament practice, this move has occurred only rarely at grandmaster level. The main line is 9.♕f4.

9...cxd4 10.♘f3 ♘c6 11.g4 ♘fe7 12.gxh5

Editor's note: 12.cxd4 has also occurred, after which 12...♕a5+ looks good, for instance, 13.♗d2 ♕a4 14.c3 b6 15.♘g5 ♗a6, and black has no complaints (Lettieri – Navaratham, Paracin 2019). Another possible continuation is 12...♕c7 13.♗d2 ♗d7 (intending 0-0-0 and f7-f6) with mutual chances (Dorawa – Uhlmann, Schkopau 1958 and O. Jacobsen – Bagirov, Helsinki 1961).

12...♕c7 13.♗f4 ♘g6 14.♕g4 ♘xf4

A serious mistake. Black should have played 14...♘gxe5 15.♘xe5 ♘xe5 16.♕xg7 ♘f3+ 17.♔f1 ♕xf4 18.♕xh8+ ♔e7 with a sharp, hard-to-evaluate position.

Editor's note: Actually, the game move is not bad at all.

15.♕xf4 dxc3

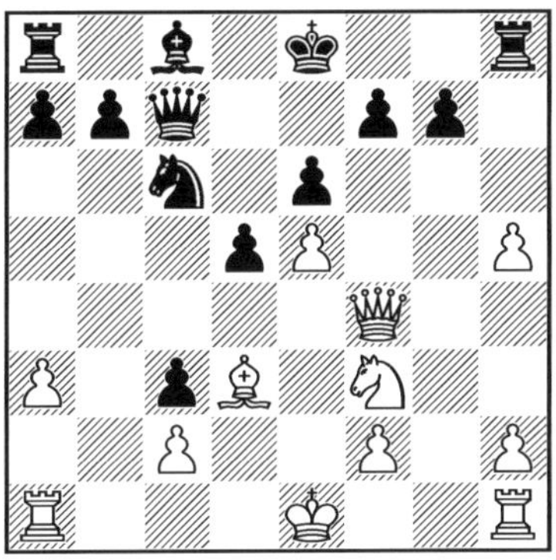

16.♕g5!

Editor's note: 16.♖g1!? is worth considering; black would meet it with 16...f6 or 16...f5 with unclear play.

16...♕e7 17.♕xg7 ♕f8

Editor's note: 17...♖xh5!? looks interesting, as played in a correspondence game Hugentobler – Dambrauskas, ICCF 1999. There followed 18.♖g1 ♕f8 19.♕f6 ♖h6 20.♕f4 ♗d7 21.♘g5 0-0-0 22.♘xf7 ♘xe5 23.♕xe5 ♕xf7 24.♕xc3+ ♔b8, and black is no worse.

18.♕g5 ♕h6

The white queen cannot be allowed to occupy such a strong position.

Editor's note: 18...♖h6 was a stronger move, with the threat 19... ♕h8. For instance, 19.♖g1 ♕h8 20.♕g8+ ♕xg8 21.♖xg8+ ♔e7 22.♖g5 ♗d7 with roughly equal chances.

19.♖g1 ♕xg5

19...♕xh5 would have been met with 20.♕f6!

20.♖xg5 ♗d7

Editor's note: Black should have first played 20...♔e7. Now, white could put his opponent in a very precarious situation after 21.h6!

21.♔e2 ♔e7 22.♔e3 ♖af8 23.♖ag1 ♗e8

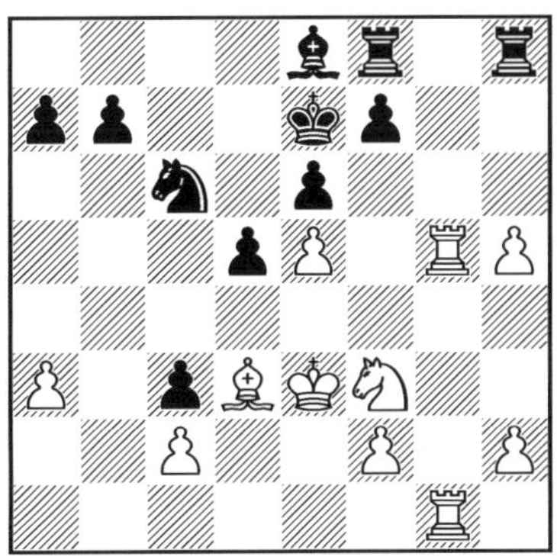

24.♘d4 f5

Black could've put up better resistance after 24...f6.

Editor's note: Actually, the game move is the decisive mistake, whereas after Koblenz's move 24... f6, black doesn't just "put up better resistance" – he shouldn't lose at all, for instance: 25.♖g7+ ♗f7 26.♘xc6+ bxc6 27.f4 ♖xh5 28.♗g6 ♖h3+ *(28...♖xh2?? 29.♖b1+−)* 29.♔d4 ♖h4 30.♔e3 ♖h3+ with threefold repetition.

25.♘xc6+ ♗xc6

Editor's note: Black can't hold after 25...bxc6 either: 26.♖b1! ♖fg8 (any capture on h5 loses to *27.♖b7+* with the subsequent *28.♖gg7*) 27.♖xg8 ♖xg8 28.♔d4, then getting the king to d6 after ♖b1-b7+.

26.♔d4 f4 27.♖g7+ ♖f7 28.♖g8 ♖xg8 29.♖xg8 ♖f8 30.♖xf8 ♔xf8 31.h6 b6 32.♔xc3 ♔g8 33.♗g6 a5 34.♔d4 ♔f8 35.c3 ♔g8 36.h7+ ♔g7 37.♗f7 ♗d7 38.♗g8

Black's position is hopeless, and the **grandmaster resigned** on move 51.

The sixth-round game was truly breathtaking.

This is a position from the game Nezhmetdinov – Tal. At that moment, Tal led the tournament.

No. 24
R. Nezhmetdinov – M. Tal
1957, Moscow, 24th Soviet Championship Final, round 6

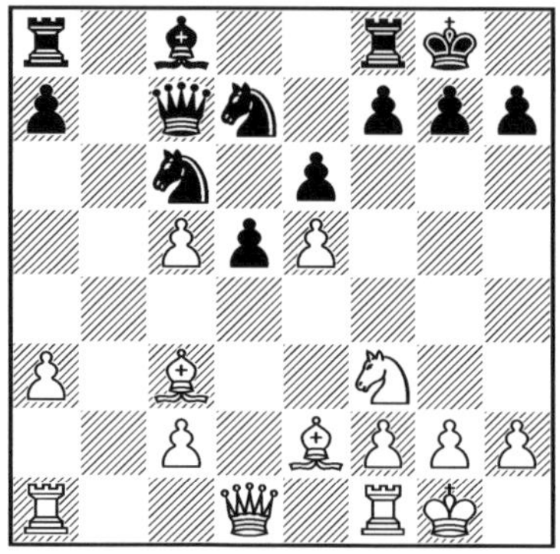

13...♘cxe5

This leads to great complications. It was impossible to fully calculate the numerous lines. Tal saw that after 13...♘xc5 14.♗d3 ♘e4! 15.♕e1 ♗b7 white couldn't capture the pawn due to 16.♗xe4 dxe4 17.♕xe4 ♘e7, and black is better. However, instead of 16.♗xe4, white could've played 16.♗b2, and Tal didn't see how to improve black's position after that.

Editor's note: After 16.♗b2, black could get a comfortable position, for instance, with 16...a5, intending ♗b7-a6

Tal created a pawn center, hoping to make it dynamic afterwards.

14.♘xe5 ♘xe5 15.♕d4 f6 16.f4 ♘c6 17.♕e3 ♖d8 18.♖ad1 e5

Editor's note: This active move leads to big trouble. Black should've made some waiting, neutral move, such as 18...♖b8.

19.fxe5 fxe5

Tal executed his strategic idea: he has created a dynamic pawn center. However, the continuation shows that it didn't bring black anything good.

20.♗b5! ♗b7

After 20...d4 21.♗c4+ ♔h8 22.♕g5! white had an attack.

Editor's note: Instead of 21.♗c4+, white had an even stronger continuation: 21.♕e4 ♗b7 *(21...dxc3 22.♕xc6+−)* 22.♗d3 g6 23.♗c4+ ♔h8 24.♖f7 ♖d7 25.♖df1 dxc3 26.♕h4+−, so black shouldn't have played 20...d4 in any case.

21.♕g3!

Editor's note: This move is actually not so good, because black could now play 21...♕e7!, getting good chances to hold the position after 22.♗xc6 ♕xc5+ 23.♖f2 ♕xc6 24.♗xe5 ♕d7 (the pawn sacrifice *24...d4!?*, activating the pieces, also deserves consideration). So, a stronger move was 21.♕g5 with a big advantage (in this case, 21...♕e7 doesn't work due to the obvious 22.♕xe7 ♘xe7 23.♗xe5+−).

21...♖d7

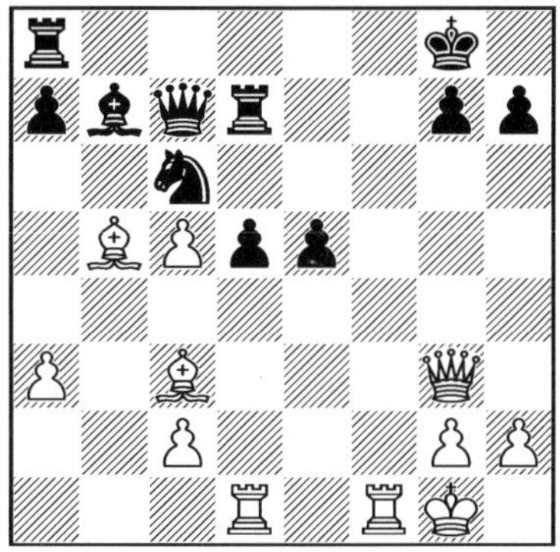

22.♖f2!

A strong move. White uses the f-file to his advantage. Also, the aggressive push of the d-pawn is now impossible. For instance, 22... d4 23.♗c4+ ♔h8 24.♖df1!, with pressure along the f-file.

22...♖e8 23.h3 ♗a8

23...d4 still doesn't work due to 24.♗c4+.

24.♗a4 ♗b7 25.♔h1 ♗a8 26.♖f5

White goes for an all-out offensive.

26...e4

There was no defense against the threat of 27.♗xc6 and ♖xe5.

27.♕xc7 ♖xc7 28.♖fxd5 e3 29.♖d7 e2 30.♗b3+ ♖e6 31.♗xe6+ ♔f8 32.♗xg7+ Black resigned.

The game with Nezhmetdinov further convinced Tal that chess principles have only a relative value. Why did black's plan to create a strong center end in failure? Here's how Tal himself explained the reason for his loss:

"The evaluation of any position is like scales. One of the heaviest weights, a dynamic pawn center, in this case ended up being lighter than the open f-file and the coordination between two white bishops and the queen."

This comparison helps to reveal the essence of Tal's creative method: he often allows his opponent to get a tangible positional advantage, but doesn't forget about his own "weights" either, always achieving some kind of trade-off. In the Nezhmetdinov game, Tal's "weight" was too light. Well, that happens.

I must admit that, the next day, I was somewhat worried: how would the loss affect my ward? But as soon as I saw Tal, my anxiety was gone. He was cheerful and happy, because his loss was deserved!

We discussed how to play against Antoshin and then went for a walk.

"Time goes so slowly," Tal said nervously. "I already want to start the game!"

In this game, Tal's play was very dynamic. Everything seemed to go well, but then the Riga master made an inexplicable mistake.

Here's the game.

No. 25, Ruy Lopez
M. Tal – V. Antoshin
1957, Moscow, 24th Soviet Championship Final, round 7

1.e4 e5 2.♘f3 ♘c6 3.♗b5 a6 4.♗a4 ♘f6 5.0-0 ♗e7 6.♖e1 b5 7.♗b3 d6 8.c3 0-0 9.h3 ♘d7

Editor's note: Currently, black most often plays 9...♘a5, 9...♗b7 or 9...♘b8.

10.d4 ♘b6

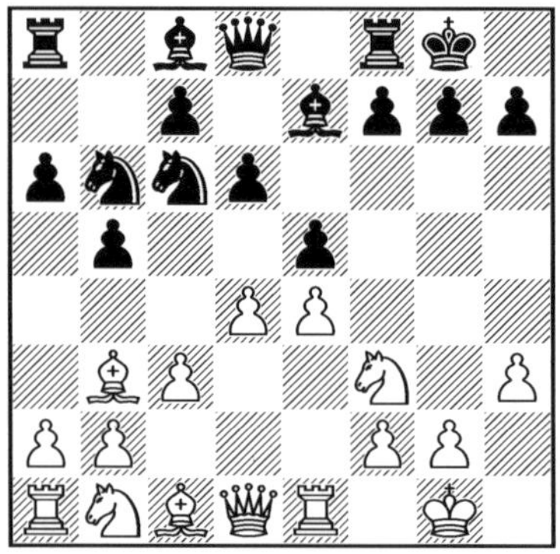

11.♗e3

Editor's note: In this position, the main line is 11.♘bd2 with the ideas ♘d2-f1-g3(-f5) or ♘d2-f1-h2-g4.

11...exd4

Theory prefers 11...♖b8.

Editor's note: The move 11...♖b8 counters dxe5 with the subsequent ♗xb6 – now black can simply take on b6 with the rook, avoiding doubled pawns. Also, in such positions white often tries to play a2-a4, which may lead to the opening of the b-file, and the rook on b8 may be useful in this case as well.

12.cxd4 d5 13.♘c3 dxe4 14.♘xe4 ♗f5 15.d5 ♘a5

A serious mistake. With 15...♗xe4 16.♗xb6 ♗xf3 17.♕xf3 ♘e5!, black could still resist. (**Editor's note:** After the subsequent 18.♖xe5 cxb6, the position is almost completely drawn: there are opposite-colored bishops on the board, white has no attacking chances, and his passed pawn can't move further.)

16.d6 cxd6

If 16...♗xd6, then, of course, 17.♗xb6. After 16...♗xe4, there's 17.dxe7 ♕xe7 18.♗xb6 cxb6 19.♘d2, winning a piece.

17.♗xb6 ♕xb6 18.♘g3 ♗e6 19.♗xe6 fxe6 20.♖xe6 ♗f6

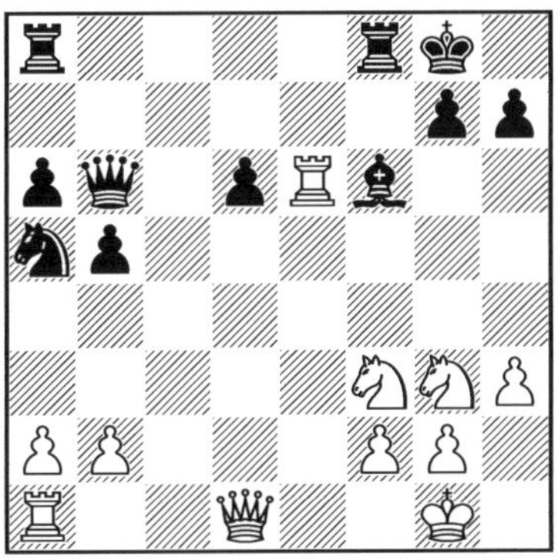

Black decides to part with the weak d-pawn and put pressure on the b2 pawn.

21.♖xd6 ♕b8 22.♘h5!

The signal to attack!

22...♗xb2 23.♖b1 ♘c4 24.♖d7 ♖a7 25.♖xb2!

Eliminating the guardian of the g7 square!

25...♘xb2 26.♕d5+ ♔h8 27.♕d4 ♖xd7 28.♕xd7 ♖g8 29.♘g5 h6 30.♘f7+ ♔h7

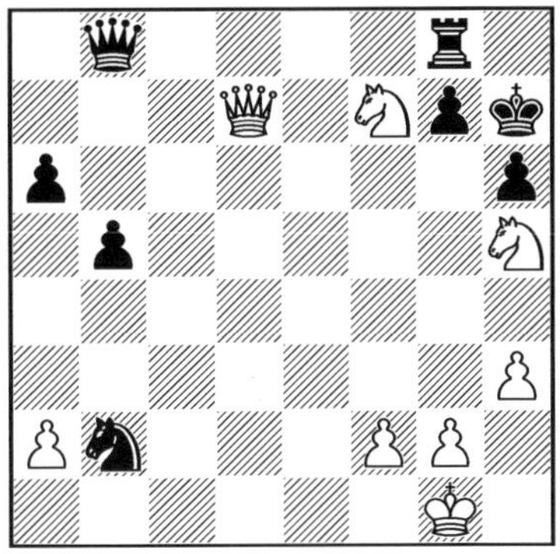

There were, as always, lots of masters and journalists in the press center. The door suddenly opened, grandmaster Geller briskly walked in, and said, "Tal has a beautiful forced win!"

And he quickly showed the line: 31.♕f5+ g6 32.♕d7 gxh5 33.♘g5+ ♔g6 34.♕e6+ ♔xg5 35.g3, and black has to resign, because after 35...h4, he gets checkmated: 36.f4+ ♔h5 37.♕f5+ ♖g5 38.g4#.

"A spectacular finish! Let's go to the hall, there'll probably be applause," said master Evgeny Zagoryansky, the press center administrator.

We went to the box seats; several grandmasters and journalists were already there.

Time went by, however, and Tal still continued to think, leaning close to the board. Almost quarter of an hour passed.

"Why is Tal thinking for so long, doesn't he see the win?" Salomon Flohr asked.

"He doesn't," Igor Bondarevsky replied.

"You really think that Tal doesn't see it?" grandmaster Andor Lilienthal argued.

However, Tal was still feverishly calculating the lines, and his opponent walked about the stage, feigning indifference. The minutes seemed endless to me. Finally, there was a flurry of whispers in the hall: the spectators also noticed the winning line.

Almost an hour passed. Finally, Tal raised his hand to make a move, and the whole hall held their breaths.

But what happened? There was no applause. The spectators groaned in disappointment.

31.h4?

How could Tal miss a simple mating combination?

"I saw it, but I thought that it wouldn't work," Tal explained afterwards. "I thought that the pawn was on g2, rather than g3, and so, g2-g4 was not a checkmate, because the opponent had 38...hxg3."

In the actual game, there followed: **31...♕c8! 32.♘f6+ ♔g6 33.♘xg8 ♕xd7 34.♘e5+ ♔h7 35.♘xd7 ♔xg8 36.♘c5 a5 37.♔f1 ♘d1 38.♘e4 b4 39.♔e2 ♘b2 40.♔d2 a4**, and a **draw was agreed**.

I tried to console Tal, to take his mind off that game, but all my efforts were in vain: he was depressed, even though this setback didn't hurt his standings in the tournament – he still led after that draw. But the young master wasn't thinking about the lost half-point: he couldn't forgive himself for the mistake that tarnished the beauty of a creative idea. Like an artist, Tal was deeply hurt by the very thought that a work of art was corrupted.

The ill-fated seventh-round game had far-reaching repercussions. Tal was psychologically exhausted and played without inspiration; he agreed four pallid draws and then lost to Boleslavsky. Only after defeating Petrosian and Klaman did he manage to finally overcome the crisis.

"Do you want to know how Tal wins? It's very simple: he places the pieces in the center and then sacrifices them somewhere," Bronstein once said.

This joke did have a grain of truth in it. Tal usually prepares his combinations quite thoroughly.

No. 26
M. Tal – K. Klaman
1957, Moscow, 24th Soviet Championship Final, round 13

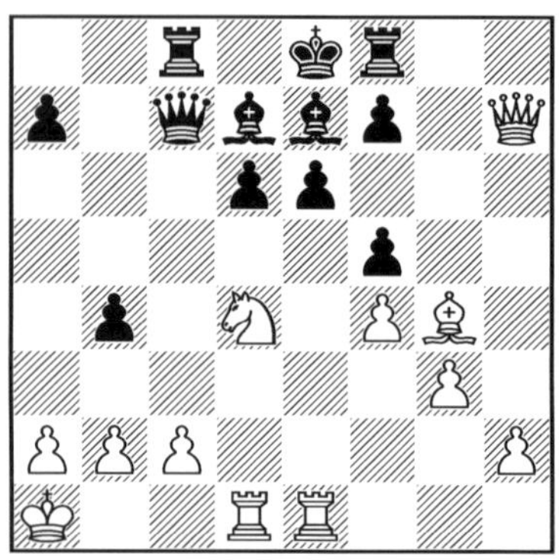

This is the position from the game Tal – Klaman, played in

round 13, right after the loss to Boleslavsky.[1]

The white pieces are positioned perfectly: the rooks and the knight are ready to land a decisive strike, and the queen has disorganized the defense. Black's pieces are positioned quite awkwardly, and the king is stuck in the center. A beautiful combination follows:

23.♗xf5!! exf5 24.♖xe7+ ♔xe7 25.♖e1+ ♔d8 26.♕h4+ f6 27.♕h6! ♕a5

The moves from 23 to 27 were made very quickly: both players obviously wanted to reach the same position.

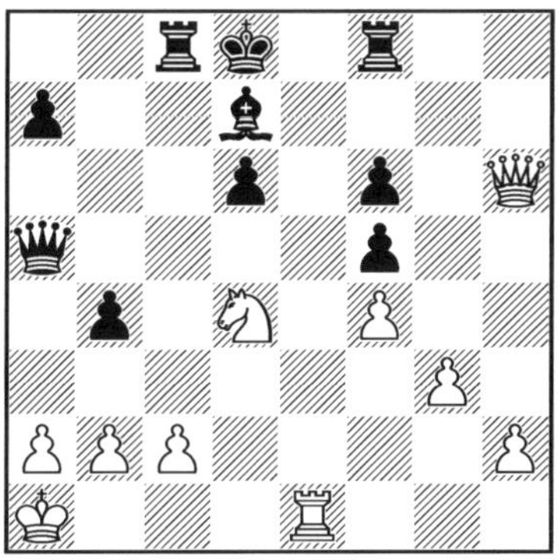

28.♘b3!

This Zwischenzug is the point of white's combination. Klaman expected the obvious-looking 28.♕xf8+ ♔c7, after which there's no 29.♕xf6 due to 29...b3! Now, however, black is quickly crushed.

28...♕d5 29.♕xf8+ ♔c7 30.♕xf6 ♖e8 31.♖c1 ♗a4 32.♕d4! ♕b7 33.♖d1 ♖e6 34.♕c4+ Black resigned (34...♔d7 35.♘c5+).

The game Tal – Aronin, from round 17, was called "the most interesting draw in the history of chess" by the ex-world champion Max Euwe.

No. 27

M. Tal – L. Aronin

1957, Moscow, 24th Soviet Championship Final, round 17

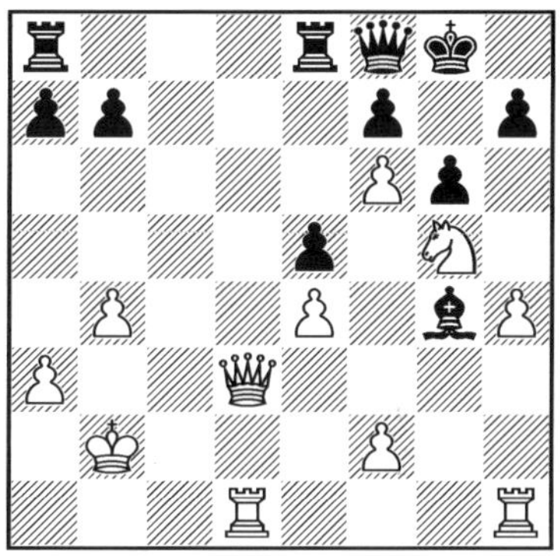

Here's the starting position of this captivating tactical struggle.

25.h5!

The only attacking resource. After the natural 25.f3, black avoided any danger with 25...♗h5. (**Editor's note:** In this case, white's position would be difficult because of the pawn's weakness and the king's compromised position. The game move leads to complicated tactical play and is best from the practical point of view, even though

[1] According to other sources this game was played in round 15

it still loses if the opponent plays perfectly.)

25...♖ad8

Editor's note: With 25...♖ed8!, Aronin could refute his opponent's plan and win. The point is, after 26.hxg6 ♖xd3 27.♖xd3, black plays 27...fxg6!, repelling the attack (the move 28.f7+ makes no sense if the rook isn't on e8) and retaining a decisive material advantage. 27.gxh7+ (instead of 27.♖xd3) doesn't help either: 27...♔h8 28.♖xd3 (hoping to create some serious threats along the g-file) – for instance, after 28...♕e8! (intending to activate the queen if possible) 29.♖g3 ♗e2! 30.♖hg1 ♗h5, there's no way for white to continue the attack.

26.hxg6! ♖xd3

26...hxg6 is bad because of 27.♕xd8 ♖xd8 28.♖xd8 ♕xd8 29.♖h8+ ♔xh8 30.♘xf7+ ♔g8 31.♘xd8 with a won endgame.

27.♖xd3

White gets only a rook for the queen, but the black king's precarious position allows him to create strong threats.

27...hxg6 28.♖h7!

Threatening 29.f3. If the bishop retreats to h5, there follows 30.♖d7, and if it goes to e6, the other rook can be transferred to the h-file through d2.

Aronin decides to eliminate the dangerous adversary, the f6 pawn, which leads to a draw by force.

28...♖c8! 29.f3 ♖c6! 30.♖xf7

30.fxg4 ♖xf6 31.♖dh3 was dangerous due to 31...♖f2+ and then ♕d6. (**Editor's note:** White is simply lost after that.)

30...♕xf7 31.♘xf7 ♔xf7 32.fxg4 ♔xf6 33.♖d7 ♖b6 34.♔c3 ♔g5 35.a4 a6 36.♔c4 ♔xg4

The opponents **agreed a draw** because of the unavoidable repetition: 37.♔c5 ♖c6+ 38.♔d5 ♖b6 39.♔c5 ♖c6+.

Before the last round, Bronstein, Tolush and Tal all led the tournament. Chess fans anxiously waited for the answer to their most important question: who's going to be the national champion?

"I'm glad to be playing Tolush! He's a true fighter, he won't avoid a sharp struggle," said Tal happily before the game.

On the way to the playing hall, he joked a lot and quoted from *The Twelve Chairs* extensively. (Analysis of this novel was later the topic of Tal's university degree dissertation.)

I walked silently and thought, "Such an important day for him, and he just jokes around!"

There were a lot of people at the entrance of the Rail Workers House of Culture. We somehow managed to squeeze into the building.

"This is a good sign!" Tal laughed

when he saw that almost all the buttons were torn from his coat.

No. 28, King's Indian Defense
M. Tal – A. Tolush
1957, Moscow, 24th Soviet Championship Final, round 21

1.c4 ♘f6 2.♘c3 g6 3.e4 d6 4.d4 ♗g7 5.f3 e5 6.♘ge2 ♘bd7

Editor's note: In modern times, strong players don't usually play this line for black. 6...0-0 is more flexible, not committing to any move of the ♘b8 just yet. However, black usually castles even one move earlier (5...0-0), getting maximum freedom in choosing the subsequent plans.

7.♗g5 c6 8.♕d2 0-0 9.d5

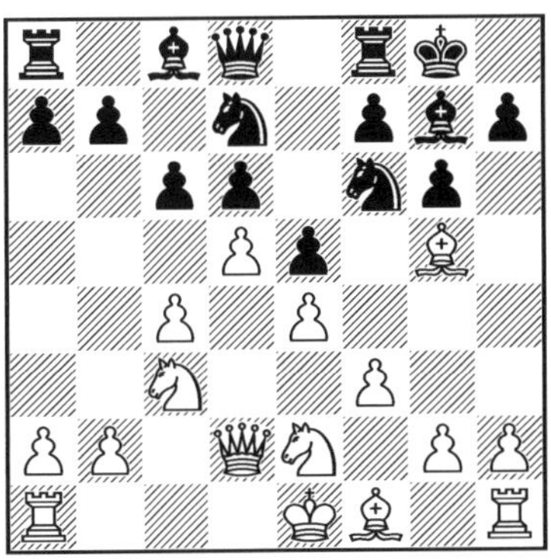

9...c5

Editor's note: This move is a big mistake that leads to a strategically lost game: by closing off the c-file, Tolush loses all chances of good counterplay and allows his opponent to fully concentrate on attacking the king. The correct move is 9... cxd5 10.cxd5 a6 or 9...h6 10.♗e3 *(10.♗xh6?! ♘xe4! 11.♘xe4 ♕h4+; 10.♗h4? ♘xe4!)* 10...cxd5 11.cxd5 a6, intending b7-b5 in both cases.

10.g4 a6 11.♘g3 ♖e8 12.h4 ♕a5

This foray is too hasty. Black should have first finished his development with 12...♘f8 and ♗d7.

13.♗h6 ♘f8 14.h5 ♕c7 15.♗d3 b5

Tolush launches a counter-attack. He hopes to create threats on the queenside after the pawn sacrifice.

16.0-0-0 b5xc4 17.♗b1!

After 17.♗xc4 ♗d7 and ♗b5, black gets counterplay. (**Editor's note:** Actually, after 17.♗xc4 ♗d7 18.♘f5!, white has a decisive attack, so black just has no time to get any counterplay. Instead of 17...♗d7, black has a stronger move 17...♗xh6 18.♕xh6 ♔h8 with the subsequent ♘f6-g8, even though his position is still very bad. However, it's possible that Tal already thought that the light-squared bishop would be more useful for him on the b1-h7 diagonal.)

17...♗h8

Editor's note: Here too, 17... ♗xh6 18.♕xh6 ♔h8, with the idea ♘f6-g8, was more resilient.

18.♖dg1

White's artillery takes up position.

18...♖b8 19.♘f5!

The cavalry goes on the attack.

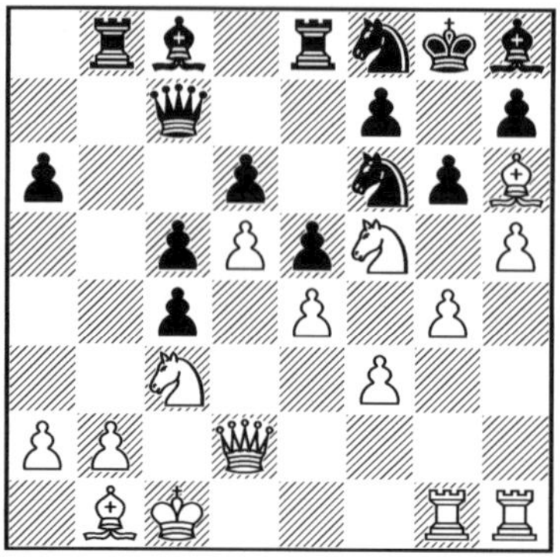

19...♘6d7

Black shouldn't accept the sacrifice: after 19...gxf5 20.gxf5+ ♘g6 21.hxg6 hxg6 22.fxg6 white opens lines for a decisive attack.

20.♗g5 ♗g7 21.♘xg7 ♔xg7 22.♗h6+ ♔g8

White already has a considerable positional advantage: the dark-squared bishop, an important defensive piece, has been eliminated, and the h-file is open for the attack. However, this advantage is not enough for a win in itself. With his next moves, white redeploys the necessary reserves to the kingside for a final blow.

23.f4!

To prevent the threat of 24.f5, black has to take the pawn.

23...exf4 24.♕xf4 ♕d8! 25.hxg6

25.♕xd6 was bad. After 25...♖b6 and 26...♘e5, black fortifies his position.

25...♘xg6 26.♕h2 ♘de5 27.♗f4

Editor's note: This move is a mistake that gives his opponent some chances to save the game. The strongest continuation was 27.♗d2! (not allowing the opponent to trade that bishop) 27...♘f8 28.♕h6, intending to get the knight to the kingside through d1 or e2. If necessary, the d2 bishop can move to c3, protecting the b2 pawn and immobilizing the e5 knight.

27...♘f8

As analysis subsequently showed, black could have put up more resistance with 27...♘xf4. After 28.♕xh7+ ♔f8 29.♕h6+ ♔e7 30.♕xf4 ♔d7, white has got nothing concrete, while after 28.♕xf4 he would have to continue the attack without the important dark-squared bishop.

28.♕h6 (threatening ♗f4-g5-f6) **28...♘eg6 29.♗g5 f6**

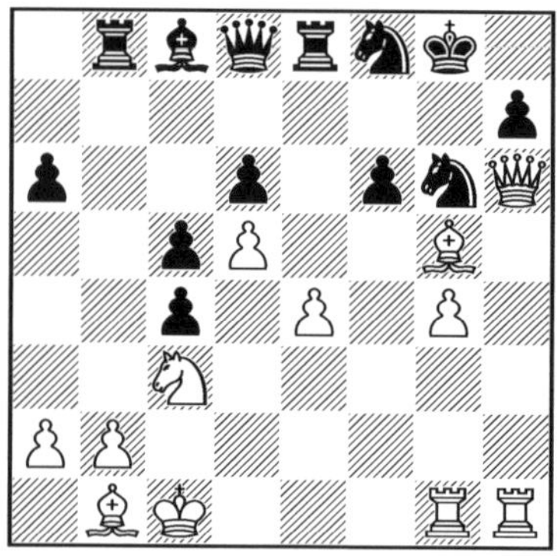

30.e5!!

This pawn move is like a stick of dynamite that blows up black's position. The bishop and the knight join the attack, and this swiftly decides matters.

30...♖xe5

After 30...fxg5, Tal intended to play 31.♗xg6 hxg6 32.♕h8+ ♔f7 33.♖h7+!

31.♗xg6 ♖b7

Black is desperately trying to defend a hopeless position. 31...hxg6 didn't help due to 32.♕h8+ and 33.♖h7+!

32.♘e4! fxg5 33.♖f1 ♖xe4

To prevent the threat 34.♘f6, black has to give up an exchange.

34.♗xe4 ♖g7 35.♖f6 ♗xg4

If 35...♘g6, then 36.♖xg6.

36.♖hf1 ♘d7 37.♖xd6 ♕e7 38.♖xa6 ♔h8 39.♗xh7! ♘b8 40.♗f5+ ♔g8 41.♗e6+! ♗xe6 42.♖xe6

Tolush stopped the clock after this move.

In the eight games against grandmasters, Tal got a brilliant result – six points. His last victory earned him the grandmaster's title as well.

Several minutes later, applause rang out in the hall again: Bronstein had agreed to a draw with Kholmov. And so, Mikhail Tal became Soviet champion.

The thunderous ovation seemed unending. The spectators wouldn't leave the hall for ages, celebrating the young player's victory.

The next morning, the new champion's room was full of journalists and newspaper photographers. Telegrams of congratulations poured in from many cities of the Soviet Union; most of them were from Riga, of course. Tal was very excited. When he saw me, he showed me one of them. It contained greetings from the Latvian Communist Party Central Committee.[2]

* * *

And then the routine days came, with mundane tasks and concerns. Tal had to finish his degree dissertation and then get a school internship as a literature teacher. He also had a lot of public duties: simultaneous displays at affiliated organizations, and lectures at factories, state entities and schools. He also had to find some time to read books and go to the theater and cinema. Should we add that the Soviet champion also had to train...

In summer 1957, Tal played in the students' world team championship and European team championship, and in the autumn he took part in the Latvian

---

2 Tal's relations with the Central Committee would become a lot more complicated a few years later, as recounted in his first wife Sally Landau's memoir *Checkmate! The Love Story of Mikhail Tal and Sally Landau* (Elk and Ruby, 2019, short-listed for the English Chess Federation Book of the Year prize) – publisher's note

players' tour in Italy. In all these competitions, Tal posted the highest individual score.

The following two games were played in the European team championship.

No. 29, Ruy Lopez
M. Tal – R. Teschner
1957, Vienna, 1st European Team Championship, round 2

1.e4 e5 2.♘f3 ♘c6 3.♗b5 a6 4.♗a4 ♘f6 5.0-0 d6 6.c3 ♗e7 7.d4

Editor's note: The main line here is 7.♖e1.

7...b5 8.♗b3 ♗g4 9.h3

Editor's note: In later games, the strongest players usually chose 9.♗e3.

9...♗xf3 10.♕xf3

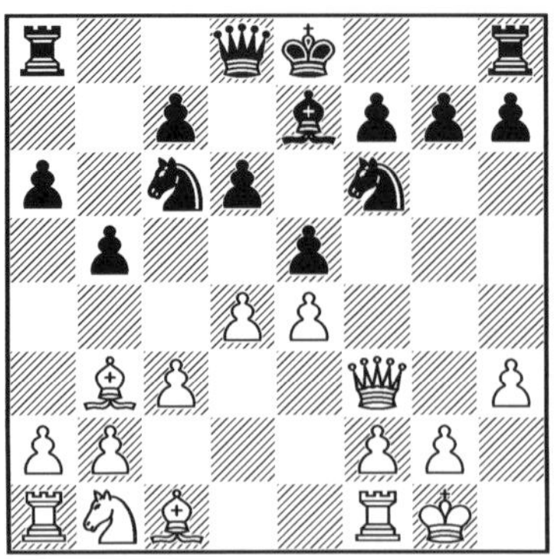

10...exd4

Black accepts the pawn sacrifice. However, the quiet 10...0-0 also allowed white great prospects in the center and on the kingside.

11.♕g3 g6

Editor's note: In most subsequent games with this line, black played 11...0-0. In this case, the main line is 12.♗h6 ♘e8 13.♗d5 ♕d7 14.♕g4! ♕xg4 15.hxg4. The stats are catastrophic for black, but that doesn't correlate with an objective evaluation of the position – analysis shows that black is only marginally worse.

12.♗d5 ♕d7 13.♗h6 ♖b8

The king voluntarily stays in the center and falls to a crushing attack. However, after 13...0-0-0 14.a4!, white's attack was dangerous as well.

Editor's note: The computer shows interesting resources: 13...♖g8!? (with the idea 14...g5, and if 14.f4, then 14...♗f8 15.♗g5 ♘xd5 16.exd5 ♘e7) and 13...g5!? (capturing the pawn with the queen, let alone the bishop, loses to 14...♖g8) – in both cases, black is alright.

14.f4

Editor's note: The stronger move was 14.♖e1!, to meet 14...♘a5 (the move that could give black good chances to resist after 14.f4) with the simple 15.cxd4, not fearing 15...c6, because after 16.♗b3, the e4 pawn is still protected.

14...♘d8

Editor's note: 14...♘a5 still gave some defending chances. If white plays 15.♘d2 like in the actual game, then 15...♘xd5 16.exd5 ♕f5 – the knight's position on a5 gives black an important defensive resource ♘a5-c4.

15.♘d2 c6 16.♗b3 dxc3 17.♕xc3 ♕a7+ 18.♔h1 ♕c5 19.♕d3!

Threatening 20.♗g7 ♖g8 21.♗xf6, then 22.e5 and ♘e4.

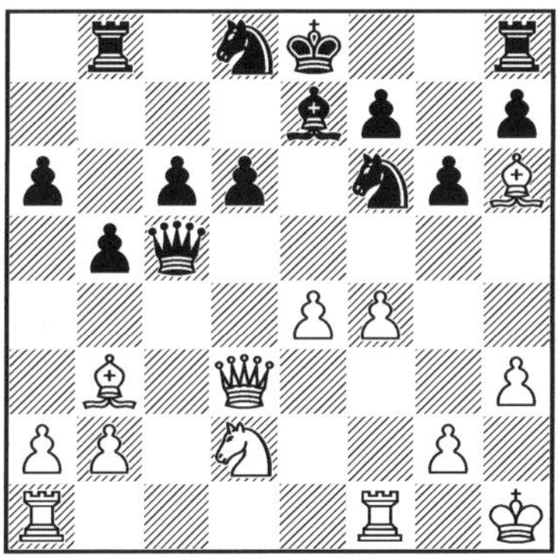

19...♘d7 20.e5! d5 (a futile attempt to avoid opening the files) **21.f5!**

Black can't capture the e-pawn: 21...♘xe5 22.♕e2 f6 23.fxg6 hxg6 24.♗g7, and white's attack is unstoppable.

Editor's note: Actually, 21...♘xe5 was the only way for black to stay in the game. Koblenz's line is not dangerous for him at all: after the subsequent 24...♖h7 25.♗xf6 *(25.♖xf6 ♘df7)* 25...♗xf6 26.♖xf6 ♖e7, he's alright. Instead of the erroneous 22.♕e2, the correct move is 22.♕g3, and after 22...f6 23.fxg6 hxg6 24.♗g7 ♘df7 *(24...♖h7? 25.♖xf6 ♖xg7 26.♕xe5+−, 24...♖h5? 25.♗xf6 ♗xf6 26.♖xf6 ♘df7 27.♖xg6+−, 24...♖g8? 25.♗xf6+− or 25.♘e4+−)* 25.♖ae1 ♕d6 26.♗xh8 ♘xh8 27.♘f3 ♘hf7 28.♗c2 ♘xf3 29.♕xd6 ♘xd6 30.♗xg6+ ♔d7 31.♖xf3 ♖g8, black has some good chances in the endgame.

So, instead of Tal's 21.f5?!, it's much better to play 21.♖ac1, first pushing the black queen to a worse position (and preventing it from reaching d6, as in the previous line), and then getting a decisive attack in all lines: 21...♕b6 22.f5+−, 21...♕a7 22.f5+−, 21...♕b4 22.a3 ♘c5 *(22...♕a5 23.f5 ♘xe5 24.♕g3+−)* 23.♕e3 ♕a5 24.f5+−.

21...gxf5 22.♕xf5 ♘f8 23.♘e4! dxe4 24.♖ac1! ♕b6 25.♖cd1 Black resigned.

International master Rudolf Teschner lost the second game to Tal as well, which was a quieter one.

No. 30, Sicilian Defense
R. Teschner – M. Tal
1957, Vienna, 1st European Team Championship, round 5

1.e4 c5 2.♘f3 ♘c6 3.d4 cxd4 4.♘xd4 ♘f6 5.♘c3 d6 6.g3 g6

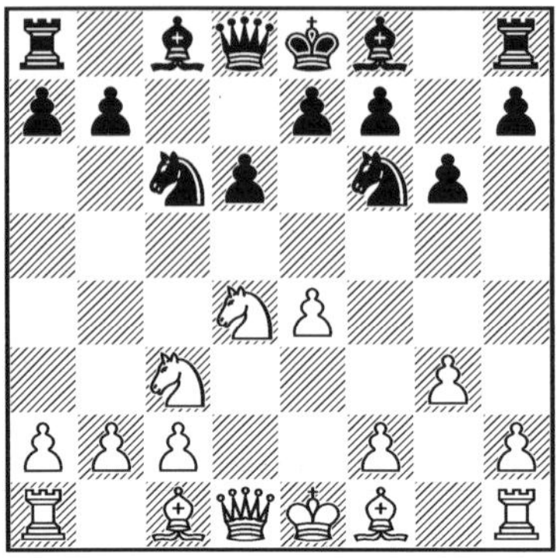

7.♗g2

Editor's note: If strong modern grandmasters go for this line, they usually place their hopes of getting an opening advantage in 7.♘xc6 bxc6 8.♗g2 or 7.♘de2.

7...♘xd4 8.♕xd4 ♗g7 9.0-0 0-0 10.♕d3 ♗e6 11.♘d5 ♖c8 12.c3 ♖e8 13.♗e3 ♕a5 14.h3

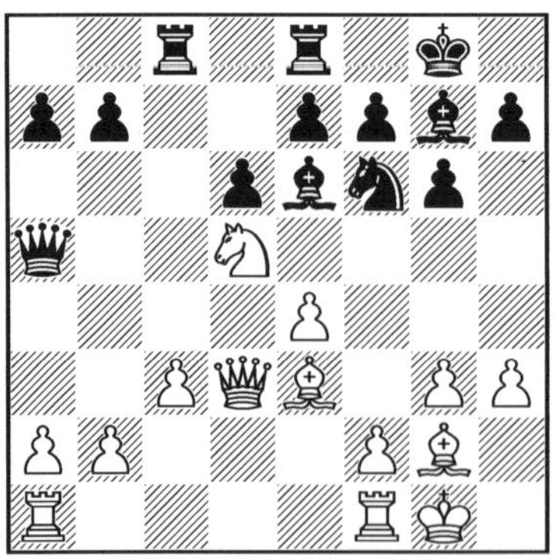

14...♕a4!

Tal wrote about this maneuver: "The most difficult move in the whole game. Black constrains white's queenside pawns even more, puts pressure on the e4 square and prepares b7-b5-b4."

15.♖fe1 b5 16.♗g5

It was better to simplify the position with 16.♘xf6+ ♗xf6 17.♗d4 ♗xd4 18.cxd4 ♖c7, even though black still had an advantage after this move.

Editor's note: Judging by Koblenz's last note, it's clear that he thinks that the position after 15...b5 is better for black, but this evaluation is too optimistic. For instance, his line can be continued with 19.d5 ♗d7 20.e5, and white is no worse. 16.♘b4!? is also worth considering, preventing the opponent's possible queenside initiative (16...a5?? 17.b3 ♕a3 18.♗c1+−) – there's no reason to believe that black has an advantage. However, the game move should've led to equality as well.

16...♘xd5 17.exd5 ♗f5 18.♕d2 b4 19.c4 ♕c2!

Finishing the maneuver that was started on move 14.

After the queen trade, the bishops will put a lot of pressure on the opponent's queenside.

20.♕xc2 ♗xc2 21.♖ac1 ♗d3

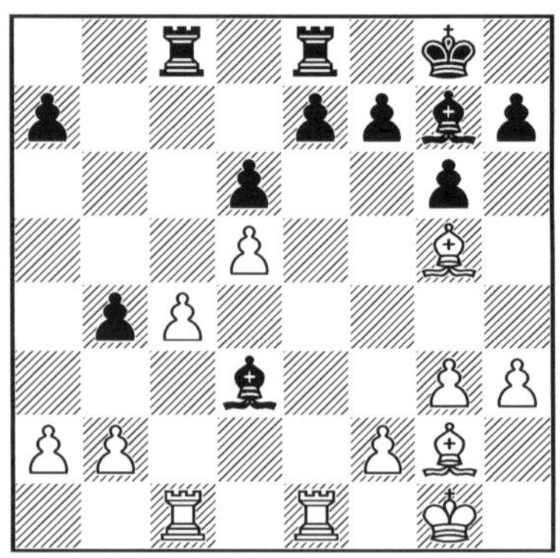

22.♖e3

Editor's note: White's last move is a mistake and leads to a lost position; however, after 22.b3 ♗b2 23.♖cd1 ♗c2 24.♖e2 ♗f6 (after *24...♗xd1?! 25.♖xb2*, only black is at risk due to big problems with the d1 bishop) 25.♖xc2 ♗xg5 26.a4 bxa3 27.♖a2, the position was completely drawn.

22...♗xb2! 23.♖xd3 ♗xc1 24.♗xc1 ♖xc4 25.♗d2 ♖b8! 26.♗e3 a5 27.♖d2 a4 28.♗f1 ♖c1 29.♖b2 ♖a1 30.♔g2 a3 31.♖c2 b3 32.axb3 a2! 33.♗e2 ♖g1+ 34.♔xg1 a1=♕+ 35.♔g2 ♖xb3 36.♖c8+ ♔g7 37.♖c4 ♕a8 38.♗d4+ e5

In this hopeless position, **white lost on time**.

Tal is often criticized for his excessively risky opening play. Indeed, he often cedes a dangerous initiative to his opponents when he plays black.

Let's look at a game played in a match in Italy.

No. 31, Modern Benoni
E. Romani – M. Tal
1957, Reggio Emilia,
Reggio Emilia-Riga Match

1.d4 ♘f6 2.c4 e6 3.♘c3 c5 4.d5 exd5 5.cxd5 d6 6.♘f3 g6

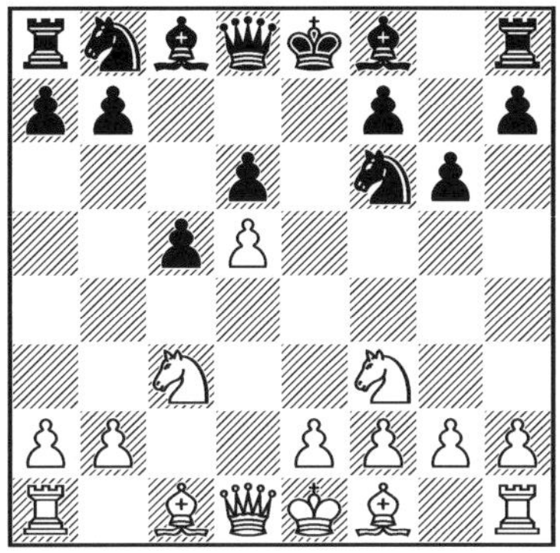

In this system, black has a weakness on d6. His opponent also gets a space advantage in the center. However, black has a chance to create counterplay with the long-range g7 bishop and queenside pawn advantage. Even though the common opinion is that this line is difficult for black, Tal often employs it in important tournaments. Such "balancing on the edge of the abyss", where even the smallest mistake made by his opponent allows him to launch a swift counterattack, always attracted Tal.

7.g3

The game can get much sharper after 7.♘d2 ♗g7 8.♘c4 0-0 9.♗f4 ♘e8 10.♕d2.

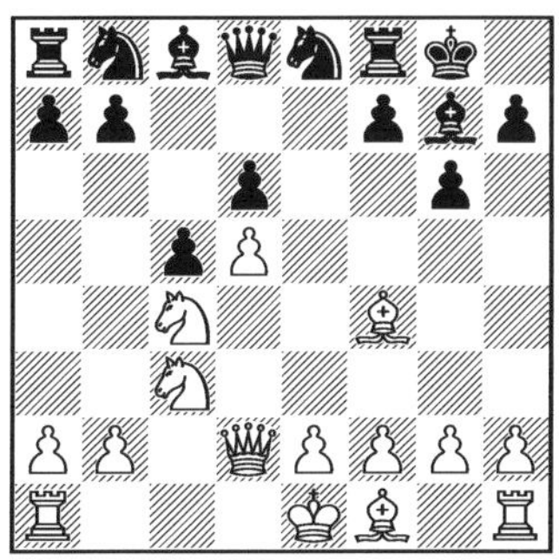

In this case, black would've played 10...b6! For instance, 11.e3 ♗a6 12.a4 ♗xc4 (**Editor's note:** Another popular move in this position is 12...f5!?, seizing kingside space, but a different move worth considering is 12...♘d7!?, as played in the game Chakravarthi – Mareco, Dubai 2018. After the subsequent 13.♗e2 ♗xc4 14.♗xc4 the white bishop got to c4, but a tempo down) 13.♗xc4 a6 14.0-0 ♘d7 15.♖ab1 f5 16.♗g3 ♕f6 17.f4 ♘c7 with the subsequent b6-b5 (**Editor's note:** Later, this unclear position with mutual chances occurred in the games Borisenko – Suetin, Riga 1958, and Lomholt Hansen – Kretschmer, corr. 1983).

Tal once played a paradoxical move 10...♗xc3 (instead of 10... b6), and after 11.bxc3 b5 12.♘b2, at the cost of trading off the important dark-squared bishop, got an opportunity to push his pawn phalanx. (**Editor's note:** Koblenz probably means the game Borisenko – Tal, Riga 1955; there followed 12...a5 13.e4 ♕e7 14.♗d3 b4. But in his other games that reached the position after 12.♘b2, Tal played 12...♗b7 – see Lebedev – Tal, Riga 1955, and Antoshin – Tal, Leningrad 1956. By the way, the idea 10...♗xc3 11.bxc3 b5 found adherents among other strong players.)

7...♗g7 8.♗g2 0-0 9.0-0 a6 10.a4 ♘bd7 11.♘d2 ♖e8

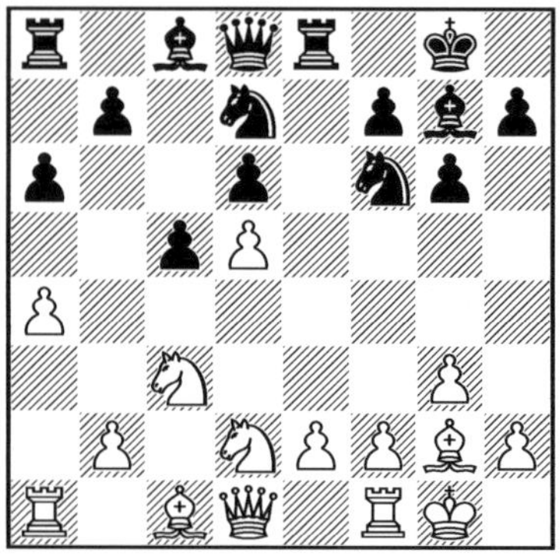

12.♘c4

12.a5 could be met with 12...b5 13.axb6 ♘xb6 14.♘b3 ♘c4! 15.♕d3 ♖b8!, and white can't implement his plan to block black's queenside with ♘a5.

Editor's note: Instead of the inaccurate 15.♕d3, white usually plays 15.♖a4, but even then after 15... ♘b6 16.♖a2 ♘c4, black is alright, and most of the games that came to this position ended with three-fold repetition (17.♖a4 ♘b6). We should also point out that today's main line is 12.h3.

12...♘b6

Preventing white from increasing the pressure on the d6 pawn with 13.♗f4.

Editor's note: In modern practice, 12...♘e5 is more popular.

13.♘e3

Editor's note: In subsequent games, white usually played 13.♘a3, which is considered the current main line in this position.

13...♘g4! 14.♕b3 ♖b8 15.h3 ♘xe3 16.♗xe3 ♘d7 17.♘e4 ♕e7 18.♗f4 ♘e5

Now everything is ready to execute black's main strategic idea: the b7-b5 pawn advance.

19.♕b6

A bad attempt to prevent b7-b5.

Editor's note: The best continuation was 19.a5, with a complicated position.

19...♘c4 20.♕b3 b5 21.axb5 axb5 22.g4

22.♘xc5 didn't work because of 22...g5!

22...♗xb2

Editor's note: The correct move is 22...f5! 23.♘xc5 g5 24.♗h2 ♘d2, winning an exchange – there's no good compensation for white.

23.♘xd6

Editor's note: The unexpected 23.♖a5!? looks interesting – after both 23...♘xa5 24.♕xb2 and 23...♗d7 24.♖a7, white has a considerable initiative for the material.

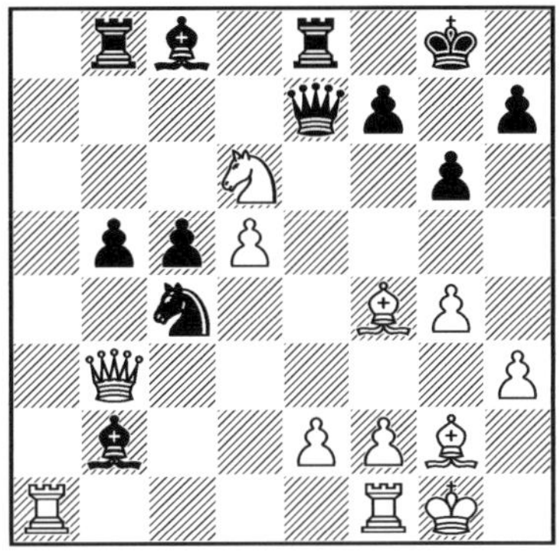

Both players have executed their plans. Black has gained a pawn advantage on the queenside, and white likewise in the center. In the subsequent stage of the game, tactics come to the fore.

23...♗xa1 24.♘xc4

24.♘xe8 is worse because of 24... ♗e5!

24...♖a8 25.♘b6

The tempting 25.♕xb5 ♕xe2 26.♗f3 was refuted by the spectacular 26...♗a6!!. (**Editor's note:** Instead of 26.♗f3, the correct move is 26.♕xc5 with enough compensation for the exchange. However, black's play can be improved as well: instead of the mistake 25...♕xe2, he had 25...♗a6 and 26...♕xe2 with an advantage.)

25...♖a5 26.d6 ♕a7 27.♗c6 ♗e6 28.♕c2

Editor's note: 28.♕f3! gave adequate compensation for the exchange, keeping the possibility to meet ♘d5 ♗xd5 with ♕xd5; also, the white queen can get to f6 from f3 in some lines. For instance: 28...

♖d8 (after *28...♖b8? 29.♘d5 ♗xd5 30.♕xd5*, black faces huge problems because of the threat d6-d7) 29.♘d5 ♗g7 30.♗g5 ♖xd6 31.♘f6+ ♔f8 (*31...♗xf6?? 32.♕xf6+–*, *31...♔h8?! 32.♕g3!*, threatening both *♕xd6* and *♕h4*) 32.♘xh7+ ♔g8 33.♘f6+ ♔f8 34.♘h7+ with perpetual check. However, after the weaker game move white still has some chances to save the game.

28...♖b8 29.♘d5 ♗xd5 30.♗xd5 ♖a4 31.e3

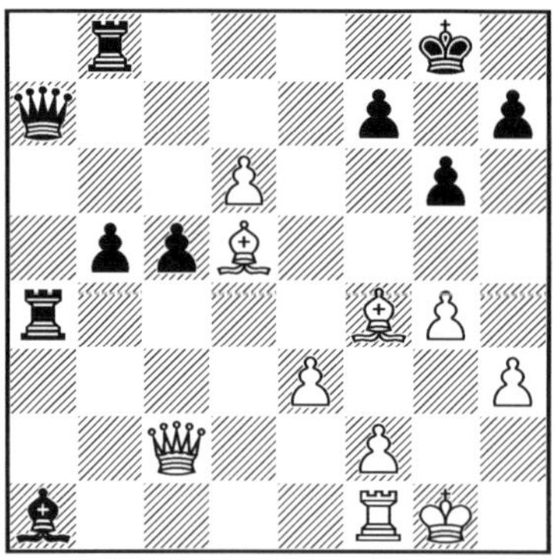

31...♗g7

Editor's note: 31...♗f6 is stronger, because after the subsequent 32.♖d1 c4 white can't play 33.d7 due to 33... ♖d8. However, if the bishop is on g7, it's all different (see the next editor's note).

32.♗c6? (32.♖d1 was better)

Editor's note: Analysis of the position after 32.♖d1 shows that in that case white had enough compensation for the exchange to draw the game. Unlike the aforementioned line 31... ♗f6, black can't now play 32...c4 due to 33.d7 – in this case, 33...♖d8 loses due to 34.♕e4! ♕xd7 35.♗xf7+ (the rook on d8 is unprotected – 35... ♕xf7 36.♖xd8+).

32...♕b6 33.♗d5 ♖xf4! 34.exf4 ♕xd6

The dangerous d6 pawn is eliminated, and the black pawns can finally march forward.

35.♕e4 ♖d8 36.♗c6 b4 37.♗a4 ♕d4! 38.♕e7 ♗f6 39.♕b7 ♕xf4 40.♗b3 c4 41.♗c2 ♗e5 42.♕g2 b3 43.♗b1 c3 White resigned.

December 1957 came. The names of the semi-final winners became known, and we were able to study the games of our future opponents, their strengths and weaknesses, and plan the championship strategy accordingly.

In the week preceding the 25th Soviet championship, we played several training games. I'll allow myself the pleasure of printing two of them.

No. 32, Dutch Opening
A. Koblenz – M. Tal
1957, Riga, Training Match, round 1

1.d4 e6 2.c4 f5 3.♘c3 ♘f6 4.g3 ♗e7 5.♗g2 0-0 6.♘f3 d6 7.0-0 ♕e8 8.♖e1! ♕g6 9.e4 fxe4 10.♘xe4 ♘xe4 11.♖xe4 ♘c6 (11...♕xe4? 12.♘h4)

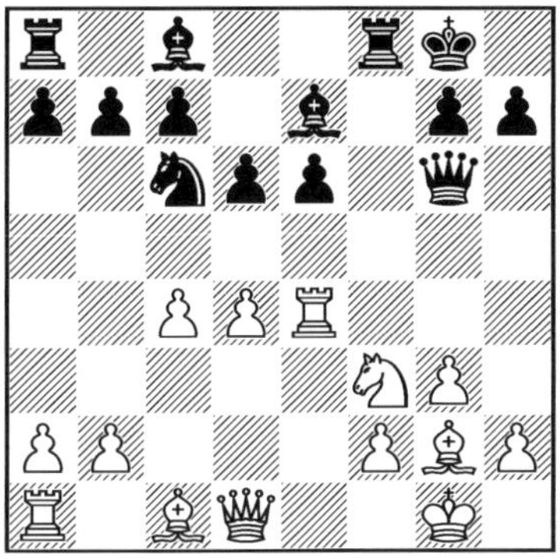

12.♖e3

At first glance, this rook retreat is illogical because it blocks the dark-squared bishop. However, as will soon become clear, the rook performs important functions on the third rank.

Editor's note: This move hasn't found much traction at grandmaster level. The current main line is 12.♕e2.

12...♗f6

12...e5 is bad because of 13.dxe5 ♗g4 14.exd6 ♗xd6 15.c5! ♗e7 16.b4! ♗f6 17.♗b2! It's easy to notice that the rook defends the knight on f3.

13.d5 exd5 14.cxd5 ♘e5

Editor's note: The aggressive 14... ♘b4!? looks like a good alternative.

15.♘xe5 ♗xe5 16.♖b3

That's the reason behind 12.♖e3. Now, after the natural 16...b6 17.♗e3, white will play 18.♖ac1 and create strong pressure along the c-file.

16...♗f5!

Launching an interesting counter-attack. Black isn't going to defend the b7 pawn!

17.♖xb7 ♗c2! 18.♕d2

The dark-squared bishop is stuck on c1 and will now hinder white's queenside development.

Editor's note: The moves 18.♕e1 and 18.♕e2 were worth considering.

18...♖ae8 19.♖xc7 ♗d3

Black avoids the trap: 19... ♗d4 20.♕xd4 ♖e1+ 21.♗f1 ♗d3 22.♗h6!!.

20.♕b4 a5! 21.♕a4 ♗xg3!

21...♖xf2 22.♔xf2 ♕f6+ gave black nothing due to 23.♔g1 (but not 23.♗f3 ♗d4+ 24.♔g2 ♗f1+) 23... ♗d4+ 24.♗e3.

22.hxg3 ♖e1+ 23.♔h2 ♗e4! 24.♗e3

Of course, not 24.♗xe4 due to a mate in two: 24...♕h5+ 25.♔g2 ♕h1#.

24...♕h5+ 25.♗h3 ♖xe3!

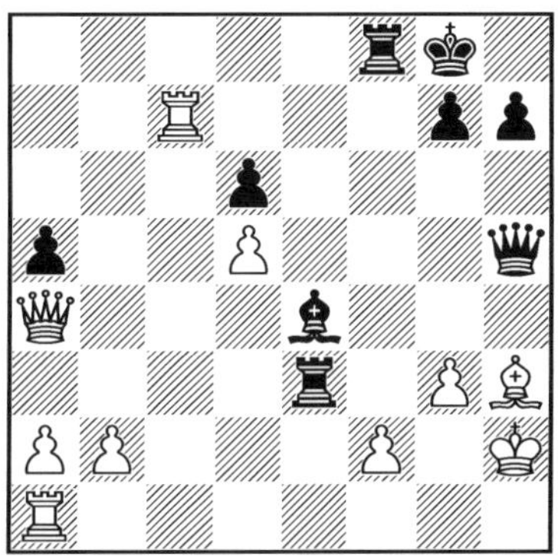

26.♖xg7+!

This rook counter-sacrifice saves white from losing. 26.fxe3 immediately lost to 26...♕e2+.

26...♔xg7

If 26...♔h8, then 27.♕d4! ♖xf2+ 28.♔g1, and the discovered check threat is decisive.

Editor's note: In Koblenz's line, instead of 27...♖xf2+, black should play 27...♖d3!, and the computer lines show that after both 28.♕xe4 ♖d2 29.♖c7 ♖dxf2+ 30.♔g1 ♕xh3 and 28.♖xh7+ ♔xh7 29.♕xe4+ ♕g6, the game ends in a draw.

27.♕d4+ ♔g8 28.♕xe3

The queen finally joins the defense, but black still has the initiative.

28...♗f5 29.g4 ♗xg4 30.♖g1 ♖xf2+!

Another rook sacrifice!

31.♔h1! ♕xd5+ 32.♗g2 ♕d2 33.♕xd2 ♖xd2 34.♗h3 h5 35.♗xg4 hxg4 36.♖xg4+ ♔f7 37.♖g2 Draw.

In the next game, our purpose was to check a line in the Sicilian Defense that Tal intended to use in the championship. I was his opponent.

No. 33, Sicilian Defense
M. Tal – A. Koblenz
1957, Riga, Training Match, round 2

After **1.e4 c5 2.♘f3 ♘c6 3.d4 cxd4 4.♘xd4 ♘f6 5.♘c3 d6 6.♗g5 e6 7.♕d2 ♗e7 8.0-0-0 0-0 9.♘b3** (**Editor's note:** The modern main line is 9.f4) **9...♕b6 10.f3 a6 11.g4 ♖d8 12.♗e3 ♕c7 13.h4 b5 14.g5 ♘d7 15.g6!**, the following position occurred.

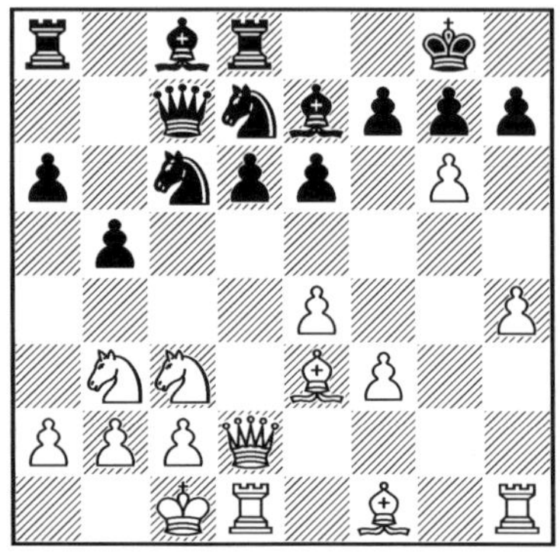

15...hxg6

After capture by the f-pawn, white still has good prospects.

Editor's note: Subsequent practice shows that 15...fxg6 is the only correct move. After 16.h5 gxh5 17.♖xh5 ♘f6, white's compensation is substantial, but this doesn't mean it will necessarily bring an advantage.

16.h5 gxh5 17.♖xh5 ♘f6 18.♖h1 d5! 19.e5!

Editor's note: There's a much simpler and quieter continuation shown by Timman: 19.♗f4! ♗d6 20.♗xd6 ♕xd6 21.f4 with the ideas 22.e5, 22.♕h2 or 22.♗d3 — white's position is won.

19...♘xe5 20.♗f4

Editor's note: This is a mistake: for some reason, white forces the black bishop to go to d6, where its position is quite good, with the black king getting a good escape square e7 in the process. The correct move was 20.♕h2 ♔f8 21.♕h8+ ♘g8 (Burgess) 22.♗d4!, and, even though great complications arise, white is ultimately able to prove that his attack is decisive.

20...♗d6 21.♕h2 ♔f8 22.♕h8+

Editor's note: The prophylactic 22.♔b1 is better, even though after 22...♔e7 white still has to prove that his activity is worth the two missing pawns.

22...♘g8

22...♔e7 was stronger, but I intended to lure the queen to h8 and get it out of play. (**Editor's note:** 22...♔e7 wasn't just "stronger" – it led to a won position; whereas, after the game move, white's compensation is adequate.)

23.♖h7 f5 24.♗h6 ♖d7 25.♗xb5! ♖f7

Editor's note: The only move was 25...♘g6. For instance: 26.♘d4 (also the only move) 26...♖e7 27.♗xg7+ ♖xg7 28.♗d7!! ♕xd7 29.♘xe6+ ♕xe6 30.♕xg7+ ♔e8 31.♘xd5 (up until now – analysis by Burgess) 31...♘8e7 32.♘f6+ ♔d8 33.♖hh1 ♗b7 34.♖he1 ♘e5 35.f4 ♘d3+! 36.cxd3 ♕xa2 37.♕f8+ ♔c7 38.♖xe7+ ♔c6 39.♕g7 ♕a1+ 40.♔c2 ♕a4+ 41.♔c1 ♕a1+ with perpetual check.

26.♖g1 ♖a7

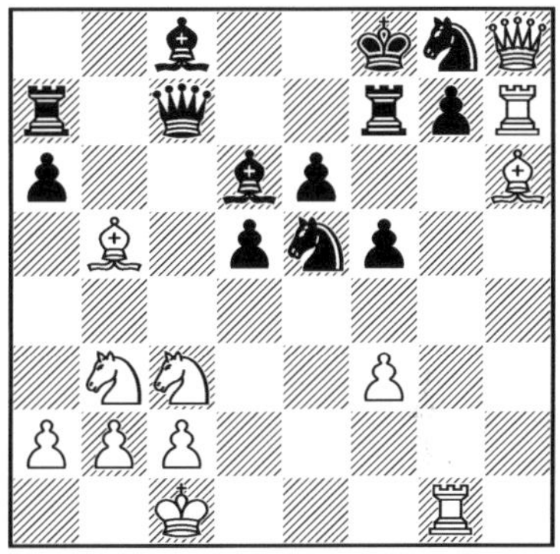

Tal wrote about this position in the *Sahs* magazine: "...The white pieces aren't positioned too well. The g7 square – the key to black's position – bends, but doesn't break. If black can bolster his position and launch an attack, then white will only manage to send a consolation telegram to his king. So white has to play very energetically."

27.♘d4

Editor's note: As Burgess pointed out, white won with 27.♗xa6! ♗xa6 *(27...♖xa6 28.♖gxg7+–; 27...♘xf3 28.♘b5+–)* 28.♘d4 ♗c8 29.♘db5+–.

27...♘g4!

The tempting 27...♕b6 was met with the brilliant 28.♗d7!

28.fxg4 ♗e5

Editor's note: The correct move is 28...♗f4+, for instance, 29.♗xf4 ♕xf4+ 30.♔b1 ♕xd4 31.♖gh1 ♖fe7 32.gxf5 (*32.g5? ♕g4* with a clear advantage for black) 32... exf5, and white has nothing decisive (according to the computer, the position is equal), or 29.♔b1! ♗xh6 30.g5 ♗xg5 31.♖xg5 ♕f4 32.♖gh5 ♖fc7 33.♘ce2 ♕f1+ 34.♘c1 axb5 35.♖h1 ♕c4 36.♖7h4 e5 37.♘e6+ ♗xe6 38.♖xc4 dxc4 with good drawing chances.

Black is a piece down, but his opponent has three pieces en prise!

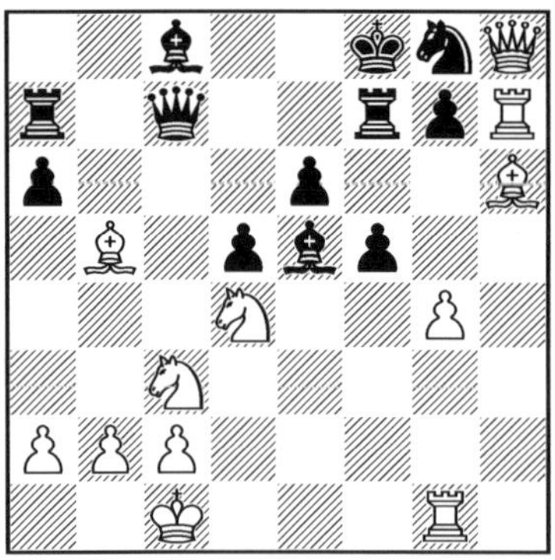

29.♘c6!!

Editor's note: 29.♘f3!! is a stronger move, with the decisive threat ♘f3-h4-g6+.

29...♗xc3

With a futile hope of launching a counter-attack after 30.bxc3 axb5 31.♘xa7 ♕xa7. (**Editor's note:** After the subsequent 32.♖h1 black still can't save the game, but instead of 31.♘xa7?!, white wins immediately with 31.gxf5 exf5 32.♖gxg7 ♖xg7 33.♘xa7+−.)

30.♗e3! d4 31.♖gh1!

Threatening 32.♕xg8+! and 33.♖h8#.

31...♖d7 32.♗g5!

Editor's note: This move gives the opponent an opportunity to defend. The correct move was 32.gxf5 (Burgess) or 32.g5 (threatening 33.♕xg8+ ♔xg8 34.g6+−) 32... ♕g3 33.g6! ♕xg6 34.♘e5 — with a decisive attack in both cases.

32...axb5 33.♖1h6!

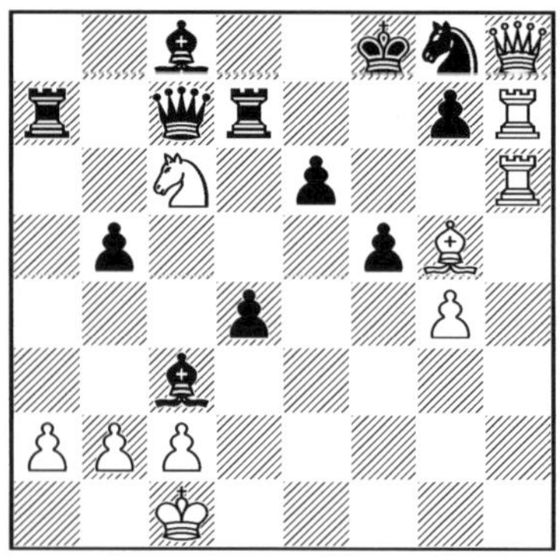

It's over – black can't defend the g7 square.

After **33...d3** (**Editor's note:** As Burgess pointed out, after 33... ♕xc6 34.♖f6+ gxf6 35.♗h6+ ♖g7 36.♗xg7+ ♔e7 black could still save the game) **34.bxc3 d2+ 35.♔d1 ♕xc6 36.♖f6+ ♖f7 37.♕xg7+ Black resigned**.

A Ticket to the Interzonal

In January 1958, the participants of the 25th Soviet championship arrived in Riga. The Science Palace became the arena for the national battle for the gold medal. Further, four representatives of the Soviet Union would qualify for the Interzonal – a world championship cycle tournament.

The decision to hold the jubilee championship in Latvia's capital was met with enthusiasm from our chess players. Riga is a city with a great chess tradition. The outstanding grandmaster Aron Nimzowitsch lived there, while the stunningly beautiful endgame studies of Hermanis Matisons were created here – he was the first Latvian chess master. Riga is the birthplace of an original opening that was named the Latvian Gambit (its inventor was Karlis Betins). Latvian chess players won many correspondence matches against other European cities. However, all these successes were the result of individual enthusiasts' efforts. The mass chess movement in bourgeois Latvia was an unattainable dream. Only in Soviet Latvia would chess finally achieve its deserved place in the republic's cultural life.

The first round. All participants are full of hope and in a combative mood.

On the third hour of play, the first applause sounded: Tal had started the championship with a win! The arbiters had a hard time trying to calm the spectators down and restore order.

The critical position occurred after move 18.

No. 34
M. Tal – A. Tolush
1958, Riga, 25th Soviet Championship Final, round 1

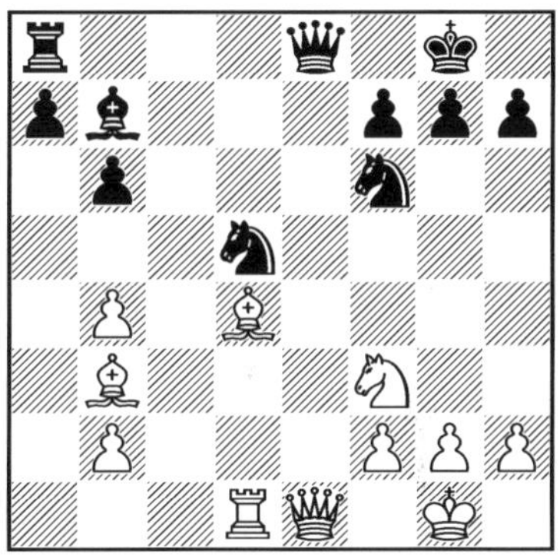

Tolush expected his opponent to exchange queens and settle for a draw. He seemed to underestimate Tal's next move.

19.♗e5! ♕b5

Editor's note: The move 19...a5!? looked good – it both activated the rook and prevented b4-b5, which could have both created a foothold on c6 for the knight and fixed the a-pawn in place. After, for instance, 20.bxa5 bxa5 21.♖d4 a4 22.♗c2 a3 23.bxa3

♖xa3 24.♕b1 ♗c6, black's position is totally defensible.

20.♗xf6 gxf6

20...♘xf6 was relatively better. However, after 21.♕e7 ♗d5 22.♗xd5 ♘xd5 23.♕b7 ♖d8 24.h4, the knight pin would be very unpleasant for black.

Editor's note: White's extra pawn after the subsequent 24...♕d7! 25.♕xd7 *(25.♕a6?! ♕e7=)* 25...♖xd7 26.♘e5 ♖d6 27.b5 ♔f8 28.♘c6 ♖d7 29.♘b4 ♘f6 30.♖xd7 ♘xd7 31.♘c6 ♔e8 32.♘xa7 ♔e7 probably can't be converted at all. The game move is the decisive mistake.

21.♕e4 ♕xb4 22.♘d4 f5 23.♕e5! ♘e7 24.♕f6 ♗d5

After 24...♖f8, Tal prepared the following line: 25.h3 ♗d5 26.♖d3 ♗xb3 27.♖g3+! ♘g6 28.♘xf5, and black can't save the game.

Now, a beautiful finale ensues.

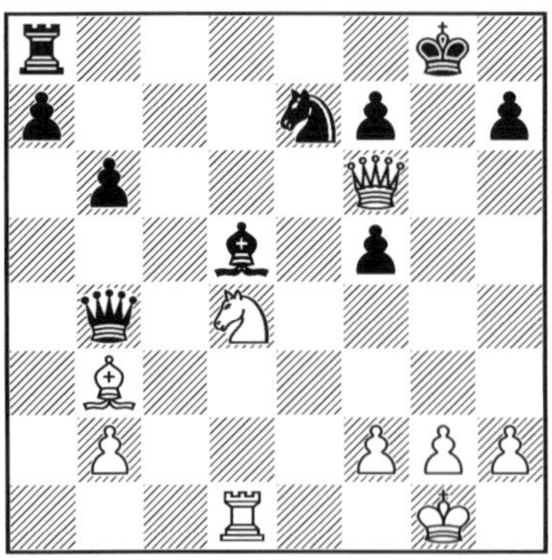

25.♘c6! ♕xb3 26.♘xe7+ ♔f8 27.♖e1 ♗e6 28.♘xf5 Black resigned.

In round 3, Isaak Boleslavsky had black against Tal. Knowing that Boleslavsky liked to play the King's Indian, Tal opted against his favorite 1.e2-e4 and started the game with the queen's pawn move: he found a new strategic plan in a well-known KID line which gave white an advantage in the opening.

The novelty was successful – Tal won a pawn.

The diagram shows the position after black's 19th move.

No. 35
M. Tal – I. Boleslavsky
1958, Riga, 25th Soviet Championship Final, round 3

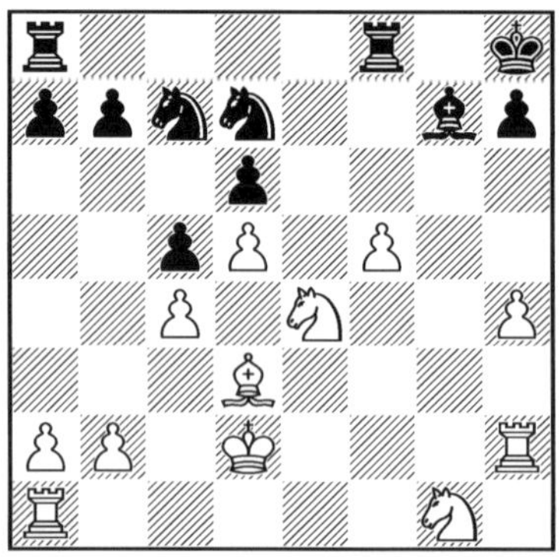

20.♖g2

This move looks very strong. White activates the rook and threatens to win the d6 pawn. However, this seemingly logical move dulled Tal's attention, and he overlooked the positional counter-threat.

20...b5!

The b-pawn movement wouldn't have been as effective had

white played 20.♖b1. In this case, 20...b5 would have been met with 21.b3.

21.♘f3

As Boleslavsky showed after the game, white could have taken on b5. After 21.cxb5 ♘xd5 22.♘xd6, he had two extra pawns. However, after 22...♘f4 or 22... ♖ad8, black seized the initiative. In case of 21.♘xd6 bxc4 22.♘xc4 (if 22.♗xc4, then 22...♖ab8!) 22...♘xd5, white retained the extra pawn, but black still had dangerous counterplay. (**Editor's note:** after Koblenz's 22.♗xc4 ♖ab8, there's 23.♖xg7!, and after 23...♔xg7 24.♖e1! ♘b6 25.♖e7+ ♔g8 26.♖xc7 ♖bd8 27.♖xc5 ♖xd6 28.b3 ♖xf5 29.♘e2, the ending is drawn. However, instead of 22... ♖ab8, black could play 22...♘e5! or 22...♘b6!, and white's position is difficult.)

The game move illustrates Tal's creative credo very well: to activate his pieces, he gladly returns the extra pawn.

21...bxc4 22.♗xc4 ♖ab8 23.♖b1

Editor's note: It was better to try 23.♖ag1 ♖xb2+ 24.♔e1 ♖xg2 25.♖xg2, for instance, 25...♘b6 (*25...♖xf5?! 26.♘fg5* with enough counterplay) 26.♗e2 ♘bxd5 27.♘xd6 and only a slight advantage for black.

23...♖xf5 24.♘fg5 ♘e5

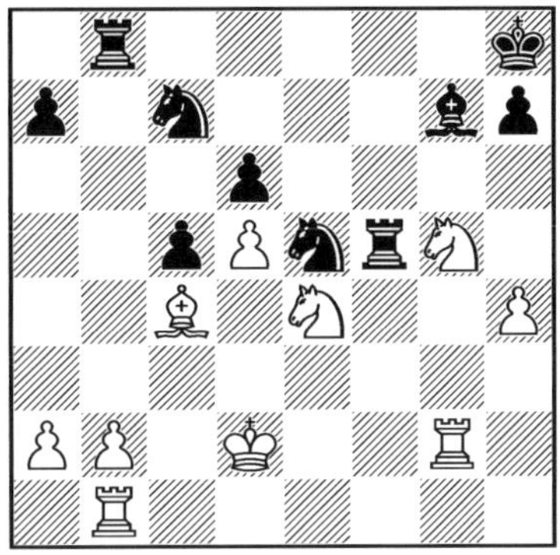

25.♗b3?

A failed attempt to complicate play. As Boleslavsky correctly pointed out, after 25.♘xd6 ♘xc4+ 26.♘xc4 ♖xd5+ 27.♔c2, black had only a minimal advantage, and white could easily draw the game. (**Editor's note:** Instead of 25... ♘xc4, black had 25...♖f6!, and after 26.♘ge4 ♖f4 27.♖e2 ♘xc4+ 28.♘xc4 ♘xd5, it's not that simple for white to equalize.)

25...c4 26.♗c2 ♘xd5 27.♘xd6

Editor's note: It was necessary to play 27.♘c3, declining to restore the material advantage, but forcing the trade of at least one pair of pieces, which made the white king's position much more comfortable and brought some hope of saving the game.

27...♖f6 28.♘f5 (28.♘de4 was better)

Editor's note: 28.♘de4 was unlikely to save the game: after 28... ♖ff8, black has an overwhelming advantage because of dangerous piece activity and white's exposed king.

28...♖d8 29.♔e1 ♘f4 30.♖g3 ♘ed3+

The white king is suddenly caught in the crossfire of his opponent's pieces.

31.♗xd3 ♘xd3+

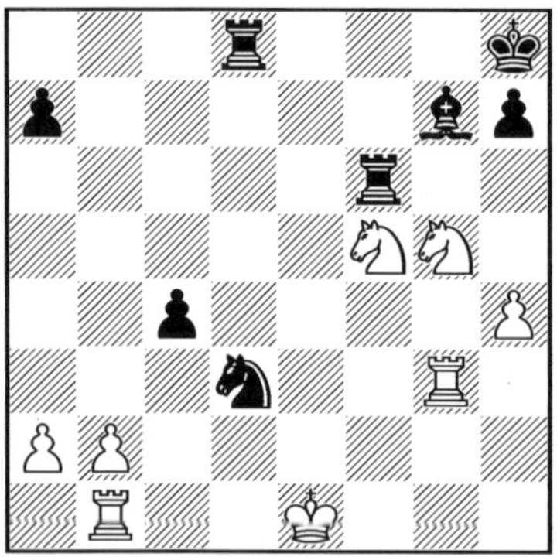

White's position is critical. Tal then sacrificed the exchange with **32.♖xd3**, but this didn't help. His opponent precisely converted his material advantage and deservedly won on move 51.

We analyzed this game for a long time, creating a "case history".

In this game, Tal fell victim to following a standard framework; he couldn't make himself delve into the concrete features of the position, which, I should say, was a rare occurrence for him. Tal was criticized for various things, but adherence to frameworks wasn't one of them. His high-risk approach, on the other hand, the fact that his sacrifices were, as a rule, unsound, was often discussed. However, anti-positional lunges at his opponent's position don't actually feature in Tal's tournament practice all that often – they were mostly seen in the return match against Botvinnik. In actuality, the overwhelming majority of Tal's sacrifices brought him success for the simple reason that they were justified.

Let's take, for instance, the game against Averbakh from the same championship. Grandmaster Averbakh represents the so-called classical school in chess, preferring quiet and clear positions. He feels less confident in sharp situations and often gets into time trouble. We decided to play Tal's "patented" sharp line in the Modern Benoni.

No. 36, Modern Benoni
Y. Averbakh – M. Tal
1958, Riga, 25th Soviet Championship Final, round 4

1.d4 ♘f6 2.c4 e6 3.♘c3 c5 4.d5 exd5 5.cxd5 d6 6.e4 g6 7.♗e2 ♗g7 8.♘f3 0-0 9.0-0 ♖e8 10.♕c2

10.♘d2 was more precise. White likely didn't anticipate that the Riga player would go for an unexpected combination just two moves later.

10...♘a6 11.♗f4

The passive 11.a3 ♘c7 12.♖e1 ♖b8 13.a4 (preventing b7-b5) 13...♘a6 allowed black to occupy the b4 square.

11...♘b4 12.♕b1

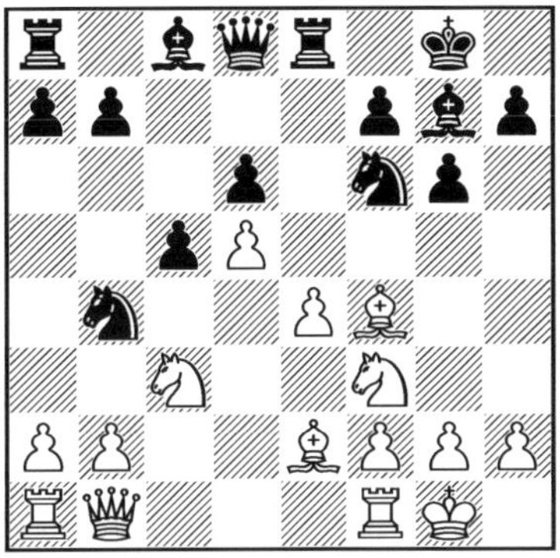

12...♘xe4!!?

This move was very controversial. After looking at the position, Petrosian and Krogius smiled skeptically. After the game, they were firmly on the side of white, thinking that the sacrifice wasn't correct. Bronstein, however, had a different opinion of this move. He wrote in the championship bulletin:

"Black's position after white's 12th move looks difficult from the strategic point of view. Tal gave 12...♘xe4 an exclamation mark and a question mark. I myself can't help but give two exclamation marks to this move.

In such cases, the question whether the sacrifice is correct is not as important as the fact that Averbakh, the quintessential positional player, had to make a drastic turn in a completely different direction.

After 13.♘xe4 ♗f5 14.♘d2 ♘xd5, white made a decisive mistake by playing 15.♗xd6 instead of the correct 15.♗g3.

It's also interesting to note that Lilienthal thought that the sacrifice was incorrect, while Tal thought that chances were equal after 15.♗g3.

Such positions contain an unlimited number of possibilities, and the player who navigates the position better and calculates more quickly and precisely has more practical chances."

Editor's note: 12...♘h5!? looks interesting (and occurred in most subsequent games), intending f7-f5.

13.♘xe4 ♗f5 14.♘fd2 ♘xd5 15.♗xd6

A grave mistake. Black regains the piece and has a material advantage.

On the back of this blunder, most commentators came to the conclusion that the sacrifice wasn't correct and was only justified with white's "help".

But let's consider what would have happened after the strongest move 15.♗g3.

Tal intended to play 15...♕e7 16.♗b5 ♗xe4 17.♘xe4 ♕xe4 18.♗xe8 ♕xe8 19.♗xd6 ♕c6 20.♗g3 c4, and black has a pawn and queenside initiative for the exchange.

The position Tal aimed for isn't to everyone's liking, of course. The move 16.♗b5 is also not the only one – there was probably a stronger continuation.

Editor's note: Instead of 16.♗b5, white had 16.♗f3, with big trouble for black.

That said, analyzing the position in quiet conditions is one thing – you can move the pieces as much as you want and have all the time in the world. You can clarify a lot of things, find the right reply to a risky move, and reinforce your conclusion with a concrete line. Making a decision during a tense tournament game, when thinking time is strictly limited and when you're facing a living opponent with their inherent strengths and weaknesses, is a whole other matter.

The player who is stronger in these difficult conditions, which are nevertheless equal for both players, will achieve success. That's how we should evaluate committal decisions that cannot be fully evaluated during a tournament game.

The fact that Tal's combination wasn't a bluff was proved by Euwe, who found the move 15...♗h6 for black with the following lines:

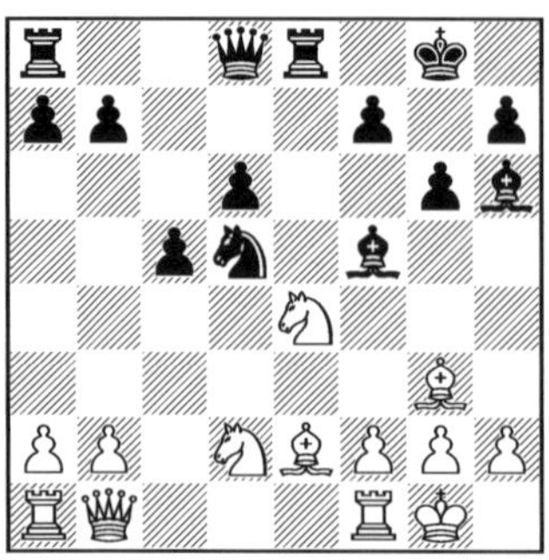

a) 16.♗d3 ♘b4 17.♖e1 ♘xd3 18.♕xd3 d5, and black wins;

Editor's note: Koblenz is wrong: white plays 19.♕xd5!, and, since 19...♗xd2 is bad because of 20.♘d6! ♗xe1 21.♕xf7+ ♔h8 22.♘xe8 ♗xf2+ *(22...♕xe8?? 23.♕f6+ ♔g8 24.♗e5+−)* 23.♗xf2 ♕xe8 24.♕xb7 with a positional advantage for white, black is forced to play 19...♕xd5 20.♘f6+ and 21.♘xd5, with a small advantage at the very most. But instead of 17...♘xd3?, black should play 17...♗xd2 18.♘xd2 ♗xd3, getting two extra pawns and a won position.

b) 16.♕d3 ♘b4 17.♕f3 (if 17.♕xd6, then 17...♗xd2 18.♕xd2 ♕xd2 19.♘xd2 ♖xc2) 17...♘c2, and white can't avoid defeat;

Editor's note: In the line with 17.♕xd6, Euwe's move 17...♗xd2 is a mistake because white wins after 18.♘f6+. The correct move is 17...♗xe4 18.♘xe4 ♖xe4 19.♗f3 ♖d4 20.♕xc5 ♘d3 with an initiative.

c) 16.f4 ♗g7, and white has no defense against numerous threats.

Editor's note: After the subsequent 17.♗b5, the position is totally unclear. However, the strongest reply to 15...♗h6 is 16.♗b5!, and after 16...♗xd2 17.♗xe8 ♕xe8 18.♘xd6 *(18.♕d1!?)* 18...♗xb1 19.♘xe8 ♗c2

20.♘d6, white gets an endgame with a minimal material advantage and some winning chances (Petersons – Khodos, Minsk 1964).

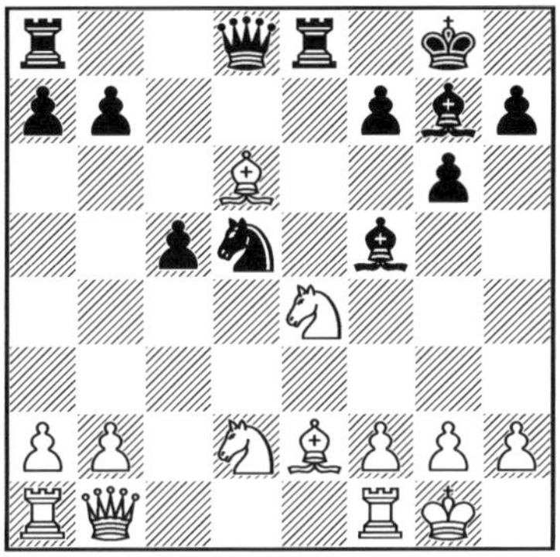

15...♘f6! 16.♗f3

Averbakh seeks to save the game with opposite-colored bishops, but the endgame is still far away. Black has a dangerous initiative.

16...♘xe4 17.♘xe4 ♗xe4 18.♗xe4 ♕xd6 19.♕c2 ♖e7 20.♗f3 ♖ae8 21.♖ad1 ♗d4 22.a4 b6 23.b3 ♖e5!

The rook is excellently placed here and can be transferred to the kingside for an attack.

24.♖d2 h5 25.♖e2

White is trying to simplify the position with trades, but this doesn't make defense any easier.

25...♖xe2 26.♗xe2 h4 27.♔h1 ♕f4 28.g3 ♕f6 29.♕d1 ♖d8 30.♗g4 ♗xf2! 31.♕e2

To attack the pinned bishop, white sacrifices a pawn, but he's in for a surprise.

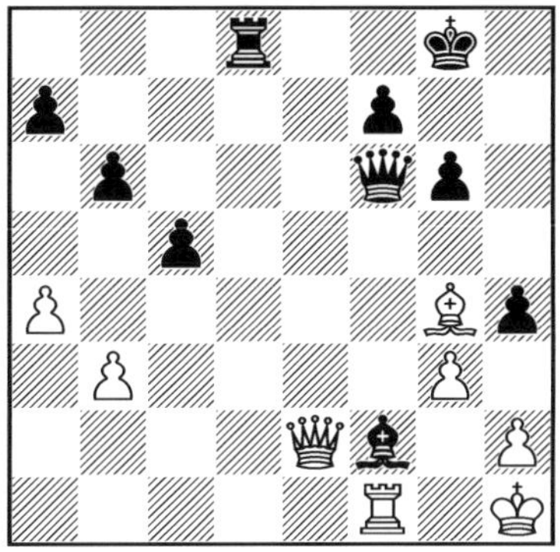

31...♖d2! 32.♕e8+ ♔g7 33.gxh4 ♕d4 34.♗h3 ♕d3!

Editor's note: 34...♕xh4–+ was stronger.

35.♗g2

After 35.♕e5+ ♔h7 36.♕f6, black won with 36...♕d5+ 37.♗g2 ♕xg2+ 38.♔xg2 ♗xd4+ (**Editor's note:** 38...♗xh4+ is even better.)

35...♖d1!

White resigned, since the endgame after 36.♕b5 ♕xb5 37.axb5 ♖xf1+ 38.♗xf1 ♗xh4 is hopeless.

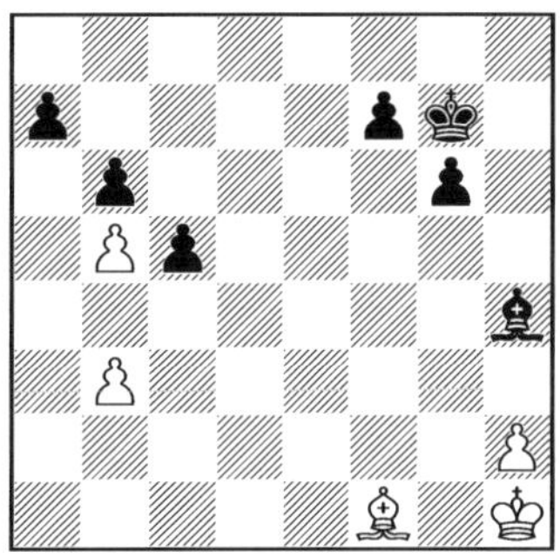

Editor's note: The bishop endgame Koblenz ends his analysis with is most likely drawn – it's probably impossible to create a passed pawn on the queenside with this pawn structure, and one passed pawn on the kingside is not enough for a win. Instead of 37...♖xf1+, black has a stronger move 37...♖d2, keeping the rooks, but the best continuation is 36...♖xf1+ 37.♗xf1 ♕e4+ 38.♗g2 ♕xh4 – with queens and opposite-colored bishops still on the board, white would have to fight off the passed pawns on both flanks and also defend his king. I think that black wouldn't have too much difficulty converting his material advantage in this case.

When beginners overlook elementary threats, they are berated by their more knowledgeable friends. The game Tal – Korchnoi showed that even grandmasters are human.

No. 37
M. Tal – V. Korchnoi
1958, Riga, 25th Soviet Championship Final, round 9

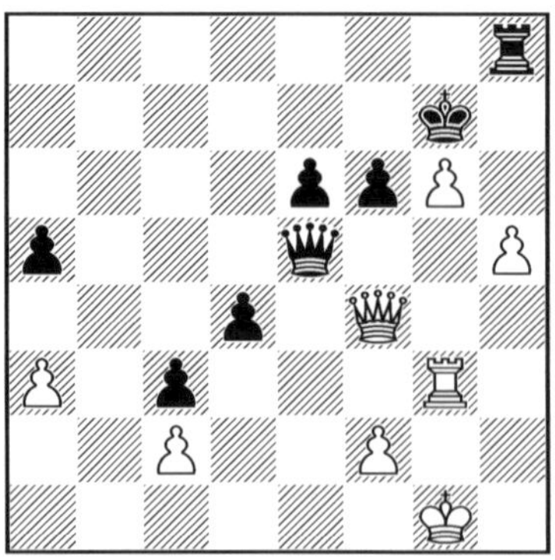

White needs to settle for a draw: 33.♕f3 ♕d5 34.♕f4 ♕e5. However, in time trouble Tal played **33.h6+? ♖xh6 34.♕xh6+ ♔xh6 35.g7 ♕xg3+!** He overlooked this Zwischenschach and so had to **resign** on the spot.

This example is a small illustration on the subject of Tal's "exceptional luck", which was quite popular a few years ago. As we know, "good luck" and "bad luck" usually go hand-in-hand in chess.

The losses to Boleslavsky, Korchnoi and Anatoly Bannik didn't break Tal's will, but to get the ticket to the Interzonal, he now had to win a lot of games.

In round 10, Tal played Kotov. He won rather convincingly with subtle maneuvering in the opening and middlegame.

Against Taimanov, Tal went for an all-out attack. Repelling the first onslaught, Taimanov offered a draw, which was declined. The game was adjourned in a rook ending with Tal a pawn up, and after an eight-hour struggle, he won.

Seeing how persistent Tal was in trying to win the rook endgame, the Moscow journalist D. Ginzburg asked, "Why is Misha trying so hard? He has no chance for fourth place!"

In the game with Geller, Tal wanted to get the initiative at all cost. He sacrificed an exchange, then a full rook.

The people in the press center said indifferently, "Sow the wind, and reap the storm." But the moves were sent to the press center with some delay; meanwhile, there was already applause in the hall.

What happened?

No. 38
M. Tal – E. Geller
1958, Riga, 25th Soviet Championship Final, round 14

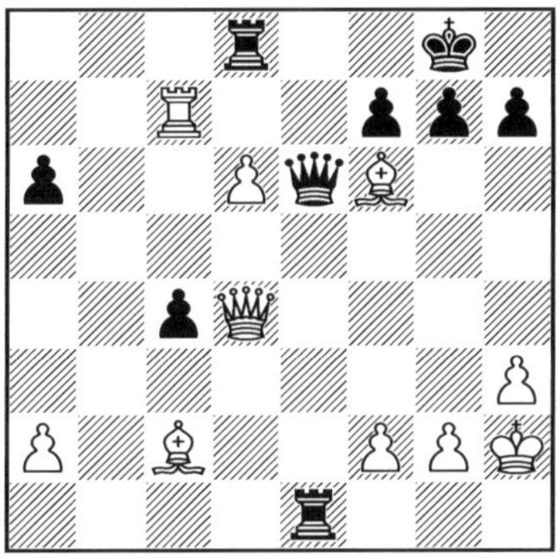

When Tal made his 25th move, the Odessa grandmaster was standing near the arbiters' table. Seeing the move on the demonstration board, he said, "If I take on f6 with the queen, the game is drawn, but I need to win!"

He headed to the board and grabbed the pawn with an energetic gesture.

25...gxf6?

Geller was absolutely right in his comment at the demonstration board: after 25...♕xf6 26.♕xf6 gxf6 27.d7, white's passed pawn equalized chances. Now, however, black is losing.

26.♖e7 ♕xd6+

26...♕xe7 didn't help due to 27.♕g4+.

27.♕xd6 ♖xd6 28.♖xe1 ♖d2 29.♖c1 ♖xf2 30.♗e4 ♖xa2 31.♖xc4 a5 32.♖c8+ ♔g7 33.♖c7 Black resigned.

This loss squashed Geller's hopes of qualifying for the Interzonal. Even scrupulous analysis couldn't refute Tal's "incorrect" idea.

How can we explain black's gross mistake in this game? I think that the main reason was that Geller wanted to win at all costs, regardless of the position.

Tal managed to improve his tournament standing somewhat after winning against grandmasters. However, he was sometimes too careless when he played against opponents who weren't competing for the top places.

In his game against Furman, Tal teetered on the brink of catastrophe.

No. 39
M. Tal – S. Furman
1958, Riga, 25th Soviet Championship Final, round 16

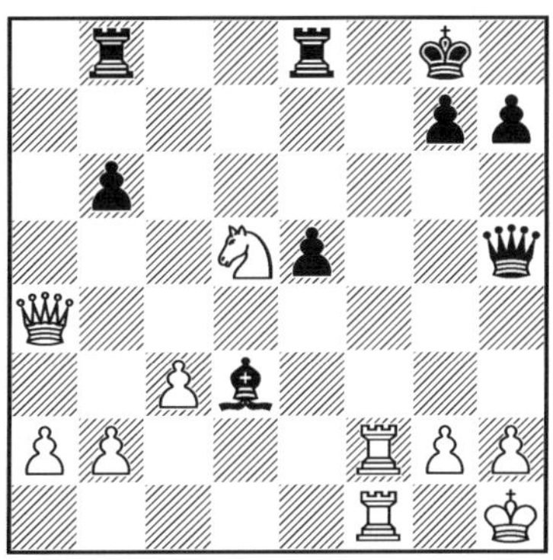

White's advantage is undoubtable. Furman also had less than two minutes for 12 moves. It seems that nothing can go wrong. However, Tal unexpectedly played the suicidal **29.g4?**

He was mainly counting on his opponent's time trouble. If black plays 29...♕h3, it's met with 30.♕xe8+, while after 29...♕g6, there's 30.♖f8+! ♖xf8 31.♘e7+ ♔h8 32.♘xg6+ and ♖xf8+. However, Furman managed to find the right move.

29...♕h4

White lost an exchange, but everything ultimately ended in Tal's favor: on move 38, Furman lost on time in a won position.

In the game against Krogius, Tal also had a bad position and only managed to draw after some help from his opponent.

Before the last round, Tal caught up with Petrosian. They led the table with 11.5 points each.

He had already clinched a ticked to the Interzonal, but the question of the new Soviet champion still remained open.

In the last round, the police had a lot of work on their plates. Hundreds of chess fans – those who failed to obtain tickets to the "chess palace" – gathered around the tall building. Only when the crowd was told that the key games would be broadcast in the Great Philharmonic Hall did they finally disperse.

The last round began.

Petrosian decided not to tempt fate and quickly agreed a draw with Averbakh.

The game Spassky – Tal became the center of attention. Tal played black and went for complications. He thought that he had better chances in a sharp struggle. Spassky played coolly and strongly. On move 23, Tal offered a draw in a roughly equal position, but Spassky declined. Just three moves later, Tal made a mistake, and his position quickly worsened.

The game was adjourned with a clear advantage for Spassky. Tal's king was threatened by his opponent's queen and rook.

No. 40
B. Spassky – M. Tal
1958, Riga, 25th Soviet Championship Final, round 19

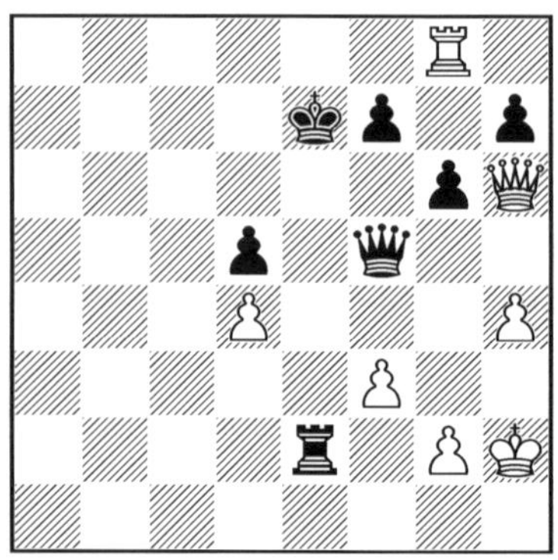

That's how the most gloomy analysis that we had ever carried out began... It continued until five in the morning. The more we studied the position, the worse the problems that we saw.

The resumption was in the morning. More than a thousand chess fans filled the playing hall. Others gathered at their TVs, eagerly awaiting the outcome of this captivating game.

48.♕f8+ ♔f6 49.♕g7+ ♔e7 50.♖a8! ♕d7

Forced, because of the threat 51.♖a7+.

Editor's note: Analysis shows that after the game move, white could win with 51.♕h8!, preventing the black king from leaving e7. Afterwards, he strengthens the position with a kingside pawn storm, which ultimately creates the foundation for a decisive attack; in many lines, ♕h8-b8 with the threat ♖a8-a7 is an important resource.

So black had to play 50...♕f4+!, and only after 51.♔h3 ♕f5+ 52.♔g3, play 52...♕d7. The principal difference is that now, with the king on g3, 53.♕h8 is met with 53...♕d6+ 54.♔h3 (if the king were on h2, white would have escaped to g1) 54...♕e6+ 55.g4 (or *55.♔h2♖xg2+!*) 55...♖h2+! 56.♔xh2 ♕e2+ with perpetual check.

51.♕f8+? ♔f6 52.♖a6+ ♖e6 53.♕h8+ ♔e7 54.♖a8 ♖e1

Editor's note: The correct move is 54...h5!, pointed out by Kasparov. After this, white has no win.

55.♔g3

Editor's note: The computer wins with 55.♖c8! (white prevents the queen check from c7, that is very unpleasant in many lines, and threatens 56.g4), and meets 55... h5 with 56.f4!!, destroying the black king's defense with f4-f5. However, the lines are very complicated.

55...h5

Preparing a safe haven for the king on f5.

Editor's note: This move again allows white to win the game. With 55...♕c7+ 56.♔f2 ♖e6, black equalizes: for instance, after 57.♕xh7 ♕c2+ 58.♔g3 ♖e2, white has to go for perpetual check (59.♖a7+).

56.♔f2 ♖e6 57.♖c8

Editor's note: As D. Eschbach later found, white got a decisive attack with 57.♕b8! ♔f6 58.g4!. The game move is weaker, but probably still doesn't miss the win completely.

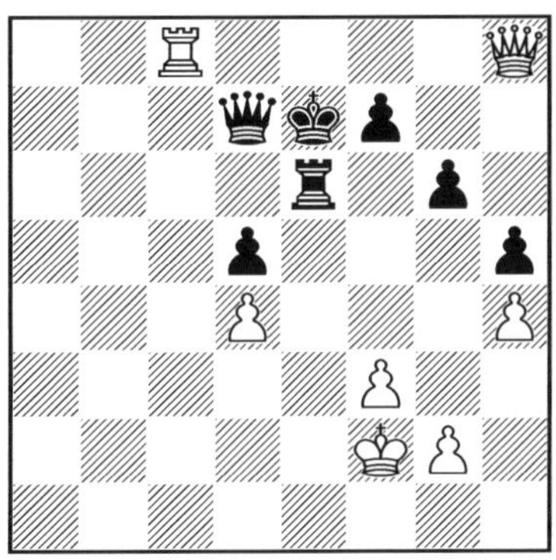

57...♖d6

Editor's note: This could have led to a quick loss, but analysis shows that even better moves were still inadequate: 57...♖c6 58.♕e5+ ♖e6 59.♕g5+ ♖f6 60.♕c1! ♕d6 61.♖c7+ ♔d8 62.♖b7 ♕f4 63.♕a1+− or 57... ♖b6 58.♕f8+ ♔f6 59.g4 ♖b2+ 60.♔g3 ♖b6 *(60...hxg4 61.fxg4 ♖d2 62.♖c3+−)* 61.♕h8+ ♔e7 62.♔f4 hxg4 63.♕f8+ ♔f6 64.fxg4 ♕d6+ 65.♕xd6 ♖xd6 66.♖e8+−.

58.♕f8+?

Vitaly Chekhover later showed in his analysis that white could win with 58.g4!.

Editor's note: Actually, this move doesn't deserve a question mark: the g-pawn could have been pushed on the next move as well.

58...♔f6 59.♖e8

Editor's note: This is a mistake. Kasparov's 59.g4! was correct, with an irresistible attack for white.

59...♖e6 60.♕h8+ ♔f5 61.♕h6 ♔f6 62.♕h8+

Editor's note: 62.♖g8! still gave white winning chances (Kasparov).

62...♔f5 63.♖d8

It's not too late to agree a draw, but Spassky only wants to win. (**Editor's note:** The best move was 63.♕h6 ♔f6 64.♖g8!, with the same position as after 62.♖g8!.)

63...♕c6! 64.♖c8?

The Leningrad grandmaster cracks under pressure. The correct move was 64.♔g3. Now Tal goes for a counter-attack.

Editor's note: This is not actually a mistake, Spassky missed the opportunity to draw only later.

64...♕a6 65.♔g3

Editor's note: This move doesn't lose yet, but Spassky's line 65.♕d8! ♕e2+ 66.♔g3 led to an easier draw.

65...♕d6+ 66.♔h3 ♖e1

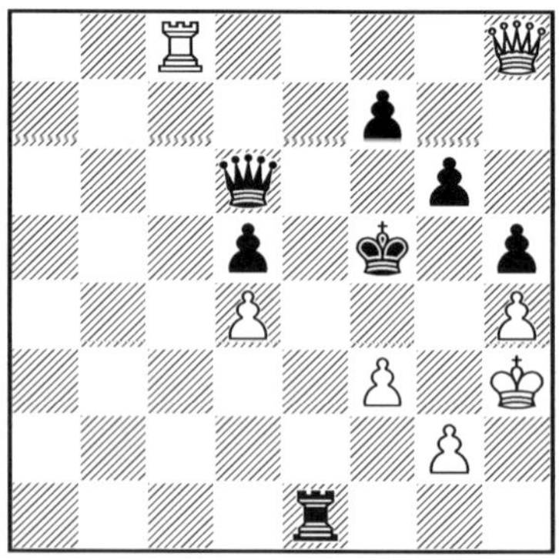

67.g3

67.g4+ hxg4+ 68.fxg4+ ♔f4 69.♕h6+ was bad due to 69...♔e4! 70.♖e8+ ♔f3

Editor's note: Actually, 67.g4+ is the only move that allows white to save the game. In this line, instead of 69.♕h6+, the correct move is 69.♖c3!, and after the subsequent 69...♖e3+ 70.♖xe3 ♔xe3 71.h5 ♔f4

72.h6 f6 73.♔g2 ♕e7 74.♕b8+ ♔g5 75.h7 ♕xh7 76.♕b3 ♕g8, there occurs a position that Kasparov also reached with a slightly different move order. However, if there were some doubts about its evaluation before, the computer now removes all of them: after 77.♕e3+ ♔xg4 78.♕f3+, white draws.

67...♖g1

Editor's note: Not a good move. 67...♕a6 won immediately.

Only now Spassky offered a draw, but Tal declined.

68.f4 ♖e1! 69.♖c2

Editor's note: Kasparov's recommendation 69.♖e8! ♖xe8 70.♕xe8 is more resilient, though it is still tough for white after 70...♕e6 due to his exposed d4-pawn.

69...♕e6 70.♖f2 ♖h1+ 71.♔g2 ♕e4+ 72.♖f3 ♔g4 73.♕c8+ f5, and **Spassky stopped the clock**.

As soon as the sign "White resigned" appeared on the demonstration board, the spectators ran to the stage. The least disciplined ones hugged Tal, then started throwing him into the air.

The whole chess world learned the news: Mikhail Tal had won the Soviet championship for the second time.

Commenting on the "final of the final", grandmaster Salo Flohr wrote in the *Ogonyok* magazine:

"'This is only an accident', the losers try to excuse themselves. But don't they think that these 'accidents' happen quite regularly with Tal? How else can you explain the fact that Tal again scored the best result against the grandmasters (7/10)?

Let's summarize: Mikhail Tal became the champion of the strongest chess country for the second time. Such great success can only be achieved by a talent as bright as the student from Riga."

Not Fearsome to his Friends

This was proved in the 1958 Latvian SSR championship. Despite Tal's huge reputation, his opponents in the republican tournament played him without fear. Many participants had played together with Tal in All-Union team tournaments or played against him in dozens of other tournaments. And so, they didn't play against grandmaster Mikhail Tal, Soviet champion – they played against Misha Tal.

From the sporting point of view, Tal's result was great – 16.5/19, however, his competitors Aivars Gipslis and Israel Zilber scored a half-point more, both defeating the Soviet champion.

The loss to Gipslis was a good lesson for Tal.

Before departing for the tournament hall, Tal started leafing through new chess magazines, and a line in the Sicilian Defense attracted his attention. He liked a novelty and decided to use it in an important game without even checking it. However, it turned out that the line was faulty.

Since then, the grandmaster has never used opening lines in important games without thoroughly checking them first.

No. 41
I. Zilber – M. Tal
1958, Riga, Latvian Championship, round 10

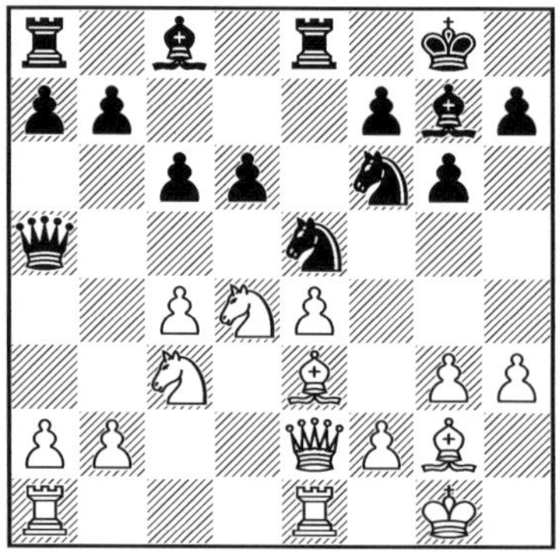

The other loss, to Zilber, is also very characteristic of Tal.

The diagram shows a complicated position with roughly equal chances. By playing 13...a6, black could have counted on some counterplay with b7-b5.

Editor's note: The position on the diagram occurred in many subsequent games. Black most often played 13...♗e6 and usually met 14.♘xe6 with 14...♖xe6, planning to create pressure on the e4 pawn with ♖a8-e8, for instance: 15.f4 ♘ed7 16.♗f2 ♖ae8 17.♕c2 ♘h5 18.♖ad1 ♘c5 (Volzhin – J. Piket, Ohrid, 2001). Koblenz's recommendation 13...a6 is not good, because it's almost impossible to create good conditions for b7-b5. For instance, in the game Ris — Bosch (Netherlands 2014), there followed 14.♖ad1 c5 (after *14...b5?*, there's *15.cxb5*, and the position is bad for black after both *15...axb5 16.f4 ♘c4 17.♘xc6* and *15...cxb5 16.f4 ♘c4 17.e5*) 15.♘b3 ♕b4? (black had to accept a difficult position after *15...♕c7 16.f4 ♘c6*) 16.♖xd6+−.

But Tal instead decides to sacrifice a piece.

13...♕b4 14.f4 ♘xc4 15.a3 ♕c5 16.b4 ♕h5 17.♕xc4 ♗xh3 18.♗f2 d5

Editor's note: The game move quickly loses, however, black didn't have enough compensation in any case.

19.exd5 ♗xg2 20.♔xg2 cxd5 21.♕d3 ♖xe1 22.♖xe1 ♘g4

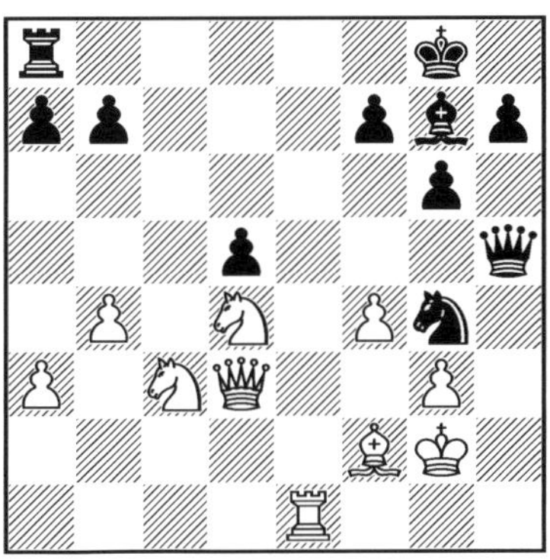

Black had placed all his hopes in this position. Tal thought that white had to play 23.♘f3, and prepared 23...♕h3+! 24.♔g1 ♕h1+! 25.♔xh1 ♘xf2+ and 26...♘xd3.

However, Zilber played **23.♗g1!**

This prosaic bishop retreat refutes black's combination. **Black resigned** on move 54.

This prompts the question: perhaps, when playing a direct competitor, it's better to avoid risky continuations and quietly wait for events to unfold?

Such decisions depend on the player's personality. If the player is bold and is not afraid to take risks, he has to follow his heart, even in the most important games.

In June, Tal traveled to Crimea for a holiday. We gradually started preparing for the Interzonal. Then one day we got a phone call. A Soviet Chess Federation representative told us that Tal had been called up to the students' national team, and he should head to Bulgaria.

Tal said goodbye to his new Crimean friends. As he boarded the plane to Varna, he felt like the happiest man alive...

The Soviet student team leader, Misha achieved a great result – 8.5/10.

On the Adriatic Sea

A few weeks after the student Olympiad, the Interzonal tournament opened in the Yugoslavian resort of Portoroz. This was an event eagerly awaited by chess players in all countries.

Previously, Tal had only played in international team events. Now, however, he had to play in a qualifying tournament for the world championship title.

Portoroz – a quiet town with five hotels and a few bars – completely transformed itself in those days. Flags of the countries whose representatives played in the tournament were displayed on the buildings facing the sea, while shop windows dazzled passers-by with bright posters and photos of the players. The grandmasters and masters fell victim to the autograph hunters. They were pestered everywhere – on the streets, in restaurants, even on the beach.

Tal defeated the Colombian player De Greiff in the first round and faced the renowned Hungarian grandmaster Laszlo Szabo in the second. Szabo played an unassuming opening and offered a draw on move 12. Tal declined the draw, and the battle intensified.

No. 42
L. Szabo – M. Tal
1958, Portoroz, Interzonal Tournament, round 2

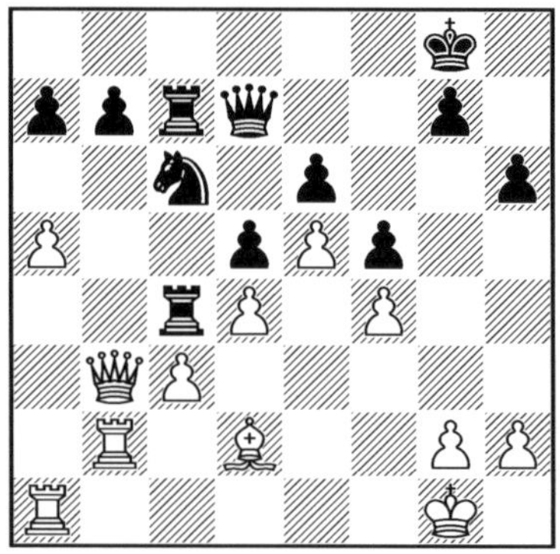

23...♔h7!

Editor's note: The purpose of this prophylactic move will become clear three moves later.

24.h3 a6

Editor's note: Black is planning ♘c6-a7-b5, attacking the weak c3 pawn.

25.♕b6 ♘e7 26.♕d6 ♕e8!

Editor's note: If the black king were on g8 right now, white would have captured the e6 pawn with check. Now, however, 27.♕xe6?? is met with 27...♖7c6, trapping the queen.

27.♖b6 ♖4c6 28.♖xc6 ♕xc6 29.♖b1 ♖d7

Black's intentions are clear – he wants to drive the opponent's queen away from its active position.

30.♕b4

White avoids the queen trade, because after 30.♕xc6 ♘xc6, black threatened ♘a7-b5 and ♖c7-c4.

30...♘c8 31.g4 g6 32.♕f8 ♖g7 33.♔f2 ♕c4! 34.♖b2

Editor's note: The correct move was 34.gxf5. Black can't play 34... gxf5, because after 35.♖g1! ♖xg1 36.♔xg1 he even loses due to the threats ♕f8–f7+ and ♗d2–e1–h4. Meanwhile, after 34...exf5, the e5 pawn becomes passed, which gives white enough counterchances. The following line is possible, for instance: 35.♔e3 ♘a7 36.♕b4 ♕c7 *(36...♕xb4? 37.♖xb4 ♘c6 38.c4!! ♘xb4 39.♗xb4 dxc4 40.d5+–)* 37.c4 dxc4 38.d5 g5 39.♕b6 ♕d7 40.♕xa7 ♕xd5 41.♕d4 gxf4+ 42.♕xf4 ♖g2 43.♕xf5+ ♔g7 44.♗e1 ♖g5 45.♕f6+ ♔g8 46.♖d1 ♖xe5+ (or *46...♕xd1 47.♕e6+*, and the king can't hide from the pursuit) 47.♔f2 ♖f5+ 48.♔g1 ♖g5+ 49.♔f2 ♕g2+ 50.♔e3 ♕xh3+ 51.♔e2 ♕h5+ 52.♔e3, and black only has perpetual check.

34...♘a7

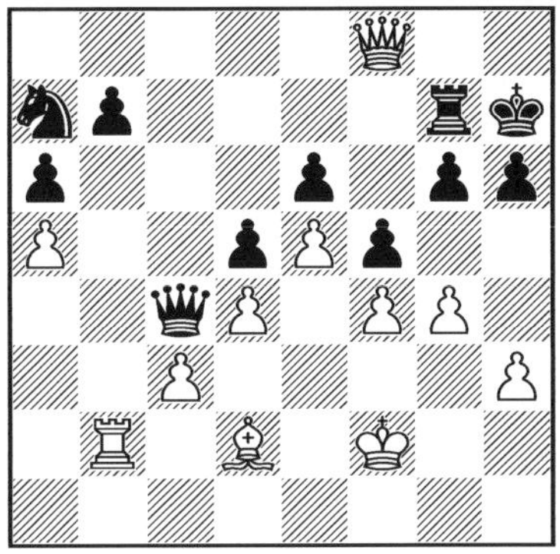

35.♖b6

Editor's note: It was necessary to go for the endgame with 35.♕c5 (perhaps after trading on f5 first) 35... ♕xc5 36.dxc5, and even though white is clearly worse, he still has some chances to save the game.

35...♘c6 36.♔e1 ♕d3! 37.g5 hxg5 38.fxg5 ♘xa5 39.♖xe6 ♘c4 40.♗c1 ♕xc3+

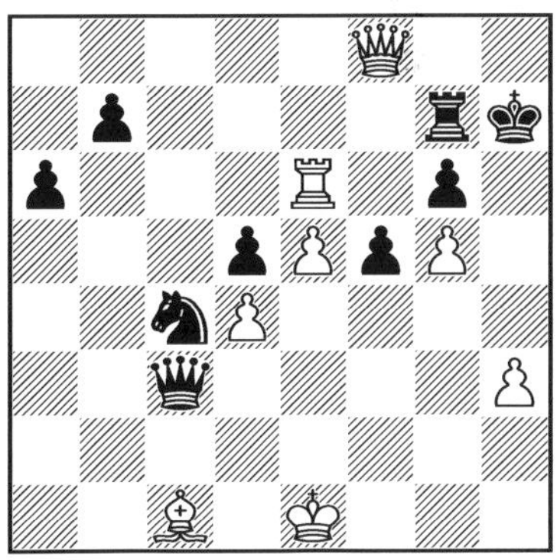

41.♔d1

There was an opinion that white could put up more resistance with 41.♔e2. However, this could be met with 41...♕xc1 42.♖e8 ♕e3+ 43.♔f1 ♘d2+ 44.♔g2 ♕xg5+ 45.♔h1 ♔h6.

41...♕xd4+ 42.♔e2 ♕e4+ 43.♔d1 ♕f3+ 44.♔c2 ♕e2+ 45.♔c3 d4+ 46.♔b4 a5+ 47.♔c5 ♖c7+ 48.♔b5 ♘xe5+ 49.♔b6 ♖c6+ White resigned.

The third round game Tal – Pachman was aptly described by grandmaster Svetozar Gligoric:

"After every knockdown punch, Pachman would get up before the referee reached the count of ten. His opponent had to start anew each time, until he, too, was out of strength."

The opponents agreed to a draw in a rook ending on move 50.

Intense emotions awaited Tal in the fourth round. His game against Aleksandar Matanovic was adjourned in the following position:

No. 43
A. Matanovic – M. Tal
1958, Portoroz, Interzonal Tournament, round 4

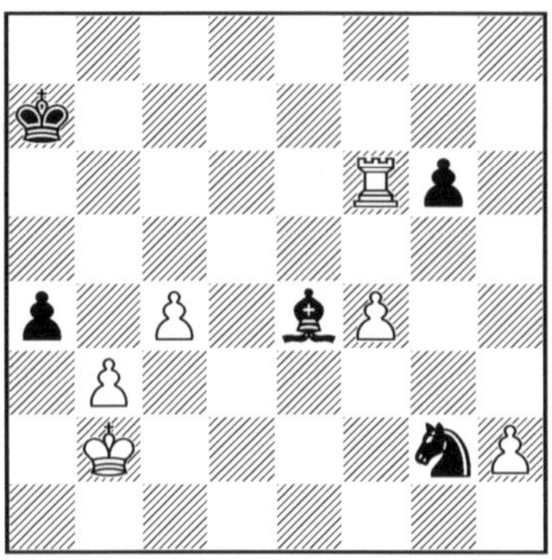

We thought that Matanovic had sealed the move 41.bxa4. It was objectively the strongest one. A long search for any way to save the game gave us nothing – the position was lost. There was no time to study other continuations in detail.

However, at the resumption we discovered that our opponent had sealed a weaker move, **41.b4**

Editor's note: It seems that the game move is also enough for a win.

41...♘e3 42.♖e6!

But not 42.♔c3 due to 42...a3 43.b5 ♘d1+ 44.♔d4 ♗b7.

Editor's note: Koblenz's line requires some corrections. Instead of 44.♔d4??, the right move is 44.♔b4, and white wins. So it's necessary to change the move order to 42...♘d1+! (instead of the erroneous 42...a3) 43.♔d4 a3!, and after 44.♔xe4 (but not *44.b5?? ♗b7*, and the position from Koblenz's note occurs, which is won for black) 44...a2 45.b5 a1=♕ 46.♖a6+ ♕xa6 47.bxa6 ♔xa6 it's a draw.

42...♘xc4+ 43.♔c3 ♗d5 44.♖xg6 ♘b6 45.h4 a3 46.b5

Editor's note: This move is a mistake that could have cost Matanovic half a point, whereas the h-pawn advance could have decided the game in just a few moves: 46.h5 ♗f7 47.♖g5 (but not *47.♖g7? ♘a4+ 48.♔c2 a2 49.♖g1 ♗xh5 50.♔b3 ♘b6 51.♔xa2 ♘d5=*) 47...♘a4+ 48.♔d4 ♔b6 *(48...a2 49.♖a5++−)* 49.h6 a2 50.♖g1 ♗g8 51.♖a1+−.

46...♗f7 47.♖g1

Here Tal thought for a while and... made a losing move.

"I was thinking about the line 47.♖g7 ♘a4+ 48.♔c2 a2," he said after the game. "I liked this pawn spurt so much that I automatically grabbed the pawn after my opponent's move. And so, I had to make this horrible move. After 47.♖g1, I planned to play 47...♘d5+ 48.♔b3 ♔b6, with good drawing chances."

After **47...a2?**, **the Yugoslavian grandmaster won**.

Tal's next opponent was the Czechoslovakian grandmaster Miroslav Filip. I knew that, after a loss, Tal would surely try and bounce back with a win, so I feared that in the game against such a careful, mature player as Filip, the desire to force matters at any cost may lead to a catastrophe.

No. 44
M. Tal – M. Filip
1958, Portoroz, Interzonal Tournament, round 5

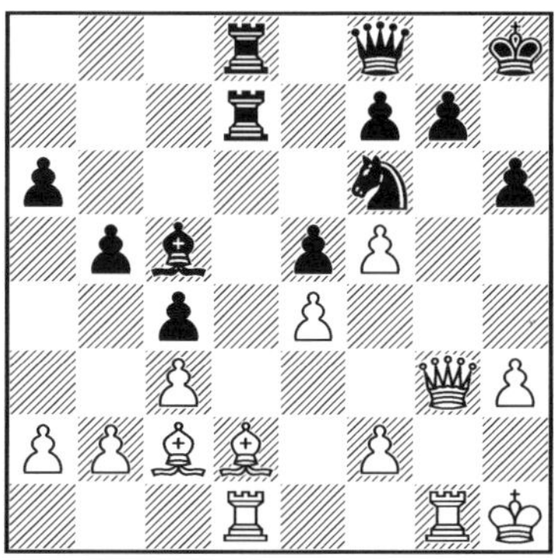

While Tal was thinking over his position, Petrosian's second, grandmaster Efim Geller, leaned in to me and said, "It seems that Misha can't do much this time!"

I realized that it wasn't easy to explode black's solid position, but I wanted to object in some way, so I answered Geller, "If Misha has an open line, there'll be a mate!"

At that moment, white sacrificed a bishop on h6.

28.♗xh6!

"After this move," Matanovic wrote, "white could have faced some problems, but we can't deny that he only won because of this sacrifice. We should respect his boldness!"

Editor's note: Actually, even the computer agrees that Tal's bishop sacrifice was the strongest move. Other continuations are much weaker: 28.♗c1?? ♖xd1 29.♖xd1 ♘xe4–+ or 28.♗e3? ♖xd1 29.♖xd1 *(29.♗xd1 ♗xe3 30.♕xe3 ♖d3–+)* 29...♗xe3 30.♕xe3 ♘h5, with the subsequent ♘h5-f4 and an overwhelming position.

28...gxh6 29.♕xe5 ♗e7 30.♖d4 ♖xd4 31.cxd4 ♔h7 32.♖d1 ♘e8?

It was better to play 32...♕g7!, and if 33.♕xe7, then 33...♖g8.

Actually, Tal planned to meet 32...♕g7 with 33.♕f4 ♖g8 34.♕f3, with roughly equal chances.

33.f6!

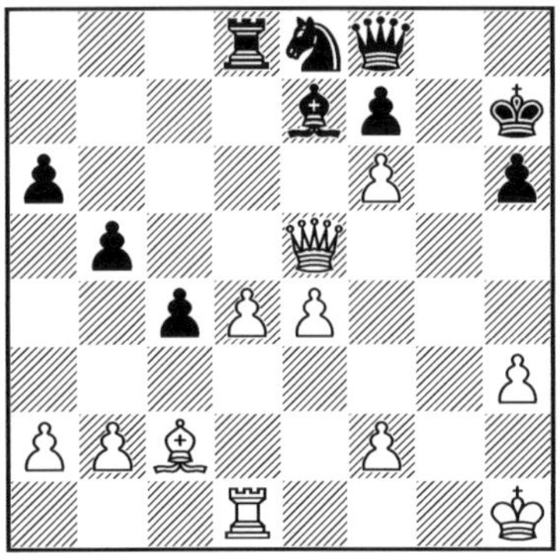

The bishop joins the attack, and black's position quickly deteriorates.

Editor's note: Actually, black could have saved the game here had he played 33...♗xf6 — after the subsequent 34.♕f5+ ♔g8 *(34...♔h8? 35.e5+−)* 35.♖g1+ (or *35.e5 ♕e7 36.♕h7+ ♔f8 37.♖g1 ♕e6 38.♖g8+ ♔e7 39.♕xh6 ♕d5! 40.♔g1 ♗g7 41.♕g5+ ♔d7 42.♗f5+ ♔c7 43.♕e7+ ♔b6 44.♖xe8 ♖xe8 45.♕xe8 ♕xd4 46.♕xf7 ♗xe5* with a drawn endgame) 35...♗g7 36.e5 ♕b4 37.e6 fxe6 38.♕xe6+ ♔f8 39.♕f5+ ♔e7 40.♕e4+ ♔f7, white only has perpetual check.

33...♘xf6 34.♕f5+ ♔h8 35.e5 ♕g7 36.exf6 ♗xf6 37.♖g1 ♗g5 38.f4 Black resigned.

In the following rounds, Tal had to settle for a draw three times. Especially frustrating was losing half a point against the Filipino player Cardoso, who was last in the tournament at that point.

Against Gligoric, Tal managed to draw the game with ingenious and inventive defense, while in the game with international master Oleg Neikirch, Tal didn't dare to decline the draw offer in a slightly worse position.

The peacefulness of the calm, always smiling master from Sofia was boundless.

"I can't play against a fifteen year-old boy. If I win, people in Sofia will say that I bullied the kid. And if I lose, I'd be ashamed to return to Bulgaria" – that's how Neikirch explained his draw against Bobby Fischer.

Master Geza Fuster performed quite badly in the tournament. In time trouble, he would lose drawn or even clearly won games.

The loss to Tal upset him the least of all of his defeats.

No. 45
M. Tal – G. Fuster
1958, Portoroz, Interzonal Tournament, round 9

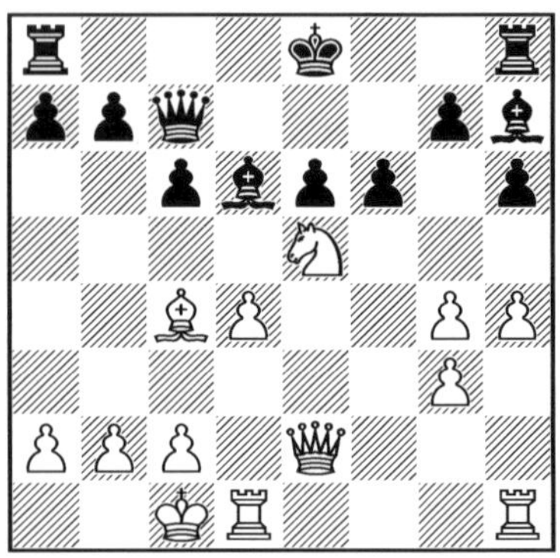

17.♗xe6! fxe5 18.dxe5 ♗e7 19.♖hf1! ♖f8 20.♖xf8+ ♗xf8 21.♕f3

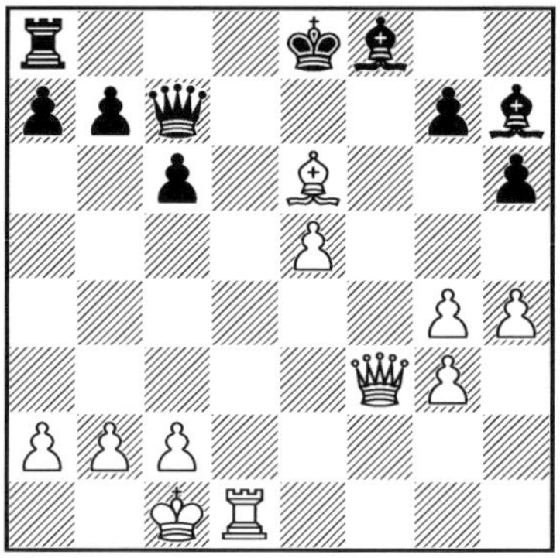

21...♕e7

Alekhine once said, "Such a pity that the execution of a beautiful plan always depends on your opponent as well!"

Here, Tal expected 21...♗c5 and had prepared 22.b4 ♗xb4 23.♖d7 ♕xd7 24.♗xd7+ ♔xd7 25.♕b3 a5 26.a3 ♗g8 27.♕b2, and black doesn't get enough compensation for the queen.

22.♕b3

With 22.♗d7+ ♕xd7 23.♖xd7 ♔xd7 24.♕f7+ ♗e7 25.♕xg7, white could transition into a won endgame, but Tal decided to set a trap for his opponent.

22...♖b8? 23.♗d7+ ♕xd7 24.♖xd7 ♔xd7 25.♕f7+ ♗e7 26.e6+ ♔d8

After 26...♔d6, there follows, of course, 27.♕f4+.

27.♕xg7 Black resigned.

After this win, Tal advanced to second place. The leader of the tournament, Tigran Petrosian, had a half-point more.

"Where did I make a mistake?" the Argentinian master Rossetto asked Tal after their game.

It was hard to answer this question. For a time, it seemed that Tal wanted to win so much that he lost the ability to assess the position objectively. At any rate, declining a draw offer while a pawn down really looked reckless.

"Without a doubt, the analysts will find where Rossetto could have played better, which move would have caused the most trouble for his inventive opponent, but this won't render the young Soviet champion's victory any less valuable," grandmasters Gligoric and Matanovic wrote in the tournament book.

No. 46, King's Indian Defense
H. Rossetto – M. Tal
1958, Portoroz, Interzonal Tournament, round 10

1.c4 ♘f6 2.♘f3 g6 3.g3 ♗g7 4.♗g2 0-0 5.0-0 d6 6.d4 ♘c6 7.♘c3 a6 8.d5 ♘a5 9.♕d3 c5 10.e4 e6

Editor's note: The main line here is 10...♖b8, intending b7-b5.

11.h3 exd5 12.cxd5 b5

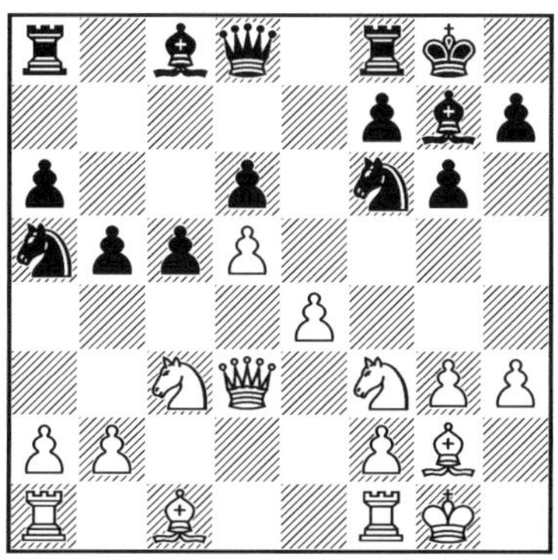

In times past, when the leading grandmasters were much stronger than masters, the tournament leader usually didn't have a hard time against weaker players. The player with the higher title would usually get an advantage out of the opening.

In our days, the leaders have a much harder time: opponents from the lower half of the table sometimes put up very stiff resistance against the favorites.

Some grandmasters try to defeat the weaker players with a sit-and-wait strategy. They expect their opponent to make a subtle positional mistake at some point. In tournaments with "mixed" line-ups, such tactics allow them to compete for high places. High places, but not first place. To finish first, pure technique is usually not enough. Only a brave tournament fighter who's not afraid to face dangers can compete for first place. That's how Tal and Korchnoi play. Even in games against weaker opponents, they face danger without fear. Of course, such a playing style requires great strength and expense of energy.

13.♗f4 b4 14.♘d1 ♖e8 15.♖e1 c4 16.♕c2 ♖a7 17.♗e3 ♖ae7

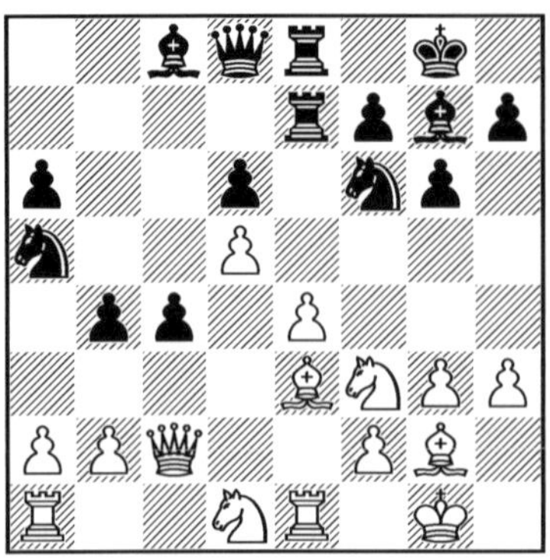

18.♘d2

White allows his opponent to launch a queenside operation. He's hoping for the chance to disperse and eliminate the advance party that has ventured too far ahead of the main forces.

In this critical moment, Tal finds an interesting tactical resource.

18...b3!

Editor's note: The computer likes 18...♗d7!? more, planning ♗d7-b5, not ceding the c3 square to white and retaining the possibility of playing c4-c3 in a number of lines. After the subsequent 19.♘xc4 ♕c7 20.♖c1 ♘xe4 21.♘b6 ♘c5 22.♘xd7 ♕xd7, the position is roughly equal.

19.axb3

Editor's note: 19.♕c1!? was worthy of serious consideration, planning ♘d1-c3 and not allowing his opponent the opportunity to carry out the tactical blow that happened on move 20. In this case, it's hard for black to find ways to develop a good initiative, while white's space and pawn advantage in the center might help him.

19...♘xb3 20.♖a4

20.♘xb3 cxb3 21.♕xb3 ♘xe4 is better for black.

20...♘xd5! 21.exd5 ♗f5 22.♕xc4 ♘xd2 23.♕xa6

Black has seized the initiative after sacrificing a pawn, but the crucial events are still ahead.

23...♘e4 24.♕b6 ♕c8

Tal decides not to trade queens: he needs his queen for a kingside attack.

25.g4 ♘c5 26.♖a7

Editor's note: Perhaps 26.♖a3!? was stronger – after the subsequent 26...♗c2 *(26...♘d3? 27.♖f1+–)* 27.♕xd6 ♘d3 28.♖f1, black must prove that his activity compensates for the lack of two pawns.

26...♖xa7 27.♕xa7 ♘d3 28.♖f1 ♗e4 29.♕a3 ♗xg2 30.♔xg2 ♕c4! 31.♕xd6 ♗f8 32.♕c6 ♕e4+ 33.♔g1

Here, white could have saved the game with 33.f3 ♕e5 34.d6 ♗xd6 35.f4. But Rossetto already had too little time: his flag was hanging menacingly.

Editor's note: The game move actually doesn't lose either.

33...♘e5 34.♘c3 ♘f3+ 35.♔h1 ♕e5 36.♔g2 ♘h4+ 37.♔g1 ♗d6 38.♖d1

Editor's note: White could have salvaged the game with 38.♗f4!, for instance, 38...♕xf4 (*38...♘f3+ 39.♔g2 ♕xf4 40.♕xe8+ ♔g7 41.♖d1 ♘e5 42.♔f1 ♗c5 43.♖d2* doesn't win either) 39.♕xe8+ ♔g7 40.♖d1 ♗c5 (after *40...♕f3?! 41.♔f1 ♕xh3+ 42.♔e2 ♕xg4+ 43.♔d3* the white king escapes the pursuit, and white retains all the extra material) 41.♘e4 ♕f3 42.♕e5+ ♔g8 (after *42...f6? 43.♕xf6+*, only black can lose) 43.♘f6+ ♔f8 44.♘d7+ with perpetual check.

38...♕h2+ 39.♔f1 ♖xe3 White resigned.

Until round 14, Tal shadowed Tigran Petrosian, staying half a point behind the leader. In round 15, he caught up with the Moscow grandmaster, and on the next day, they switched places – Tal took the lead.

In round 17, Petrosian played Sanguinetti. After losing in the previous round, the grandmaster looked tired, but he played very coolly, gradually increasing his positional advantage.

Tal played against the Argentinian grandmaster Oscar Panno. At first, Tal watched his rival's game carefully, but then the events of his own game had him in deep thought.

Panno, usually a quiet player, was unrecognizable in this game. He chose an original defensive system, creating a real storm on the board.

The game was still on, but I was already receiving consolations.

David Bronstein approached me first.

"Don't be upset if Misha loses today," he whispered to me. "You'll see, he'll bounce back for sure!"

"Panno has a whole bunch of pieces for his queen!" Vladimir Simagin, Yuri Averbakh's coach, sighed.

"Could you tell me where Tal made a mistake?" a Yugoslavian journalist asked me as he passed by. "I'm sorry, I'm hurrying to the telegraph. Panno will win for sure, and there'll be a long queue later..."

What happened in that game, anyway?

No. 47, Ruy Lopez
M. Tal – O. Panno
1958, Portoroz, Interzonal Tournament, round 17

1.e4 e5 2.♘f3 ♘c6 3.♗b5 a6 4.♗a4 ♘f6 5.0-0 ♗e7 6.♖e1 b5 7.♗b3 d6 8.c3 0-0 9.h3 ♘d7

Editor's note: In modern practice, there are much more popular moves for black: 9...♘a5, 9...♗b7 and 9...♘b8 (with the idea of ♘b8-d7 and ♗c8-b7).

10.d4 ♘b6

Editor's note: In subsequent games, black usually played 10...♗f6 in this line.

11.♗e3

Editor's note: The current main line in this position is 11.♘bd2.

11...exd4 12.cxd4 ♘a5 13.♗c2 c5

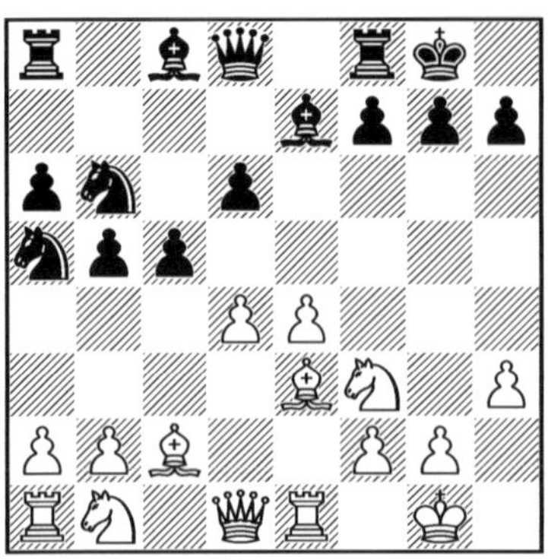

14.e5!

White has to play energetically, otherwise black will seize the initiative, for instance, after the quiet 14.♘c3 ♘ac4 15.♗c1 cxd4 16.♘xd4 ♗f6.

Editor's note: The computer evaluates the situation differently: it says that white is slightly better in Koblenz's line (the weakness on d6 is rather glaring, and the active c4 knight can be kicked away with b2-b3), while the game move leads to a roughly equal position.

14...dxe5!

The Argentinian player avoids the trap 14...♘ac4 15.exd6 ♕xd6, which Tal planned to meet with 16.♗g5!.

Editor's note: The position from Koblenz's line is not dangerous for black: after the subsequent 16...♗xg5 17.♘xg5 h6 18.dxc5 ♕xd1 (*18...♕xc5? 19.♘h7! ♘xb2 20.♕e2* drops an exchange, because black can't play *20...♖d8* due to *21.♕e8+*) 19.♗xd1 *(19.♖xd1?! ♘xb2)* 19...hxg5 (black is all right after *19...♘d7* or *19...♘xb2*) 20.cxb6 (or *20.b3 ♗b7*=) 20...♘xb2, the position is equal. However, instead of 15.exd6, white has a stronger reply 15.♕d3, and after 15...g6 16.exd6 ♗xd6 (perhaps *16...♕xd6* is the lesser evil, even though it loses a pawn after *17.dxc5 ♕xd3 18.♗xd3*) 17.♗g5, white has a very dangerous initiative.

15.♘xe5 ♘bc4 16.♕d3

Declining the draw — 16.♕h5 g6 17.♘xg6 fxg6 18.♗xg6 hxg6 19.♕xg6+ ♔h8 – and willingly diving into complications that are hard to calculate completely.

16...f5

Editor's note: 16...g6, intending ♗c8-f5, was worthy of serious consideration.

17.♗b3! f4

Editor's note: This move is a mistake. Instead of it, Panno had a number of good resources, including the immediate 17...♘xb3, for instance: 18.♘c6 (or *18.♕xb3 ♗e6*, and *19.dxc5* is bad due to *19...f4* with the subsequent *20...♗xc5*) 18...♕d6 19.♘xe7+ ♕xe7 20.axb3 ♘xe3 21.♖xe3 ♕g5, and black is no worse (22.dxc5? f4).

18.♗d2 ♘xb3!

A great reply! After 19.♕xb3 ♗f6 20.♘xc4 bxc4 21.♕xc4+ ♔h8, white faces considerable trouble, while in the line that happened in the game, black gets more than enough compensation for the queen.

Editor's note: In Koblenz's line, instead of the erroneous 20.♘xc4, white has a stronger reply 20.♘a3, and analysis shows that after the subsequent 20...♗e6 21.♘axc4, the position is equal.

19.♘c6 ♘xa1 20.♘xd8 ♗f5 21.♕f3 ♖axd8 22.♖xe7 ♗xb1 23.♗xf4

Editor's note: 23.♗e1! was a much stronger move, with black facing great difficulties due to his uncoordinated pieces, for instance: 23...♘c2 24.♕g4 ♖f7 25.♕e6 ♖df8 26.♖xf7 ♖xf7 27.dxc5, and, because of the dangerous passed c-pawn and weak a6 pawn (and if it falls, the b5 pawn will likely fall as well), black might not hold, or 23...cxd4 24.b3 ♖fe8 25.♗b4 ♘e5 26.♕b7 ♖xe7 27.♕xe7 ♘f7 28.♗a5 ♖f8 29.♕e1 ♗xa2 30.♕xa1 ♗xb3 31.♕xd4 ♘g5 32.♗b4 ♖e8 33.♕xf4 — white has a material advantage now, and it's black who has to struggle for a draw.

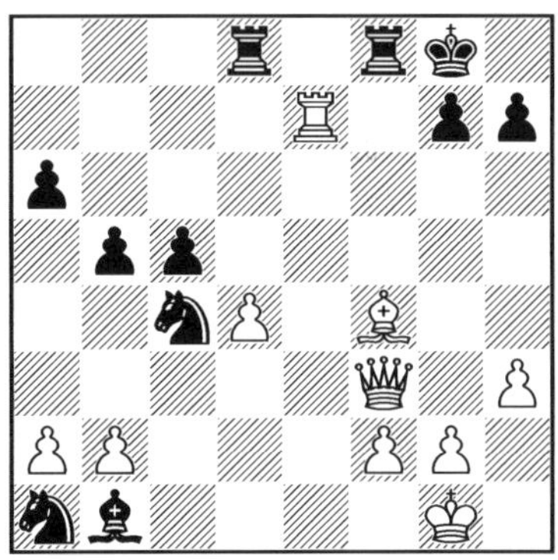

23...♖xd4

In the opinion of the Yugoslavian theoretician V. Vukovic, black should have won after 23...cxd4, however, after 24.b3 ♗g6 25.bxc4 d3 (threatening 26...♖xf4), white has the move 26.♕g4, and if 26...d2, then 27.♖d7 (**Editor's note:** The computer insists on 27.♗xd2! ♖xd2 28.c5 instead and proves that the passed c-pawn wins the game for white). After 26...♖xf4, there's 27.♕xf4 d2 28.♖xg7+! ♔h8 29.♖d7!, and white wins.

Editor's note: In the above line, instead of 26.♕g4, white has an even stronger move: 26.♕g3! d2 27.♗xd2! ♖xd2 28.♕c3 ♖d1+ 29.♔h2 ♗f7 30.c5+−. But, at any rate, instead of the erroneous 24...♗g6, the correct move is 24...♘d6, for instance: 25.♖e1 ♗e4 26.♕g3 ♘c2 27.♗xd6 ♘xe1 28.♗xf8 ♖xf8 29.♕e5 ♗xg2 30.♕xe1 ♗xh3 31.♕e4 ♖f6 *(31...♖d8? 32.♕h4)* 32.♕xd4 h6 with an obvious draw. But instead of 24.b3, white has an interesting resource 24.♕g3!? – after the subsequent 24...♗g6 25.b3 ♘b6 26.♗e5 ♖d7 27.♖xd7 ♘xd7 28.♗xd4 ♘c2 29.♗b2 black can be satisfied from the material point of view, but the white pieces are very active, the g7 square needs protection, the c2 knight is placed very awkwardly, and the a6 pawn is very weak and will likely fall soon, so it's only white who can play for a win here.

24.♕g4! ♗g6 25.♕e6+ ♗f7 26.♕f5 ♘c2

The knight is stuck deep behind enemy lines and has to be brought back into play. After 26...♗g6, Tal intended to play 27.♖xg7+ ♔xg7 28.♗h6+ ♔xh6 29.♕xf8+ with the subsequent 30.♕xc5+ and ♕xd4.

Editor's note: The game move wasn't the only move; another good reply was 26...♖d5 27.♕e4 *(27.♕b1?! ♗g6 28.♕e1 ♘c2 29.♕e6+ ♗f7 30.♕xa6 ♖d1+ 31.♔h2 ♘d4* gives black dangerous counterplay and is risky for white) 27...♖d4 28.♕f5 ♖d5, with repetition.

27.b3 ♗g6

Editor's note: This move is a mistake. The correct reply was 27...♖d1+ 28.♔h2 ♘d2 – analysis shows that the position is dynamically equal: 29.♗xd2 ♖xd2 30.♕xc5, and then, for instance, 30...h6 (a useful luft) 31.♖a7 ♖e8 32.♖xa6 ♘d4 33.♖a7 ♖ee2 34.♕c8+ ♖e8 35.♕c3 ♖ee2 36.♕c8+ ♖e8, with repetition.

28.♖xg7+

This sacrifice doesn't win. However, black has to be very careful to repel the numerous threats.

Editor's note: Actually, black is already lost.

28...♔xg7 29.♗h6+ ♔xh6 30.♕xf8+ ♔g5 31.bxc4 bxc4 32.g3

Editor's note: This is a mistake. White could have won with both 32.g4, intending ♔g1-h2-g3, and 32.♔h2, with the idea g3-g4 and ♔h2-g3. For instance: 32.g4 ♖d7 33.♔h2 ♖f7 34.♕d6 ♔h6 *(34...♖xf2+ 35.♔g3 ♖f7 36.♕e5+ ♔h6 37.♔h4+−)* 35.♕xc5 ♔g7 36.♕e5+ ♔g8 37.f4

♗d3 38.♕g5+ ♔f8 39.♕d8+ ♔g7 40.♕d6 a5 41.a4 ♘b4 42.f5 – white will soon capture the a5 pawn and win the game with a combined pawn push on both flanks.

32...♗e4 33.h4+ ♔g4 34.♔h2 ♗f5!

Had black retreated his bishop with 34...♗d5, he would have gotten checkmated after 35.f3+! ♗xf3 36.♕c8+ ♔h5 37.♕f5+.

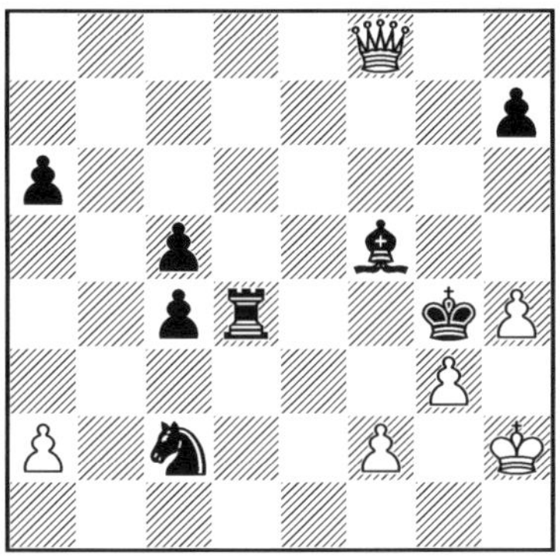

There were only a few minutes left until time control, but Tal was in deep thought.

"Why is he thinking?" the spectators murmured. He seemed to have only one move: 35.f3+. But Tal played a different move.

35.♕f6!

After 35.f3+? ♔xf3 36.♕xf5+ ♔e3 37.♕xh7 c3, it's white who has to scramble for a draw now!

Editor's note: Analysis leaves no doubt that the position resulting from Koblenz's line is indeed won for black.

35...h6 36.♕e5 ♖e4 37.♕g7+ ♔f3 38.♕c3+ ♘e3

With 38...♔xf2 39.♕xc2+ ♔f3, black could have easily drawn. At this moment, both players were completely exhausted. Drops of sweat ran down Panno's face. And, as the reader can see, there was a reason for this exhaustion!

39.♔g1! ♗g4 40.fxe3 h5 41.♕e1!

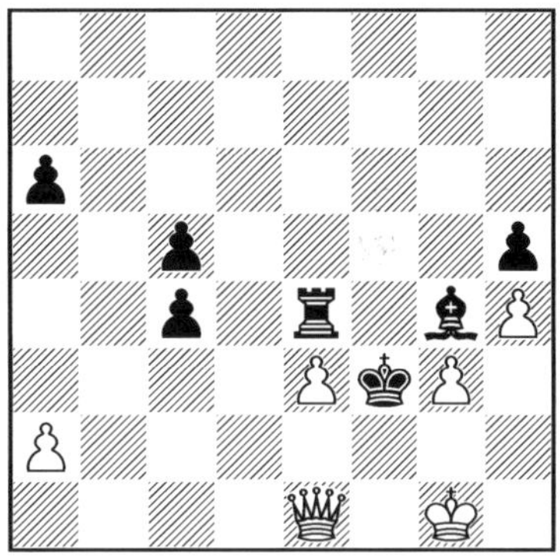

41...♖xe3

The decisive mistake. Black could have drawn with 41...♖e6!. (**Editor's note:** One of the possible lines after 41...♖e6! is, for instance: 42.e4 c3 43.♕xc3+ ♔xe4 44.♕xc5 ♔d3, and, no matter what the computer says, there's a fortress on the board.)

The game was adjourned here. Here's how it ended on the resumption day:

42.♕f1+ ♔e4 43.♕xc4+ ♔f3 44.♕f1+ ♔e4 45.♕xa6 ♔d4 46.♕d6+ ♔c4 47.a4 ♖e1+ 48.♔f2 ♖e2+ 49.♔f1 ♖a2 50.♕a6+ ♔d4 51.a5 c4 52.♕b6+ ♔d5 53.a6 ♖a1+ 54.♔f2 c3 55.a7 c2 56.♕b3+

♔**d6 57.**♕**d3+**, and **black resigned**, because he can't take the a7 pawn without losing his rook.

This game shows just how energetic and inspired Tal's play was in double-edged positions.

While Tal's theoretical knowledge, endgame technique and persistence in defense are not superior to that of other leading grandmasters, his dynamic style, rich imagination and quickness of calculation undoubtedly make him stand out even among the most renowned chess players.

Tal is able to create more and more difficulties for his opponents. Sometimes, his opponent manages to repel a whole series of attacks and avoids numerous traps, but difficult defense exhausts him so much that he ultimately makes a mistake.

For the spectators who sit comfortably in their tournament hall chairs, this mistake may seem random and inexplicable... In actuality, this is a consequence of the great strain.

Tal drew his last three games in Portoroz. He took first place, earning the right to continue his quest for the world championship title.

The Absolutely Best Result

At the 13th Chess Olympiad in Munich, the Soviet Union team emerged victorious again, winning the world champions' cup.

Mikhail Tal was the first reserve player, but he played 15 games. His result, 13.5/15, was the best individual result at the whole Olympiad.

Before the match with England, a journalist asked Tal which combination at the Olympiad he considered his best.

"I hope to play one soon," Tal joked.

It's up to the reader to decide whether this hope came true.

No. 48, Caro-Kann Defense
M. Tal – H. Golombek
1958, Munich, 13th Olympiad Final, round 8

1.e4 c6 2.d4 d5 3.e5 ♗f5 4.c4

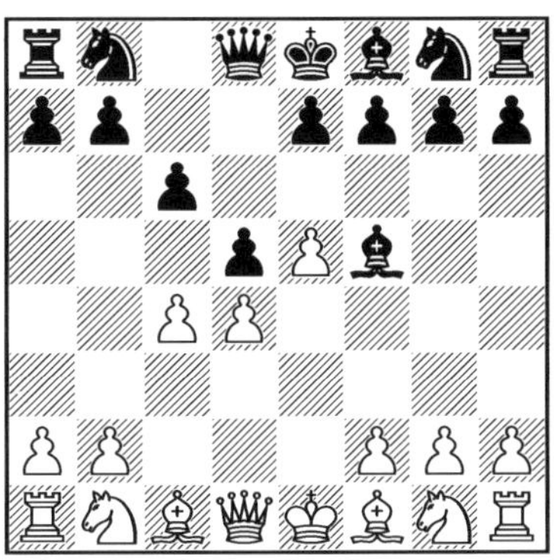

4...e6

Black is right to decline this pawn sacrifice. After 4...♗xb1 5.♖xb1 ♕a5+ 6.♗d2 ♕xa2 7.c5! b5 8.♖a1 ♕xb2 9.♘e2 b4 10.♕a4 b3 11.♘c1! it's quite hard to repel the threat 12.♗d3 with the subsequent ♖b1.

Editor's note: In addition to 12.♗d3, white has other threats: 12.♖a3 (with the subsequent ♖xb3) and even 12.♗b5. The computer leaves no doubt about Koblenz's evaluation of the final position: white wins.

5.♘c3 dxc4 6.♗xc4 ♘e7 7.♘ge2 ♘d7 8.0-0 ♘b6 9.♗b3 ♕d7

9...♘ed5 with the subsequent ♗e7, completing development, was worth considering.

10.a4 a5 11.♘g3

Editor's note: In a modern grandmaster game Stukopin – Maceija (Greensboro 2015), white preferred 11.♗e3 with unclear play.

11...♗g6

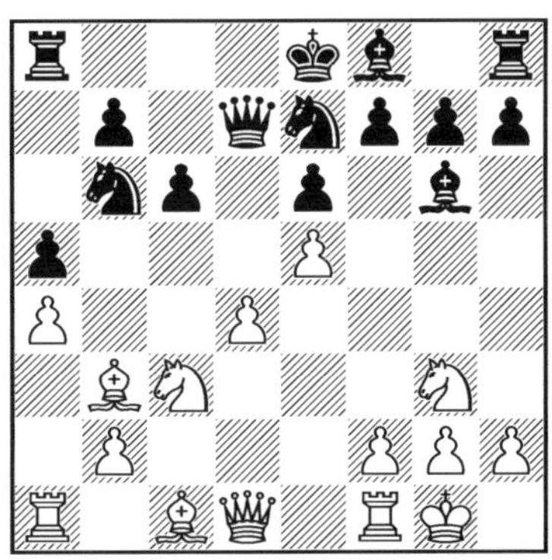

12.♗c2!

A subtle positional maneuver. After the bishop trade, the black king loses an important defender; in addition, the white knight can reach the important e4 square.

12...♗xc2 13.♕xc2 ♘ed5

The central pawn shouldn't be captured. After 13...♕xd4 14.♗e3 ♕d8 15.♘ce4 ♘ed5 16.♗c5!, white's attack is unstoppable.

Editor's note: Koblenz's evaluation is not confirmed by analysis: after the subsequent 16...♘b4 17.♕c3 ♘6d5 18.♕c4, black doesn't even have to offer a draw by repetition with 18... ♘b6 (which white should probably agree to): he can even try to prove that his extra pawn is worth more than his opponent's activity, for instance: 18... ♗xc5 19.♕xc5 b6 20.♘d6+ ♔d7 with the subsequent 21...♕e7 — his strong knight on d5 hinders the development of his opponent's initiative. One of the possible improvements for white in this line is 15.f4 (with the idea of f4-f5), and there are other possibilities as well.

14.♘ce4 ♘b4 15.♕e2 ♘6d5 16.f4! g6 17.♖a3 ♗e7 18.♗d2 ♘c2 19.♖d3 ♘db4 20.♗xb4 ♘xb4 21.♖dd1 ♖d8 22.♔h1 h5 23.♘f6+

Editor's note: The last move is a mistake that could have led to a very dubious position for white. A better move was, for instance, 23.♖f3 (with the idea of activating the g3 knight with ♘g3-f1-e3), with roughly equal chances.

23...♗xf6 24.exf6 ♔f8

24...0-0 didn't work due to 25.♘xh5!

Editor's note: Black had a much stronger move 24...h4 25.♘e4 ♕c7, with the idea ♔e8-d7-c8. In this case, white has no dangerous initiative, and his pawn weaknesses are rather obvious.

25.♘e4 h4

It was better to involve the knight in defense with 25...♘d5.

Editor's note: It's quite possible that the game move, which gives black an opportunity to get the rook into the game with ♖h8-h5 in many lines and also creates the idea h4-h3, was indeed the strongest.

26.♘c5

Editor's note: 26.♖f3 was a stronger reply, activating the rook on the third rank (with resources such as ♖f3-h3 or ♖f3-c3-c5) and maintaining the possibility of ♘g3-e4-g5, which counters both the possible activation of the h8 rook and h4-h3.

26...♕c8

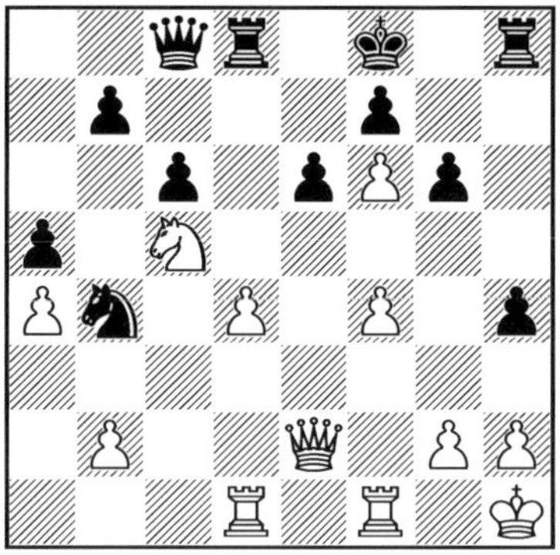

27.f5! gxf5

Editor's note: After 27...exf5! 28.♕e7+ ♔g8 29.♕xb7 ♘d5 30.♖fe1 h3 31.♕xc8 hxg2+ 32.♔xg2 ♖xc8 33.♘d7 ♖c7 34.♘e5 ♘xf6 35.♖c1 ♔g7 36.♖xc6 ♖b7 37.♖e2 ♘d5, black gets an endgame with a clear advantage because of his dangerous kingside pawns and white's pawn weaknesses.

28.♕e3! b6

Editor's note: A blunder that loses the game. After 28...♘d5 (preventing ♖f4) 29.♕g5 ♖h7, with the idea of ♖d6 and ♕d8 (with the possible inclusion of b6), the game is unclear.

29.♕g5 ♖h7 30.♖f4! bxc5 31.♖xh4 ♖xh4 32.♕g7+ ♔e8 33.♕g8+ ♔d7 34.♕xf7+ ♔d6 35.♕e7+ Black resigned.

Casual chess lovers are usually enchanted by the amount of sacrificed material. More knowledgeable fans can also appreciate a subtle sacrifice of a pawn – a humble footman of the chess army.

A pawn sacrifice often serves as a signal for the attack – the spark that creates the fire for the onslaught.

No. 49
A. Beni – M. Tal
1958, Munich, 13th Olympiad
Preliminaries, round 2

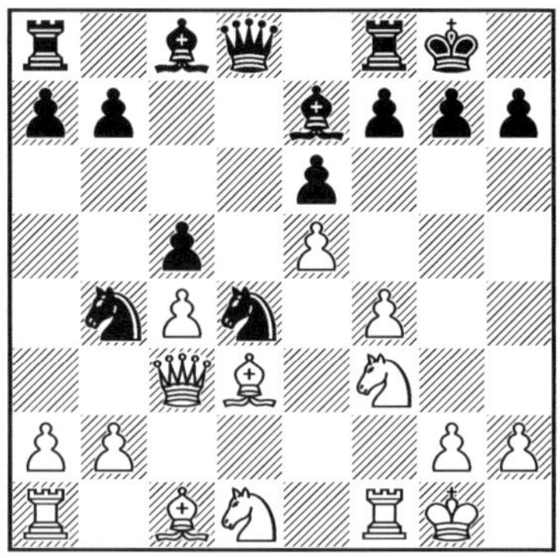

Black could have just completed development with 14...b6 and ♗b7, but this plan gave white great freedom of action. To seize the initiative (to develop the light-squared bishop and create a base on d5), Tal sacrifices a pawn.

14...b5! 15.cxb5 ♗b7

Editor's note: 15...♘xd3 16.♘xd3 a6! led to a big advantage.

16.♗c4 (16...♘xf3+ was a threat) **16...♘d5 17.♕d2 ♘b6 18.♗e2 ♕c7**

Editor's note: The best move here is probably 18...♘xe2+! 19.♕xe2 a6, with a dangerous initiative and clear compensation for the sacrificed pawn.

19.♘xd4 cxd4

A dangerous passed pawn replaces the knight.

20.♗d3 ♘d5 21.a3 a6

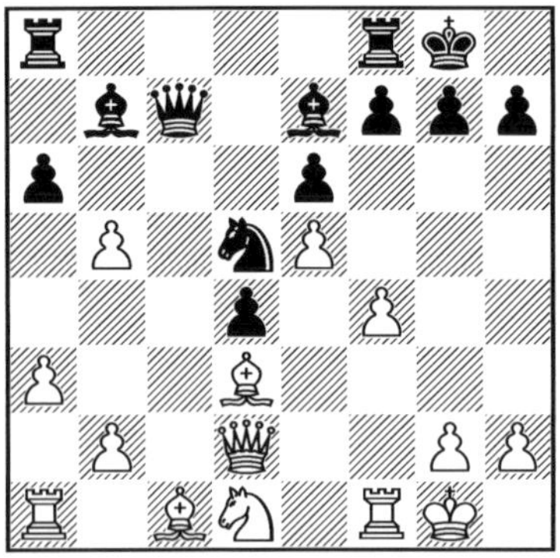

If now 22.bxa6 ♗xa6 23.♗xa6 ♖xa6 24.♔h1, then 24...♕c4, and, due to the threat 25...♖fc8 and ♘b4, it's hard for white to contain black's pressure in the center and on the queenside.

Editor's note: In Koblenz's line, instead of 24...♕c4, there's a stronger move 24...♖c6!, and black wins because of the idea ♖c6-c2. However, instead of 24.♔h1?, white has 24.♕d3, and if 24...♖c6, then 25.♗d2 – black has decent compensation, but it doesn't give him any advantage. So white did have to play 22.bxa6, whereas after the game move his position quickly unravels.

22.♕e2 axb5 23.♗xb5 ♕b6 24.♔h1 ♘b4 25.a4 d3

Editor's note: There was no need to hurry with this move. Black had a great opportunity 25...♖ac8 with a strong initiative that ensured a big advantage. After the game move 25...d3, on the other hand, white could play 26.♕f2!, and the position becomes unclear (after 26...♗c5, there's 27.♗e3).

26.♕g4? ♘c2 27.♖b1 ♖fd8 28.♗d2 ♕d4

Editor's note: This move could have lost all the advantage. A better alternative was 28...♘d4!, for instance, 29.♗e3 (*29.♘c3* can be met with *29...♘f5!,* intending *30...♘h4*) 29...d2!, and white's position is difficult (*30.♗xd2??* loses immediately to *30...♘xb5*).

29.♗c3

Editor's note: White shouldn't have called off the blockade of the d3 pawn. After 29.♕h3, with the ideas ♘d1-c3, ♘d1-f2 and f4-f5, the position is unclear (and completely equal from the computer's point of view).

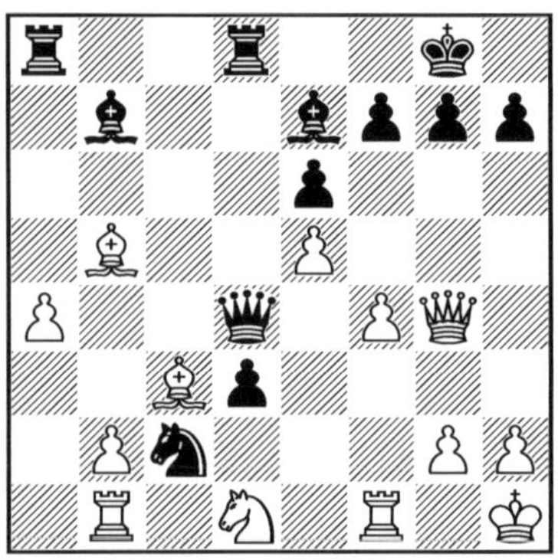

29...♕d5

Editor's note: A much better move was 29...♕e4 30.♘f2 *(30.♗d2? ♕e2!–+)* 30...♕e2! 31.♕xe2 dxe2 32.♗xe2 ♘e3 33.♖g1 ♖xa4 with strong pressure.

White now had to return his bishop to d2 on his next move, getting good chances to hold, but he makes a decisive mistake instead.

30.♖f3 d2 31.f5

A desperate attempt to complicate play.

31...exf5 32.♕xf5 ♘e1! 33.♖g3 ♘xg2 34.♔g1 ♗c5+ 35.♔f1 ♘f4! 36.♖xg7+ ♔f8 37.♕xf4 ♕h1+ 38.♔e2 ♕e1#

Petrosian's Victory

The 26th Soviet championship was held in Tbilisi.

In the first half of the tournament, Tal lost to Yakov Yukhtman and Eduard Gufeld, but then won nine games, which almost allowed him to catch up with the leader. He trailed Tigran Petrosian by a point.

Tal won an interesting game in round 17.

No. 50, Sicilian Defense
A. Nikitin – M. Tal
1959, Tbilisi, 26th Soviet Championship Final, round 17

1.e4 c5 2.♘f3 d6 3.d4 cxd4 4.♘xd4 ♘f6 5.♘c3 a6 6.♗g5 ♘bd7 7.♗c4 ♕a5 8.♕d2 e6

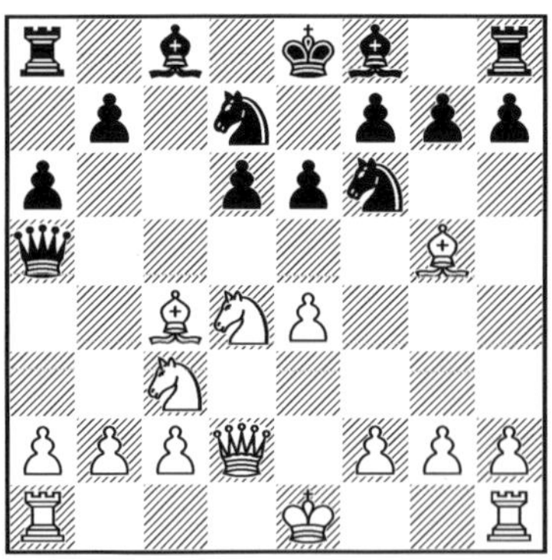

9.0-0

Editor's note: Elite players today usually castle long here.

9...h6 10.♗h4 ♗e7 11.♖ae1

Editor's note: The current main line in this position is 11.♖ad1.

11...♘e5 12.♗b3

Editor's note: 12.♗e2? is bad due to 12...♘xe4!, winning a pawn.

12...g5 13.♗g3 ♗d7

Editor's note: Black's position is also fine after 13...♘h5!, forcing the trade of his opponent's dark-squared bishop: Firat – Sakaev (Rijeka 2010) and Padmini – Kotanjian (Manila 2010).

14.f4 gxf4 15.♗xf4 ♕c7! 16.♘f3 0-0-0 17.♔h1 ♖hg8 18.♗e3 ♗c6 19.♕d4 ♖g6 20.♖e2 ♖dg8 21.♕a7

Black's pieces have assumed threatening positions, and Nikitin wants to trade queens to weaken his opponent's onslaught. But he's in for a big surprise.

21...♘xe4

This leads to a tempest of complications, which ultimately result in black's decisive advantage in the endgame.

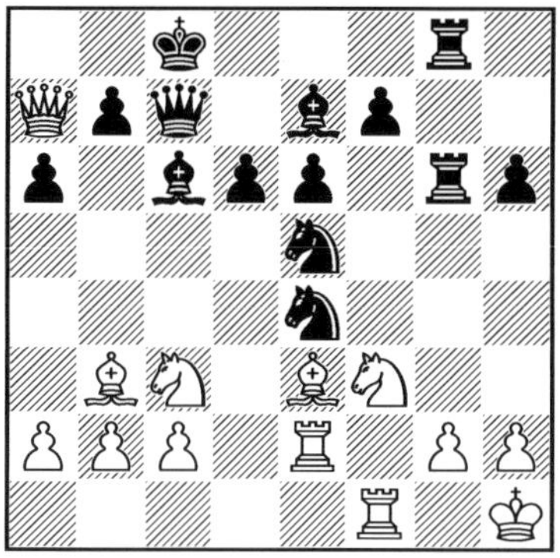

Editor's note: Actually, Tal's move could have led to big trouble had white played 22.♘xe4, for instance: 22...♗xe4 23.♗b6 ♘c6 *(23...♗xf3? 24.♗xc7 ♖xg2 25.♖xf3 ♖g1+ 26.♕xg1 ♖xg1+ 27.♔xg1 ♘xf3+ 28.♔f2 ♘d4 29.♗b6 ♘xe2 30.♔xe2+−)* 24.♕a8+ ♔d7 25.♕xg8 ♖xg8 26.♗xc7 ♗xf3 27.♖xf3 ♘d4 *(27...♔xc7? 28.♖xf7+−)* 28.♖ff2 ♘xe2 29.♗b6! ♘c1 30.♗a4+ ♔c8 31.♖xf7 ♖f8 32.♖xe7 ♖f1+ 33.♗g1 ♘e2 34.h4 ♖xg1+ 35.♔h2 and a clear advantage for white. However, Nikitin makes a grave mistake instead, which leads to a lost position.

22.♗b6 ♘xc3! 23.♗xc7 ♘xe2 24.♗b6 ♖xg2

Editor's note: 24...♘d7! led to a quick win, forestalling the idea of ♗b3-a4 and intending to capture the g2 pawn in better conditions.

25.♗a4!

The threat 26.♕a8+ and 27.♕xb7+ requires black to play very energetically.

25...♖g1+! 26.♗xg1 ♖xg1+ 27.♕xg1

Not 27.♖xg1 due to 27...♗xf3+ 28.♖g2 ♘f4.

27...♗xf3+!

Not 27...♘xg1 because of 28.♗xc6!

28.♖xf3 ♘xg1 29.♖c3+ ♔d8 30.♔xg1 d5

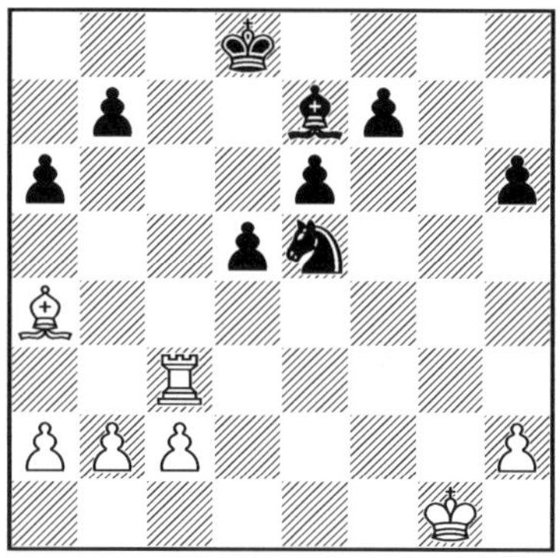

This is the position Tal meant to reach when he made his 21st move. White manages to repel the mating threats, but he has only minimal chances of holding the endgame.

31.♖g3 ♗g5 32.b4 b5 33.♗b3 f5 34.c3 ♔e7 35.a4 f4 36.♖h3 ♘c4 37.axb5 axb5 38.♔f2 ♔d6 39.♔e2 e5 40.♗xc4 bxc4 41.♖h5 e4 42.h4 f3+ 43.♔d1 ♗f4 White resigned.

This win was loudly celebrated by the excitable Georgians.

The tournament in the Georgian capital showed that Tal's play had become more universal. The Riga grandmaster wasn't avoiding endgames anymore; moreover, if the position demanded, he would gladly go for the ending.

No. 51, Modern Benoni
E. Geller – M. Tal
1959, Tbilisi, 26th Soviet Championship Final, round 4

1.d4 ♘f6 2.c4 c5 3.d5 e6 4.♘c3 exd5 5.cxd5 d6 6.e4 g6 7.♘f3 ♗g7 8.♗g5

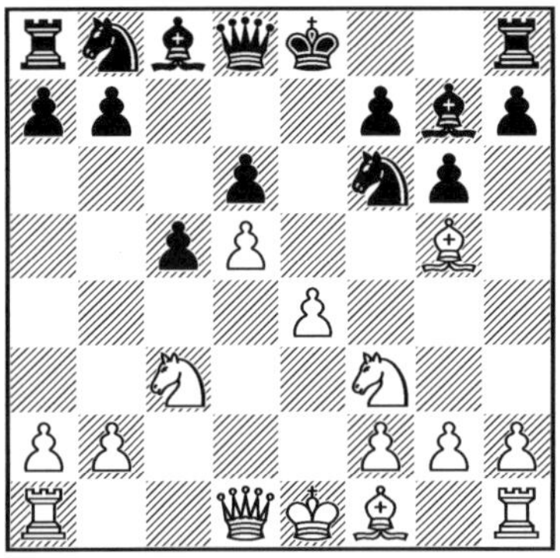

8...a6 9.a4

Editor's note: Including the moves a7-a6 and a2-a4 allows black to avoid the checks along the a4-e8 diagonal, which are quite unpleasant, for instance, in the lines 8...h6 9.♗h4 g5 10.♗g3 ♘h5 11.♗b5+! ♔f8 *(11... ♗d7 12.♗xd7+ ♕xd7 13.♘e5! and a clear advantage for white)* 12.e5! (as we know, this pawn sacrifice is very good for white) or 8...♗g4 9.♕a4+! *(9.♗b5+!?)* 9...♗d7 *(9...♘bd7? 10.e5!)* 10.♕b3. Note that the line 8.♗g5 is rarely played these days.

9...h6 10.♗f4 ♗g4

Editor's note: Since black has played h7-h6, the continuation 10... g5!? looks more logical (11.♗g3 ♘h5 or 11.♗e3 ♘bd7).

11.♗e2 0-0 12.0-0

Editor's note: This position (after a different move order) occurred in a number of later games, most notably Beliavsky – Kudrin, Wijk aan Zee 1985, and Mamedyarov – Bacrot, Skopje 2015. Both these games continued 12...♘h5 13.♗e3 with complicated play; in the opinion of the Hungarian analyst Krisztian Szabo, white is slightly better.

12...♖e8 13.♕c2

Editor's note: As the game's progress showed, white achieves nothing with this move. 13.♘d2 ♗xe2 14.♕xe2 (with the ideas f2-f4 and ♘d2-c4) was worthy of serious consideration; this line was tested in some later games.

13...♕c7 14.♖fe1 ♘bd7

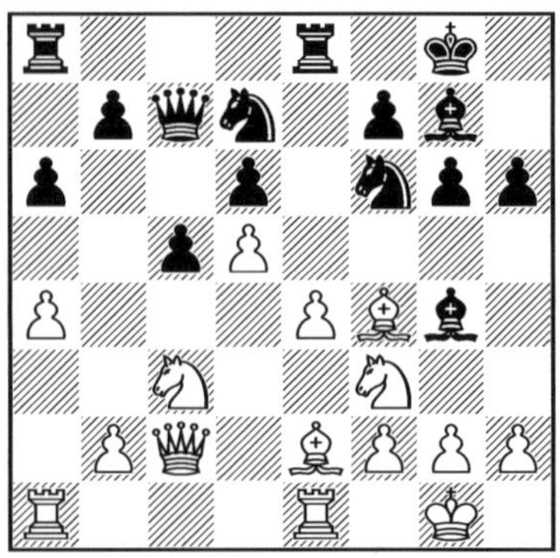

15.h3

After 15.♖ad1, there's 15...♗xf3 16.♗xf3 ♖ab8, and if 17.e5!?, then 17...♘xe5 18.♗xe5 dxe5 19.d6 ♕d7, and black repels his opponent's threats.

15...♗xf3 16.♗xf3 c4! 17.♗e2 (preventing 17...♘c5) **17...♖ac8 18.a5 ♘c5**

Easily agreeing to swap the c-pawn for the e-pawn; after this, the game simplifies, and black gets a positional advantage.

19.♗xc4 ♘fxe4 20.♘xe4 ♖xe4 21.♖xe4 ♘xe4 22.♕xe4 ♕xc4

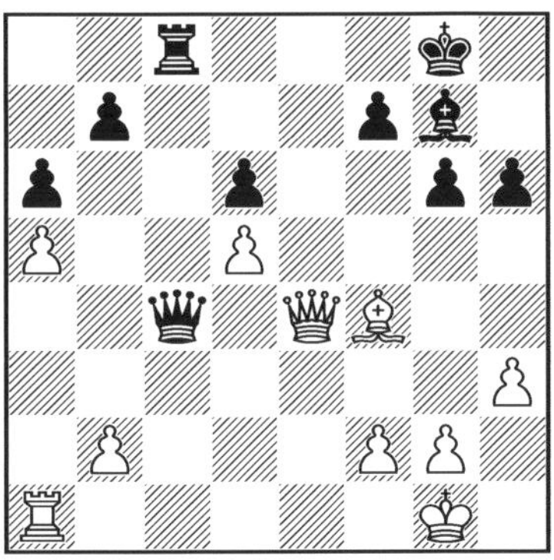

23.♕f3

After the queen trade, black's advantage would have still been substantial, but with 23.♖a4!, white could still hold.

23...♕b4!

Now white can't avoid material losses. There followed: **24.♕g3 ♕xb2 25.♖e1 ♕b5 26.♕f3 ♗f8! 27.h4 ♕xa5 28.♖b1 b5 29.h5 g5 30.♕g3 ♕a2 31.♖d1 ♕e2 32.♖d3 ♗g7 33.♕h3 ♖c2 34.♗xd6 ♖c1+ 35.♔h2 ♕xf2 36.♖f3 ♕g1+ 37.♔g3 ♕e1+ 38.♔h2 ♗e5+ 39.♗xe5 ♕xe5+ 40.♕g3 ♕xd5 41.♖d3 ♕c5 42.♕g4 ♕e5+ White resigned**.

Still, Tal couldn't catch up with the leader. Petrosian won the tournament without a single loss. Tal shared 2nd–3rd place with Spassky.

It's Good That You Weren't There!

Tal traveled to the Zurich international tournament alone. After his return, we, the Riga chess players, listened to his story about the "battle in Switzerland".

"It's good that you weren't there," Tal told me. "My play in Switzerland would have perturbed you too much."

Indeed, Tal's play in Zurich was more than risky. However, the majority of his opponents was weaker than him, and the Riga grandmaster managed to get away with a lot of things.

Let's look at one of Tal's games in this tournament – it's a great illustration of his ability to use the psychological factor in his games.

No. 52, Queen's Gambit Declined
M. Tal – D. Keller
1959, Zurich International, round 7

1.♘f3 ♘f6 2.c4 e6 3.♘c3 d5 4.d4 c6 5.♗g5 dxc4 6.e4 b5

So, his opponent decided to go for the complicated Botvinnik system. Trusting that Keller was well-prepared, the grandmaster made an unexpected decision.

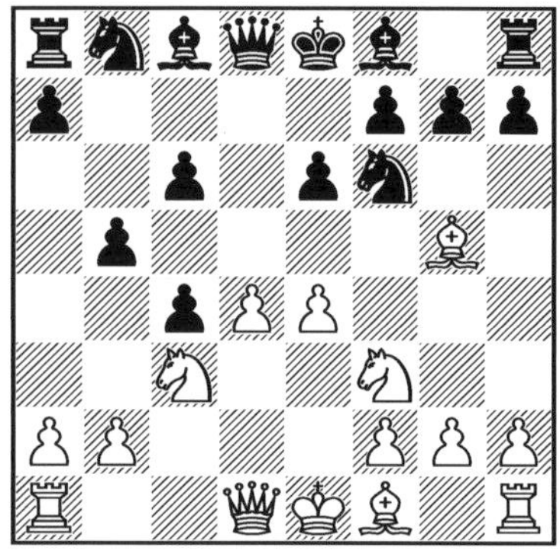

7.a4

"This move was obviously prepared beforehand," Tal's opponent seemed to think. But that was not the case. We never analyzed this line at all. When Tal moved his a-pawn forward, he knew that this move didn't give white any advantage; its only purpose was to make his opponent face an unfamiliar opening situation.

Editor's note: 7.e5 is a much more popular move.

7...♕b6

Tal's unusual move 7.a4 achieved its goal. Black's first independent move is already a mistake.

Editor's note: Today, 7...♕b6 is not considered a mistake – it's one of the main lines.

7...♗b4 was worth considering, after which David Bronstein

recommended 8.e5 h6 9.♗d2 ♘d5 10.♘e4! ♗e7!

Editor's note: Practice showed that after 7...♗b4 8.e5 h6 9.♗d2, instead of Bronstein's move 9...♘d5, black can play 9...♗xc3 followed by 10...♘d5, with a good game. So, instead of 9.♗d2, white usually prefers 9.exf6 hxg5 10.fxg7 ♖g8 11.g3 (or 11.h4).

8.♗xf6

Editor's note: This move has occurred the most often in practice, but grandmaster Reiner Knaak points out that 8.♗e2 is more precise – after 8...♗b7 9.0-0 a6 10.d5 cxd5 (importantly, *10...♘bd7* is bad due to *11.dxe6 fxe6 12.e5 ♘d5 13.♘d4 ♘c5 14.♗g4*) 11.♗xf6 gxf6, we get to the same position as in the actual game after move 11. Tal's move order, however, gives a good additional resource to his opponent – see the editor's note to move 11.

8...gxf6 9.♗e2 a6

It was better to start preparing to castle with 9...♗b7.

Editor's note: Modern theory does not consider 9...a6 a bad move.

10.0-0 ♗b7 11.d5!

Black is behind in development, so Tal hurries to open lines for an attack!

11...cxd5

Editor's note: Black has an interesting alternative 11...♘d7!?. Reiner Knaak thinks that black is even slightly better after this move (that's why he recommended 8.♗e2), and stats support his point of view.

12.exd5 b4

Editor's note: This move is a mistake, and black is now worse. The correct move was 12...♘d7 with the main line 13.axb5 axb5 14.♖xa8+ ♗xa8 15.♘d4 ♗c5 16.♘dxb5 ♘e5. Based on the games Gorelov – Kishnev, Barnaul 1984, and Hillarp Persson – Robson, Reykjavik 2008, we can surmise that black can likely hold.

13.a5 ♕c7

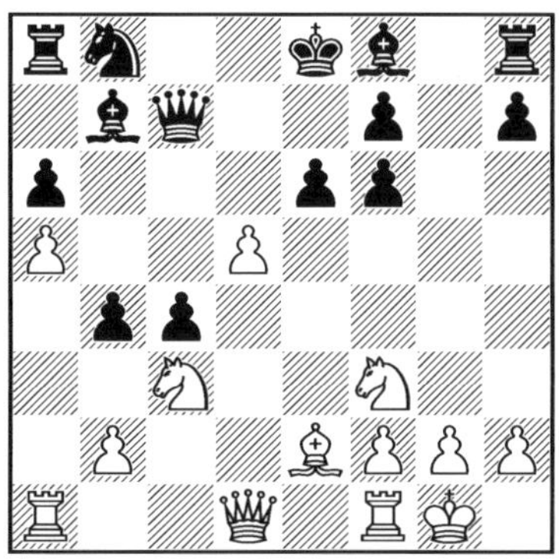

14.dxe6!

Only this way! White sacrifices a piece to keep the enemy king in the center. The knight retreat 14.♘a4 could be met with 14...♘d7, and if 15.dxe6 fxe6 16.♘d4, then 16...0-0-0!

Editor's note: In Koblenz's line, black's last move (16...0-0-0) is a mistake, because he can't defend after 17.♖c1. The correct reply is 16...♖g8 17.♗h5+ ♔e7 18.g3 ♕xa5, with unclear play.

14...bxc3 15.♘d4 ♖g8 16.♕a4+ ♔d8 17.g3 ♗d5 18.♖fd1

Editor's note: Tal puts the wrong rook on d1: the correct move was 18.♖ad1, with a decisive attack. The key difference is shown in the line 18...cxb2 19.exf7 ♕xf7 20.♗c4!, and then, for instance, 20...♖g5 21.♗xd5 ♖xd5 22.♖fe1 ♘d7 23.♕c6+−.

18...♔c8

The black king finds no safe haven here.

Editor's note: As grandmaster Robert Huebner noted, black should have played 18...cxb2 (attacking the rook!) 19.♖ab1 c3 – computer analysis shows that white had enough compensation for the sacrificed material, but little else.

19.bxc3

It was more precise to drive the black king to the b-file first with 19.♕e8+ ♔b7 and only then play 20.bxc3.

Editor's note: Actually, white's last move is not just an inaccuracy – it's a serious mistake that gives his opponent a chance to save the game.

19...♗c5!

After 19...♔b7, Tal had prepared the following line: 20.♖ab1+ ♔a7 21.exf7 ♕xf7 22.♗xc4 ♗xc4 23.♕c6!!, and black can only resign.

20.e7 ♘c6

The Swiss master decides to complete development. After 20...♗xe7 21.♘f5 ♗e6 22.♘xe7+ ♕xe7 23.♗f3 ♖a7 24.♖db1, white had strong pressure along the b-file.

Editor's note: Analysis shows that, for instance, after 24...♖d8 (there are other good moves as well), the pressure along the b-file mentioned by Koblenz is not enough for white to even draw. So, instead of 22.♘xe7+?, white should play 22.♘d4 with enough compensation after 22...♗d7 23.♕c2 or repetition after 22...♗d5 23.♘f5.

21.♗g4+ ♔b7 22.♘b5

Editor's note: This is a mistake that could have led to white's defeat. Tal had several continuations that gave him adequate compensation for the piece (but not more); one of the possible lines is: 22.♘f5 ♗e6 (Huebner's recommendation *22...♕e5* is met with *23.♖xd5! ♕xd5 24.♖d1+−*) 23.♖ab1+ ♔a7 24.♗f3 ♗xf5 25.♕xc6 ♕xc6 26.♗xc6 ♗xb1 27.♖xb1 ♖ac8 28.♖b7+ ♔a8 29.♖c7+ ♔b8 30.♖xc8+ ♔xc8 31.e8=♕+ ♖xe8 32.♗xe8 ♗d6 33.♗xf7 ♗e5 34.♗xc4 ♔b7, with a draw.

22...♕e5 23.♖e1

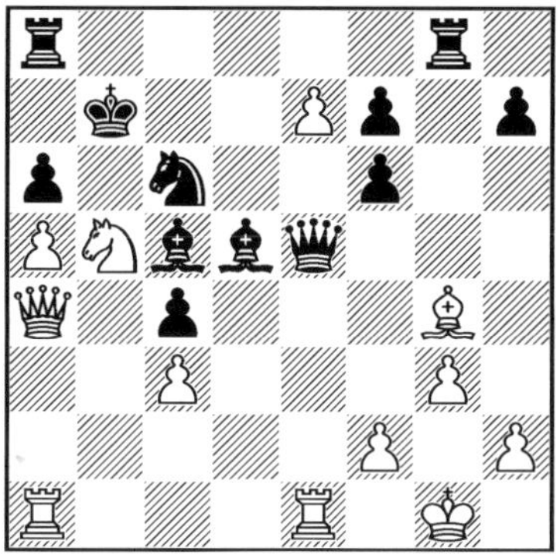

23...♗e4

Editor's note: After 23...♕g5, black won, for instance: 24.♖ab1 ♕xg4 25.♘d6+ ♔c7 26.e8=♘+ ♖axe8 27.♘xe8+ ♖xe8 28.♖xe8 ♕f3−+ (Unzicker).

24.♖ab1! ♖xg4

After 24...♗xb1, instead of 25.♖xe5, white would have played 25.♖xb1 with a strong attack. (**Editor's note:** black's position is indefensible in this case.)

25.♖xe4 ♕xe4 (if 25...♖xe4, then, of course, 26.♘d4+) **26.♘d6+ ♔c7 27.♘xe4 ♖xe4 28.♕d1**

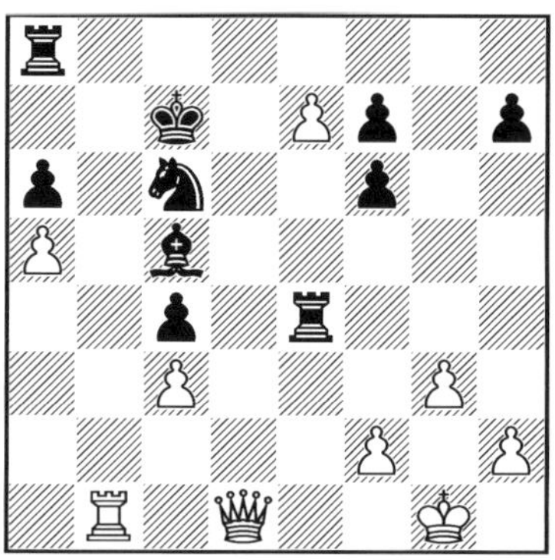

28...♖e5?

Black misses his opponent's combination. After 28...♖xe7, the battle was still to come.

Editor's note: Instead of 28... ♖xe7, black has 28...♗xe7, and after the subsequent 29.♕d5 ♖e5, the capture 30.♕xf7 happens (unlike in the line 28...♖xe7 29.♕d5 ♖e5) without a check (this was pointed out by Huebner). The computer evaluates this complicated position as equal.

I must say that Tal's opponents would often make such mistakes.

"Tal hypnotizes his opponents," said those who didn't want to delve deeper into the reasons behind the "inexplicable" blunders of the grandmaster's opponents. And Pal Benko found a "practical answer": at the Candidates Tournament, he played his last two games against Tal wearing sunglasses...

Let's remember that some of Emmanuel Lasker's opponents, including Siegbert Tarrasch, also explained the ex-world champion's wins by hypnosis.

Keller's mistake is similar to Efim Geller's mistake at the 25th Soviet championship or Panno's mistake at the Portoroz Interzonal. In these cases, the Riga player's opponents also lost drawn position "in strange ways".

However, we shouldn't forget that these mistakes were made after Geller and Panno had withstood a barrage of attacks from Tal. They just cracked under the pressure, and their concentration lapsed momentarily. And it's enough to make just one mistake in chess to nullify all the previous efforts.

We should also keep in mind that Tal forces his opponents to play positions that need a great deal of time to think over, and so they often suffer from severe time trouble.

This game illustrates all those points. Up until now, Keller had bravely fought off all these problems, but just when white's combination resources seemed to be over, he got tired and missed a simple rook sacrifice that immediately won the game.

There followed:

29.♖b7+! ♔xb7 30.♕d7+ ♔b8 31.e8=♕+ ♖xe8 32.♕xe8+ ♔b7 33.♕d7+ ♔b8 34.♕xc6 and **Black resigned**.

The Yugoslav Marathon

On 2nd September 1959, Tal took the plane to Yugoslavia. In August, he had played in the USSR Spartakiad, and his performance was dismal (2.5/8). Then he went to Riga for an urgent appendicitis operation, with only two weeks before the tournament! His friends were very concerned. The Candidates Tournament required great effort. Each participant of this truly marathon competition had to play 28 games!

The first-round loss to the ex-world champion Vasily Smyslov didn't alarm Riga too much. The fans were already used to Tal's starting losses (such as in Tbilisi and Zurich). However, when he also lost in round 3, his friends got worried.

I came somewhat late to the tournament.

I was in Belgrade during round 4 and Tal played against Fridrik Olafsson that day. After a sharp struggle, the Riga player managed to win.

The games were held in Bled and broadcast in Belgrade. Tal's win was met with loud applause. However, Svetozar Gligoric then resigned to the 16 year-old Bobby Fischer, and the hall abruptly fell silent.

I got to Bled the next day; Tal was despondent. The loss to Paul Keres in round 3 was especially disappointing for the grandmaster. When he showed me how it happened, he said, "This game could have been my greatest win in Bled."

No. 53
P. Keres – M. Tal
1959, Bled/Zagreb/Belgrade,
Candidates Tournament, round 3

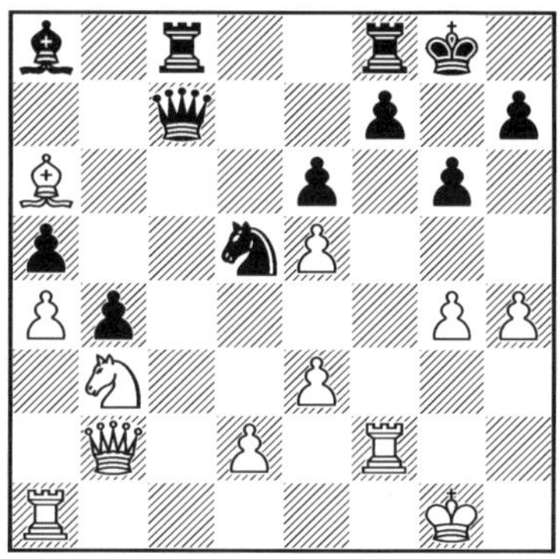

28...♘xe3! 29.♖c1

White can't capture the knight immediately due to the threat 29...♕c6.

29...♕e7!

Editor's note: Black had an even stronger reply: 29...♕d7! 30.dxe3 ♖xc1+ 31.♕xc1 *(31.♘xc1 ♕c6)* 31...♕d5 32.♖b2 f5!–+.

30.dxe3 ♕xh4 31.♔f1 ♕h3+ 32.♔e2 ♕xg4+ 33.♔d2 ♖fd8+ 34.♘d4 ♕g3 35.♖f4

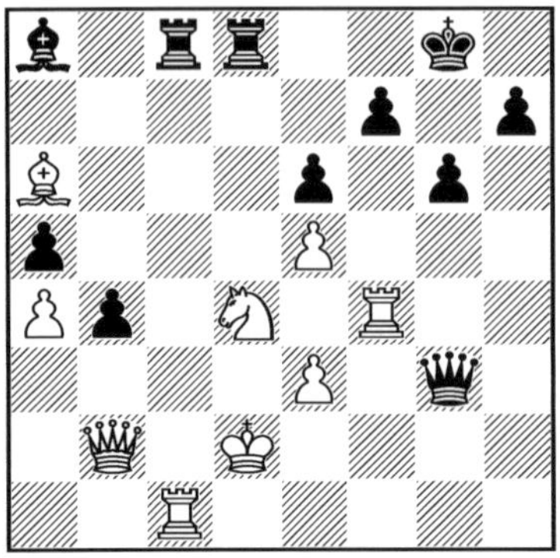

35...♖xc1?

A serious mistake. After 35... ♕g2+! 36.♗e2 ♕d5, black could capture the fourth pawn and maintain the attack.

Editor's note: The computer thinks that 35...♕h2+ is the strongest move and evaluates the position after 36.♗e2 ♗d5 (with the threats ♗c4 and g6-g5) as won for black.

36.♕xc1 ♕g2+ 37.♗e2 ♕d5 38.♕c7! ♖d7 39.♕c4 ♔g7 (39...h5 was better)

Editor's note: Actually, Tal's move doesn't deserve any criticism – the mistake was made later.

40.♕xd5 ♗xd5 41.♗b5 ♖c7 42.e4 ♗a8

The game was adjourned here. The resumption started with **43.♔e3 ♖c3+ 44.♗d3**

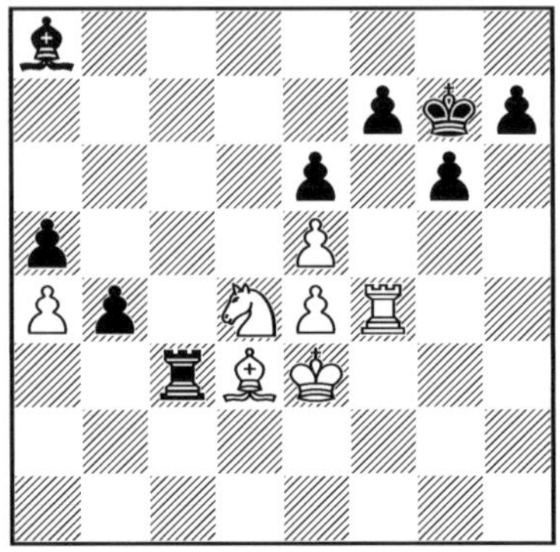

44...b3

Editor's note: This move leads to a lost position. The correct move was 44...♗c6, and after the subsequent 45.♘b5 ♗xb5 46.axb5 a4, the position is equal, for instance: 47.♔d4 ♖c8 48.♖f1 b3 49.♖a1 ♖d8+ 50.♔c4 b2 51.♖xa4 ♖xd3 52.♖b4 ♖d8 53.b6 (there's no time to capture the b-pawn yet: after *53.♖xb2? g5 54.b6 g4 55.b7 ♖b8 56.♔d4 ♔g6 57.♔e3 ♔g5* black manages to prevent the white king from getting to f4 and wins) 53...g5 54.b7 ♖b8 55.♔d4 h5 *(55... ♔g6 56.♔e3!)* 56.♖xb2 (now it's possible to capture this pawn) 56... Kg6 57.♔e3 h4 *(57...g4 58.♔f4=)* 58.♔f3 ♔h5 59.♖b1 g4+ 60.♔f4 g3 61.♖b2, with a draw. The interesting point here is that it was white who had to achieve the draw.

45.♖f1

Editor's note: 45.♘b5! was much stronger, to first get the knight to d6, attacking the f7 pawn, and only then take care of the b-pawn. For instance: 45...♖c8 46.♘d6 ♖f8 47.♖f1 h5 48.♗c4 b2 49.♖b1 ♖b8 50.♗b5+−.

45...♖c5 46.♘xb3 ♖xe5 47.♖c1 ♖h5 48.♖c7

Editor's note: The correct move was 48.♔d4, immediately activating the king and not committing the rook yet. Even so, it's unclear whether white would win.

48...♔f6

Editor's note: After 48...♖h3+ 49.♔d4 e5+ 50.♔c4 h5, black got strong counterplay, which, in the computer's opinion, is enough to draw the game.

49.♘c5 ♔e5 50.♘d7+ ♔d6 51.♖a7 e5 52.♖xa8 ♔xd7 53.♖xa5, and **white soon won**.

Tal drew with Tigran Petrosian, and then defeated Pal Benko and Bobby Fischer; with 4.5 points after the first leg, he caught up with Petrosian and Keres, who lost one game each.

The second leg started. It was no secret to Smyslov that Tal was bent on revenge. Indeed, the position was complicated from the very beginning. The foreign journalists ran to their phones to tell their editors that Tal had sacrificed a piece. Smyslov's second, the usually calm grandmaster Igor Bondarevsky, was anxious too.

When Tal sacrificed his queen, the spectators realized that the end was near. The ex-world champion resigned on move 26.

The Riga grandmaster's combination became a topic for a heated discussion. The Yugoslavian master Vladimir Vukovic, dubbed "the greatest skeptic of the 20th century" by his friends, would approach grandmaster Vyacheslav Ragozin, the head of our delegation, every day, trying to prove again and again that Tal's sacrifice was unsound.

No. 54, Caro-Kann Defense
M. Tal – V. Smyslov
1959, Bled/Zagreb/Belgrade, Candidates Tournament, round 8

1.e4 c6 2.d3

We had planned to use this modest move against Botvinnik at the 2nd USSR Spartakiad, but the game didn't take place. The purpose of this move is to avoid known theoretical lines.

2...d5 3.♘d2 e5 4.♘gf3 ♘d7

Editor's note: The modern main line is 4...♗d6, which is most often met with 5.g3.

5.d4! dxe4 6.♘xe4 exd4 7.♕xd4 ♘gf6 8.♗g5 ♗e7 9.0-0-0 0-0 10.♘d6 ♕a5

Black could simplify the position with 10...♘b6, but Smyslov isn't thinking about a draw.

11.♗c4

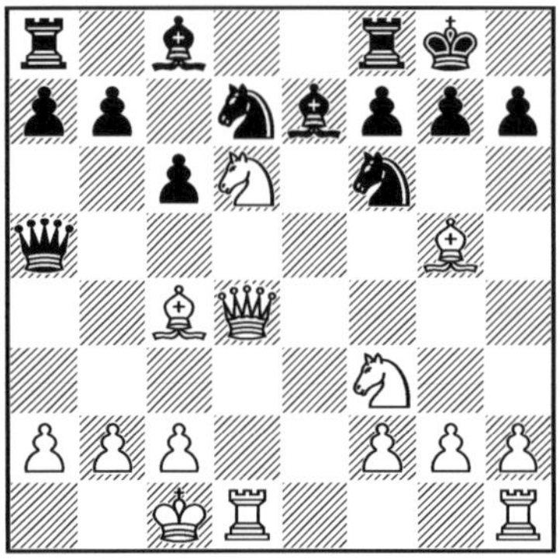

I must admit that I didn't like this move. "What is he doing?" I fumed. "He's helping black to organize a queenside attack."

Smyslov quickly made his move, and I was still angry at Tal for his carelessness.

11...b5 12.♗d2!

Nobody expected this move. White is planning to transfer the bishop to c3, freeing up the g5 square for the queen. Here, I "forgave" Tal.

12...♕a6 13.♘f5! ♗d8 14.♕h4!

A sudden change of "decoration". White goes on the offensive.

14...bxc4 15.♕g5

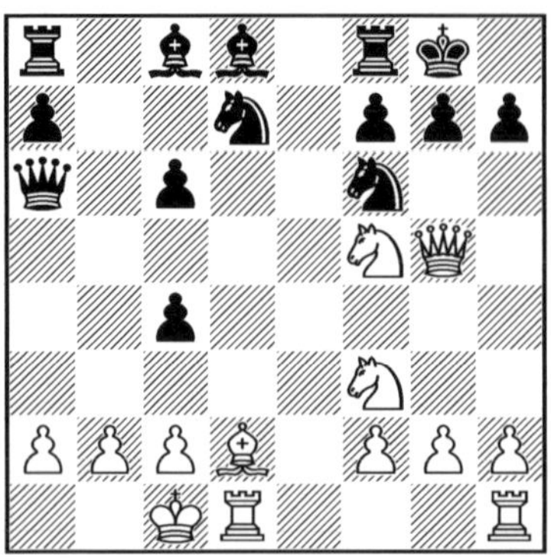

15...♘h5

The ex-champion returns the sacrificed piece and prepares a counter-attack. After 15...g6, Tal planned to continue the attack with 16.♘h6+ ♔g7 17.♗c3 ♕xa2 18.♖he1.

16.♘h6+ ♔h8 17.♕xh5 ♕xa2

This seemingly active move is a mistake. It was later found that the correct move was 17...♗f6. Tal saw this and planned to play 18.♗c3! ♗xc3 19.♘g5! g6 20.♘hxf7+ ♖xf7 21.♘xf7+ ♔g7 22.♕f3 ♗f6 23.♘d6 with strong threats.

Editor's note: Actually, 18.♗c3 is a mistake, because after 18...♗xc3 19.♘g5, instead of 19...g6?, black has 19...♗xb2+!, and after the subsequent 20.♔xb2 ♕b5+ 21.♔c1 gxh6 22.♕xh6 ♕f5, white's attack is repelled, and black keeps his extra pieces (found by Kasparov). And so, instead of 18.♗c3?, white should have gone for another line shown by Tal, which led to a somewhat better endgame: 18.♘xf7+ ♔g8 19.♘7g5 h6 20.♘e4 ♕xa2 21.♘xf6+ ♘xf6 22.♕a5 ♕xa5 23.♗xa5 and a slight advantage for white.

18.♗c3 ♘f6

Now 18...♗f6 didn't work due to 19.♘xf7+ ♔g8

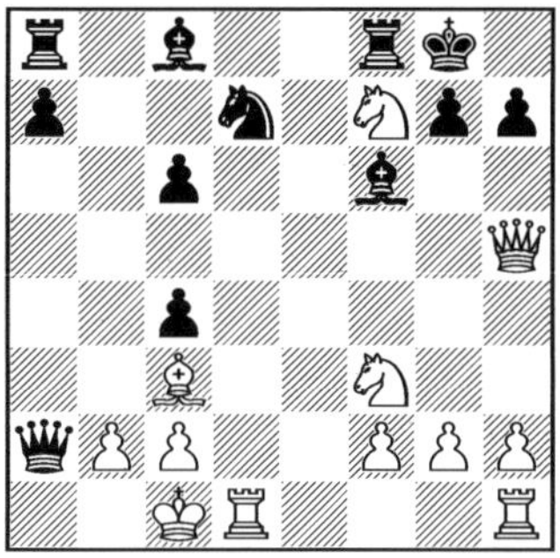

20.♘3g5 ♗xg5 21.♘xg5 h6 22.♕g6! (found by David Bronstein).

Editor's note: This line contains several mistakes: 1) Instead of 21...h6, black should play 21...♘f6! 22.♗xf6 ♗f5! (Kasparov), after which it's white who has to scramble to save the game, because black threatens 23...♕a4, and his bishop is hanging; 2) Instead of 21.♘xg5?!, the correct move is 21.♕xg5! ♖xf7 22.♖he1, and the only approach that gives black chances to survive is returning the piece and going for a clearly worse endgame after 22...h6 23.♖e8+ ♔h7 24.♕h5 ♘e5 25.♖xe5 ♕a1+ 26.♔d2 ♖d7+ 27.♔e1 ♕xd1+ 28.♕xd1 ♖xd1+ 29.♔xd1 ♖b8; 3) Instead of 20...♗xg5?, the correct move is Kasparov's 20...♕a1+! 21.♔d2 ♗xc3+ 22.bxc3 ♘f6! with better chances for black; 4) Instead of 20.♘3g5?, white should play 20.♘7g5, for instance, 20...♕a1+ 21.♔d2 ♗xc3+ 22.bxc3 ♘f6 (Kasparov) 23.♕f7+!? ♖xf7 24.♖xa1, with a drawn endgame.

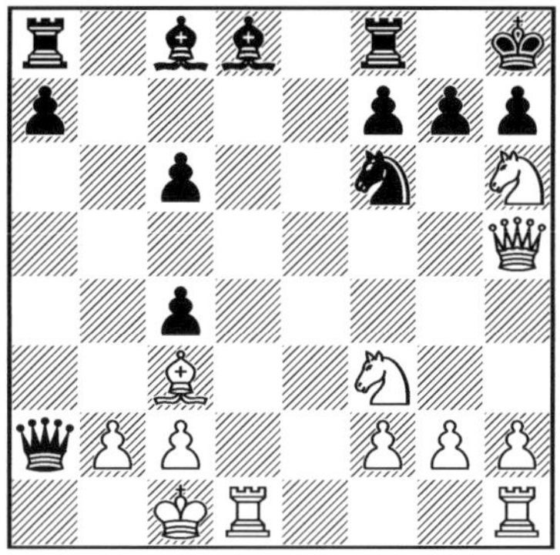

19.♕xf7!

This queen sacrifice wins.

19....♕a1+ 20.♔d2 ♖xf7 21.♘xf7+ ♔g8 22.♖xa1 ♔xf7 23.♘e5+ ♔e6 24.♘xc6 ♘e4+ 25.♔e3 ♗b6+ 26.♗d4 Black resigned.

The game was awarded a special prize.

Both I and Tal's official second, Yuri Averbakh, were quite satisfied with his play in Bled. Tal was just half a point behind the leader, grandmaster Paul Keres. We were glad to see that living in Bled, which is located in a beautiful mountain region, was beneficial to Tal – he looked noticeably healthier and fresher.

The next leg was played in the capital of Croatia, Zagreb. The results of the first half of the tournament were evaluated differently by the players.

Fischer was disappointed because of his many losses and the organizers' "tactlessness": he received children's soap in pretty wrapping as a gift.

Benko was sad to part with the fun casino and dancing. The grandmaster complained that he was unable to find a better coach. His second, Yugoslav master Maric, said, "Like player, like coach."

Olafsson and his three coaches were especially unhappy. The Icelandic grandmaster sadly contemplated his return to the homeland, which had organized a special fundraiser to help him travel to the tournament.

Tal was secretly mad at me: I had asked the table tennis lovers not to play him because of his recent operation. However, film footage showed Tal waving the little bat anyway...

The cinema people were rather happy. They managed to film Petrosian as a gondolier during a boat ride on the lake with his second, grandmaster Isaak Boleslavsky. The cameras caught Olafsson and Gligoric in the swimming pool, and Keres out fishing.

And then, we boarded the bus heading to Zagreb. Fischer seemed to have left his worries behind. In answer to Tal's question about whether he'd ever been to an opera, the American sang the smugglers' march from *Carmen* in a soprano.

"Tell me, Bobby," Tal continued his interrogation, "how do you like Volpert's game style?"

Fischer thought for a bit, then answered very seriously, "She's too cautious. But you have another woman player, Dmitrieva, I like her games!"

When the grandmasters disembarked at the fashionable Zagreb hotel Esplanada, they were immediately surrounded by a crowd of chess fans.

The first round in the Croatian capital yielded some unexpected results. Keres blundered in an equal position against Fischer and had to resign. Petrosian lost to Olafsson.

The influx of spectators was so huge that the organizers had to place a demonstration board on the balcony of the playing hall. Thousands of people watched the battle between the candidates, and one of the streets in the center was closed off for a few hours.

The game between Tal and Smyslov attracted the most interest.

It was broadcast in Riga by phone. At first, the people were happy, but then, when the middlegame started, they began to ask anxious questions:

"How do you evaluate Tal's position? Will he be able to survive?"

I couldn't say anything good. Tal's loss seemed inevitable. However, he was still putting up fierce resistance in severe time trouble. Each of Smyslov's moves saw an immediate, lightning-fast reply. And then, the ex-world champion, who usually keeps his cool even in the most difficult conditions, suddenly lost concentration. He got into time trouble as well, missed a simple tactical threat, and Tal saved the game with perpetual check.

Here's how the finale of this dramatic game played out.

No. 55
V. Smyslov – M. Tal
1959, Bled/Zagreb/Belgrade, Candidates Tournament, round 15

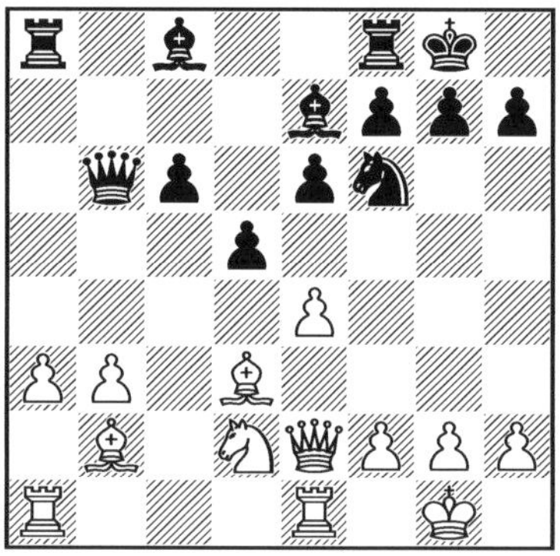

At this point, Tal considered his position quite tenable, but just several moves later, he started to think a lot. As the subsequent play showed, he had every reason for that.

15.exd5 cxd5 16.b4 ♘d7 17.♘b3! e5

Black's active operations in the center don't reach their intended goal. With several precise moves, Smyslov manages to attain a decisive advantage.

18.♗f5 e4 19.♖ec1!

A typical "Smyslov" move – simple and yet very strong. The threat 20.♖xc8 and 21.♗xd7 doesn't leave much choice for black.

19...♕d6 20.♘d4

After this move, Tal thought for 40 minutes. The threats 21.♖c6 and 21.♗xh7+ with the subsequent 22.♘f5 are very unpleasant.

20...♗f6 21.♖c6 ♕e7 22.♖ac1 h6

22...♗e5 didn't work due to 23.♗xh7+ ♔xh7 24.♕h5+ ♔g8 25.♘f5, and if 25...♕d8, then 26.♖xc8!. (**Editor's note:** Instead of 26.♖xc8, white could win much more rapidly: 26.♖h6! gxh6 27.♘xh6+ ♔g7 28.♘f5+ with a quick mate.)

23.♖c7!

Now black can't avoid material losses.

23...♗e5 24.♘c6 ♕g5 25.h4

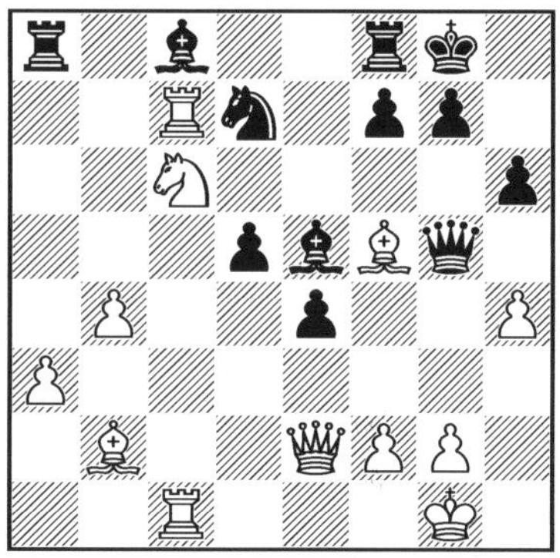

It seems that nothing can save black from a loss. Among other things, he had just two minutes left to make fifteen moves.

25...♕xh4 26.♘xe5 ♘xe5 27.♖xc8

Of course, the simplest move was 27.♗xc8, and after 27...♘d3 – 28.♗b7. After the game move, black has some chances to continue the struggle...

27...♘f3+ 28.gxf3 ♕g5+ 29.♔f1 ♕xf5 30.♖xf8+ ♖xf8 31.fxe4 dxe4

After getting an extra piece, Smyslov started playing without confidence.

32.♕e3 ♖d8 33.♕g3 g5 34.♖c5

34.♕c3 f6 35.♕b3+ with the subsequent 36.♖c6 won immediately.

34...♖d1+ 35.♔g2 ♕e6 36.b5 ♔h7

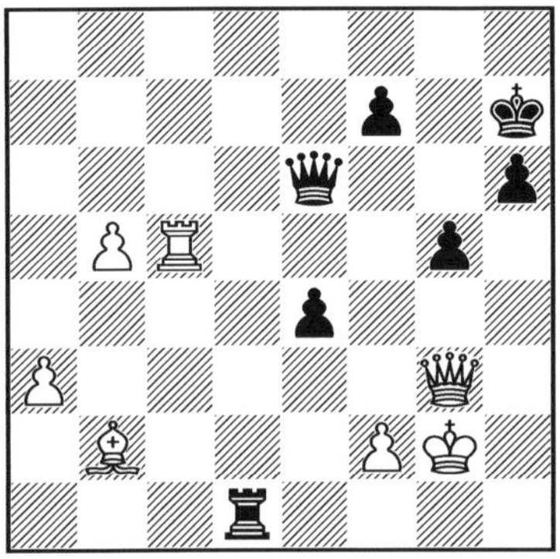

37.♖c6

Editor's note: White's last move is a mistake (the correct reply was 37.♖c3, controlling the third rank), which Tal could have exploited with 37...♕f5! (instead of 37...♕d5?), not just with the ideas 38...♕xb5 and 38...♖d3, but also forcing the opponent's queen to guard the f3 square (38.♕h2?? ♕f3#). After the subsequent 38.♖c1 ♖d3 39.♕e5 ♕g4+ 40.♔f1 ♕h3+ or 38.♖c3 ♕xb5 39.♕h3 ♕f1+ 40.♔g3 ♕b5 41.♔g2 (*41.♗c1? e3! 42.♗xe3 ♕e5+*, winning) 41...♕f1+ *(41...♕xb2?? 42.♖c6+−)* 42.♔g3 ♕b5, the game ends with a threefold repetition.

37...♕d5

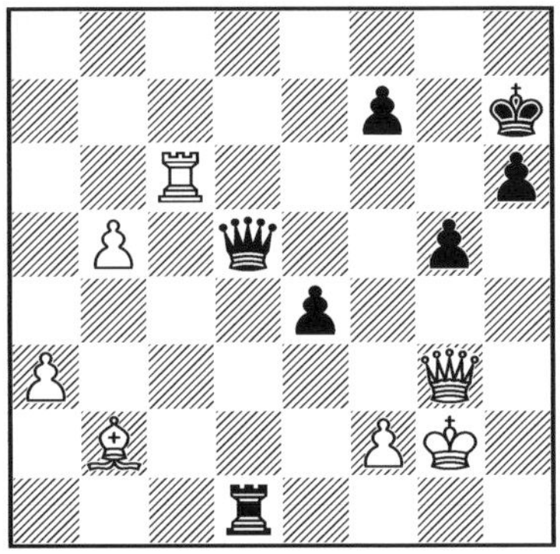

38.♕e5?

Smyslov, who was in time trouble too at this point, misses a simple tactic. After 38.♕e3 ♖d3 39.♕b6! e3+ 40.♔h2, black had to resign.

Editor's note: Actually, 38.♕e3 is no good either: it is met with 38...♕f5! (threatening 39...♕g4+ 40.♕g3 ♕e2−+), and white has no way to win: 39.♖f6 ♕g4+ 40.♕g3 ♕h5 41.♕h2 ♕g4+, 39.♕e2 ♖d2! 40.♕xd2 ♕f3+, or 39.♖c1 ♖d3 40.♕e2 ♖d2! 41.♕xd2 ♕f3+, with a draw in all lines.

There was a good move 38.♖c1! – after the subsequent 38...♖xc1 *(38...e3+ 39.♕f3+−)* 39.♗xc1 ♕xb5 40.♕d6 white should win after overcoming some technical difficulties. However, the strongest continuation was 38.♕h2!! (threatening to take on h6) 38...e3+ 39.♔g3, and black is defenseless.

38...♖g1+ 39.♔h2 ♖h1+ 40.♔g2 ♖g1+

Taking the rook results in perpetual check, and so the opponents agreed to a **draw**.

In round 16, Tal defeated Gligoric, and Keres drew with Smyslov. Thus, Tal overtook the Estonian grandmaster by half a point. It seemed that the Riga player, who had black against Keres in round 17, could just settle for a draw. But Tal declined the peace offer made by his opponent on the 18th move. This was a critical decision. The position was incredibly sharp, but Tal was going exactly for that. If he won, he could increase his lead further.

No. 56
P. Keres – M. Tal
1959, Bled/Zagreb/Belgrade, Candidates Tournament, round 17

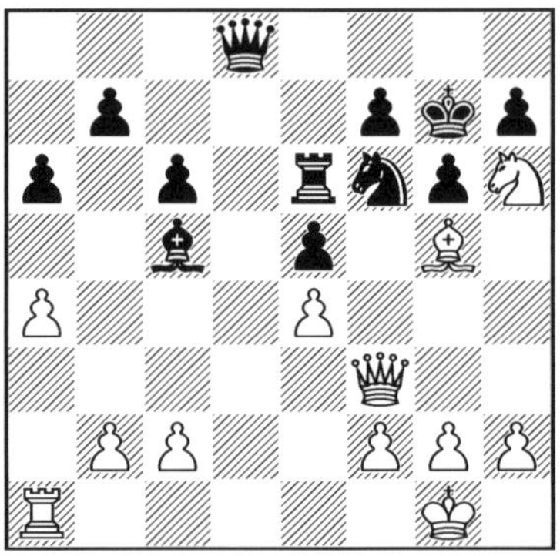

19...♕d4!?

Of course, 19...♗e7 was more solid.

20.h4 ♕xb2 21.♖d1 ♗d4 22.♖d3 ♕xc2 23.♖xd4! exd4 24.e5 ♔f8! 25.exf6

Without a doubt, Keres saw that he could force a draw with 25.♗xf6 ♕c1+ 26.♔h2 ♕xh6 27.♗g5 ♕g7 28.♗f6 ♕h6 29.♗g5, but he preferred to play for a win.

Editor's note: Keres' move is a mistake that leads to a lost position for white.

25...♕c3! 26.♕g4 ♕e1+ 27.♔h2 ♕xf2 28.♕h3 ♕e1 29.♕b3 b5 30.axb5 cxb5 31.♕a3+ b4 32.♕b3 ♕e5+ 33.♔h1 ♕e1+ 34.♔h2 ♕e5+

Both opponents were in time trouble at that point.

35.♔h1 ♕d6 36.♔g1 d3

36...♕c5 was more cautious, and if 37.♗d2, then 37...a5.

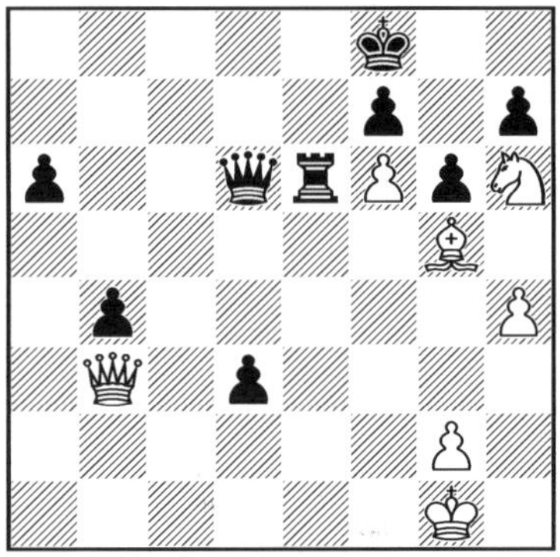

37.♕d1

Many commentators pointed out that white had the move 37.♕c4 available. Then 37...d2 is bad due to 38.♗xd2!, and black can't play 38...♕xd2 due to 39.♕c8+ ♖e8 40.♕c5+, mating. Further, after 37...b3 38.♕c8+ ♖e8 39.♕c4 ♖e6 40.♕c8+, white forces a draw. (**Editor's note:** After 39.♕c4, black doesn't have to play 39...♖e6; instead, he can play 39...♖e1+ 40.♔f2 ♖e2+ 41.♔f1 ♕e6 42.♕b4+ ♔e8 43.♕b8+ ♔d7 44.♕b7+ ♔d6 45.♕b6+ ♔d5 46.♕xb3+ ♔d4

47.♕b4+ ♕c4 48.♕xc4+ ♔xc4 49.♘xf7 ♖e6 50.♘d8 d2 51.♗xd2 ♖xf6+ 52.♔e2 ♔b5, maintaining winning chances, even though white probably should hold. However, instead of 39.♕c4?!, white has a much better move: 39.♕b7, forcing black to give perpetual check with 39...♕d4+ 40.♔h2 ♕e5+ etc.) However, Tal's intended 37...♕b6+ 38.♔h2 ♕b5! 39.♕c8+ ♖e8 still won.

37...♕c5+ 38.♔h1 ♕c2 39.♕f3 d2 40.♗xd2 ♕xd2 White resigned.

In round 20, Tal won his third game against the U.S. champion.

No. 57
M. Tal – B. Fischer
1959, Bled/Zagreb/Belgrade,
Candidates Tournament, round 20

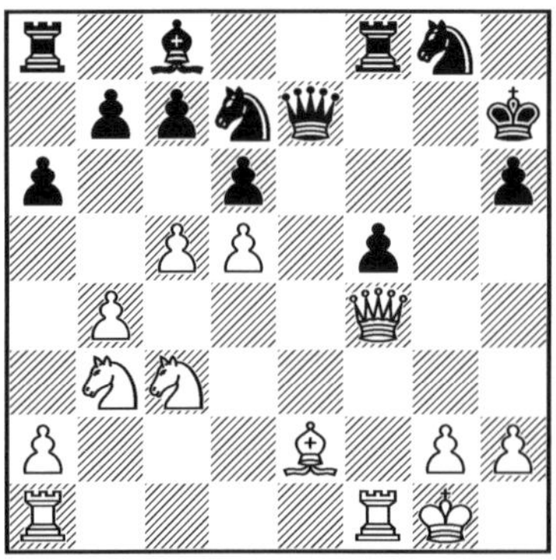

Black played **20...dxc5** without much thought. The seconds of foreign grandmasters exchanged knowing smiles. They, like Fischer, thought that Tal had just lost a pawn. However, just a few moves later, it turned out that Fischer had lost a lot more...

21.♗d3! cxb4 22.♖ae1 ♕f6 (22...♕d6 was better). **23.♖e6**

Editor's note: 23.♘a4 was a stronger move with the threats 24.♗xf5+ and 24.♕xc7 and a big advantage. Had Fischer now continued correctly, it would have turned out that the white rook's position on e6 was not ideal: if the knight leaves d7, it falls under attack.

23...♕xc3

Editor's note: The only correct move was 23...♕g7, still protecting the h-pawn with the queen. It's also important to note that the queen would have covered the f8 rook and attacked the c3 knight, and the c7 pawn was also protected after the knight left d7. There could follow: a) 24.♗xf5+ ♔h8 25.♕xb4 a5! 26.♕d4 (*26.♘xa5? ♘c5!*) 26...♕xd4+ 27.♘xd4 ♘c5; b) 24.♕xb4 a5! 25.♘xa5 ♘c5 26.♖e3 *(26.♕xc5? ♗xe6 27.dxe6 b6 with a clear advantage for black)* 26...♘xd3 27.♖xd3 ♖a6; or c) 24.♖f3 ♘df6 25.♖g3 ♕f7 26.♗xf5+ ♔h8 – black should probably hold in all cases.

24.♗xf5+ ♖xf5 25.♕xf5+ ♔h8 26.♖f3!

Now black is defenseless. After **26...♕b2 27.♖e8 ♘df6 28.♕xf6+ ♕xf6 29.♖xf6 ♔g7 30.♖ff8 ♘e7 31.♘a5! h5 32.h4 ♖b8 33.♘c4 b5 34.♘e5**, the **American grandmaster resigned**.

Tal bolstered his tournament standing with wins against Benko and Olafsson. After round 21, he had scored 15.5 points, Keres had 14, and Smyslov and Petrosian were on 11.5 each.

On 15th October, the last, decisive leg of the tournament started in Belgrade. There was an eye-catching headline in the evening newspaper that reported on the tournament: "Seven grandmasters approaching Belgrade, Tal approaching Botvinnik!"

The interest in the Candidates Tournament in Belgrade was huge. The tournament hall couldn't accommodate everyone. The games were demonstrated on the streets.

It was rather hard for Tal. Each evening, the grandmasters were surrounded by hundreds of chess enthusiasts at the exit. The supporters walked with Tal to the hotel, and the grandmaster had to answer questions and give autographs all the way.

Tal had every chance to gain first place, but the battle hadn't yet ended. The games of the Zagreb leg drained much of his strength, and now, at the finishing line, Tal was noticeably tired.

In the game against Smyslov – the first round of the last leg – he played too riskily and lost a knight. Only Smyslov's weak play in time trouble saved the leader from defeat.

Before the game with Keres, Tal resolutely declined advice to calmly play for a draw against the Estonian grandmaster.

"Keres has two and a half fewer points, and I have no moral right to avoid a fight."

These weren't just words. Even though Tal couldn't play at his full strength because of his tiredness, he didn't avoid complications. Keres exploited his opponent's opening mistake and won convincingly.

Tal drew his next two games, against Petrosian and Olafsson, and then won his fourth game with Fischer out of four. We should point out that Tal barely avoided big trouble in this game: his risky opening play allowed Fischer to create a strong attack.

Before the last round, Tal had one point more than Keres. His opponent was Benko. As I said earlier, Benko came to the game against the leader wearing sunglasses – he had found his remedy against hypnosis!

Tal's countermeasure caused a merry stir in the hall. He greeted his opponent, sat down and, before making a move, also put sunglasses on.

When Tal offered Benko a draw in a better position, the latter pretended not to hear his opponent. However, peace was agreed after some time. In a winning position, Tal forced a perpetual check. He had won the Candidates Tournament!

At the press conference, Tal said, "I have dreamed of playing at least one game against the world champion for quite a while, and I'm happy that I will get to play a whole match against him!"

Reactions after the Candidates Tournament

The results of the Candidates Tournament and Tal's victory were discussed by chess players throughout the world. Despite the young grandmaster's brilliant successes in recent years – two Soviet championship wins and first place at the Portoroz and Zurich tournaments – many chess fans were still surprised when the 23 year-old Riga player triumphed at the Candidates.

Tal's ascent to the very top was truly rapid. In just nine years, the young player had progressed from first-category player to world championship candidate!

In his article "Modern Chess", the ex-world champion Max Euwe wrote, "We cannot talk about modern chess without mentioning Tal's name. The incredible combinations that arise in his games as though summoned by a magic wand are something more than just brilliant fireworks. This is a manifestation of the new style. With his efforts, Tal, despite his youth, has taken an important part in building the strong edifice of chess art, the foundation of which was laid more than a hundred years ago."

In the article "M. Tal's Victory", published in *Shakhmaty v SSSR*, grandmaster Alexander Kotov highlighted that "...Tal's example will help our chess youth to understand the beauty of chess, to understand how they should play."

"What's most characteristic of Tal's playing style? The desire to create unclear, double-edged positions and seize the initiative at any cost, without regard to sacrifices," said grandmaster Vyacheslav Ragozin, FIDE Vice-President, at the Candidates Tournament closing ceremony.

Here are some examples that illustrate these features of Tal's creative style.

No. 58
M. Tal – S. Gligoric
1959, Bled/Zagreb/Belgrade, Candidates Tournament, round 16

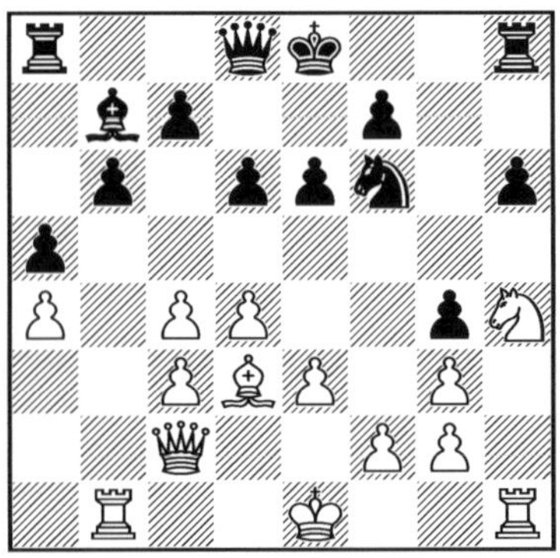

It looks like both sides are going to castle and then begin long positional maneuvering. However, Tal's next move changes the situation drastically.

16.d5!

Editor's note: This move could have led to a very unpleasant position for white.

16...♕e7

Gligoric refuses to accept the pawn sacrifice, because after 16... exd5 17.cxd5 ♗xd5 (if 17...♘xd5, then 18.♗e4!) 18.c4 ♗c6 19.♘f5, white has a threatening initiative.

17.0-0 ♘d7

Editor's note: After 17...0-0-0! black seizes the initiative. The point is, after 18.dxe6? (white wins an exchange this way, but the opponent's bishop becomes rather dangerous) 18...fxe6 19.♘g6 ♕g7 20.♘xh8 ♖xh8, black pushes the h-pawn forward, creating a very dangerous (and probably decisive) attack. Instead of 18.dxe6, white has a stronger move 18.e4, but after 18...♘d7 with the subsequent ♘c5 black is in the driver's seat: the a4 and c4 pawns are weak, the idea f7-f5 is in the air, and white has no way to create any activity.

18.dxe6 ♕xe6 19.♗f5! ♕xc4

Editor's note: As it soon transpires, the queen is positioned badly here. The right move was 19...♕e5, with unclear play.

20.♖fd1 ♘f6 21.♖d4 ♕c6

It seems that the first wave of the attack is over – it's unclear how white can increase the pressure. However, Tal finds an elegant combination maneuver, and black's position soon becomes very difficult.

22.♗e6!

Editor's note: Actually, this move allows black to consolidate, whereas after 22.♗d3! (not just threatening 23.♗b5, but with a lot of other ideas as well, such as, ♖f4, ♖c4 and ♘f5), white has an overwhelming position.

22...♖g8 23.♗c4! ♔f8

Editor's note: Analysis shows that after 23...0-0-0!, the position was dynamically equal. One example line: 24.♕f5+ ♘d7 25.♕xf7 ♖gf8 26.♕e6 h5 27.♗b5 ♕xc3 28.♗xd7+ ♖xd7 29.♘g6 ♖xf2! 30.♕e8+ ♖d8 31.♘e7+ ♔b8 32.♕xd8+ ♔a7 33.♔xf2+ ♕c2+ 34.♔e1 ♕xb1+ 35.♖d1 ♕b4+ 36.♖d2 ♕c3! 37.♘f5 ♕c1+ 38.♖d1 ♕c3+ with perpetual check.

24.♗b5 ♕c5 25.♖c4 ♕e5 26.♖xc7 ♗e4 27.♗d3 d5 28.♖c6 ♖b8 29.c4, and, gaining a great positional advantage, **white won** on move 64.

After Tal took the lead, he could have afforded to play quietly, but, even in the last rounds, he still preferred to take risks.

In another game against Gligoric, in the fourth leg, Tal chose a double-edged line in the King's Indian. After 18 moves, the following position occurred on the board:

No. 59
S. Gligoric – M. Tal
1959, Bled/Zagreb/Belgrade,
Candidates Tournament, round 23

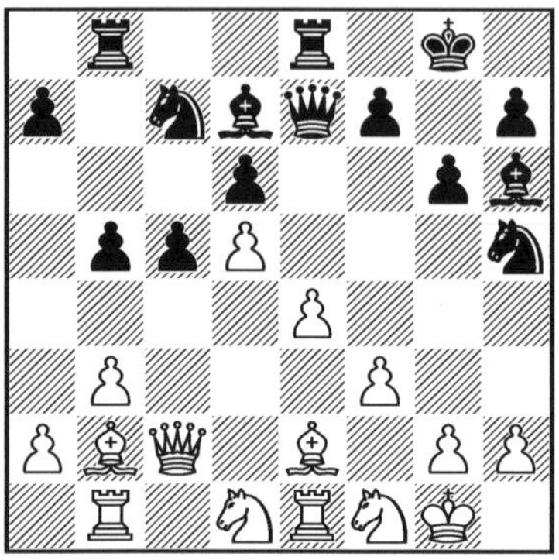

18...♘xd5

Black doesn't get enough material compensation for the sacrificed knight, but pressure along the e-file helps him maintain a long-term initiative. White faced many difficulties while neutralizing this pressure, and he ultimately cracked.

19.exd5 ♗f5 20.♕c3 ♗g7 21.♕c1 ♗xb1 22.♗xg7 ♔xg7 23.♕xb1 ♘f4 24.♘de3 ♕e5

Gligoric makes the right decision: he returns the piece to get some freedom in maneuvering.

25.♗xb5 ♖xb5 26.♘f5+

Editor's note: The correct move was 26.g3 with a roughly equal position after 26...♔f8 (the king evades a possible ♘f5+) 27.gxf4 ♕xf4.

26...gxf5!

Editor's note: Objectively speaking, Tal's move is questionable. 26...♕xf5 27.♕xf5 gxf5 28.♖xe8 ♘xd5 was stronger, getting an endgame with a tiny material advantage. On the other hand, even though only black would have chances of winning, they were actually quite marginal because of his compromised pawn structure. Tal's move leads to an equal but complicated position that suits his style much better.

27.♖xe5 ♖xe5

Black gets enough compensation for the queen.

28.g3 ♘e2+ 29.♔f2 ♔g8?

The first consequence of time trouble. Black should have played 29...♘d4.

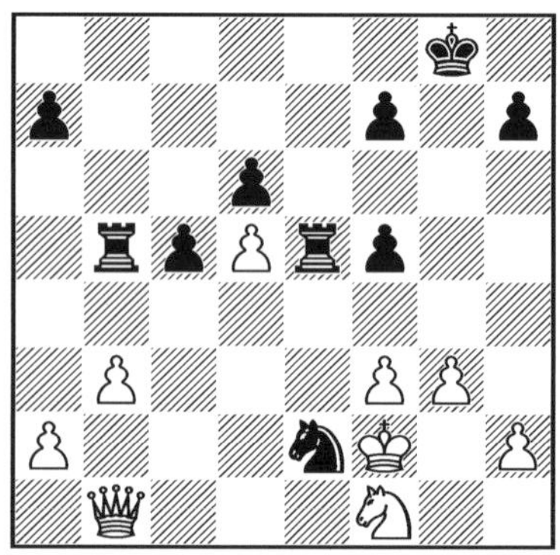

30.♘e3?

White, affected by the pressure, makes a mistake too. After 30.f4! ♖e8 (if 30...♖e4, then 31.♘d2) 31.♕xf5, he got a material advantage.

30...♘d4 31.f4 ♖e4 32.g4??

Suicide! The necessary move was 32.♘xf5!, with equal chances.

32...♖xf4+ 33.♔g2 fxg4 34.♘c4 ♘f3 35.♕c1 ♖f6 36.♕e3 ♔f8 37.♕e4 ♖b8 38.♕xh7 ♖e8 39.♕h8+ ♔e7 40.♕g7 ♘h4+ 41.♔g1

Time trouble has ended, but white can't do anything – his position is hopeless.

41...♘f3+ 42.♔g2 ♖g6 43.♕c3 ♘d4 44.b4 ♔f8 45.♘e3 g3! 46.h3 ♖f6 White resigned.

In addition to his attacking skills, Tal showed his great defensive technique at the Candidates Tournament.

No. 60
F. Olafsson – M. Tal
1959, Bled/Zagreb/Belgrade, Candidates Tournament, round 11

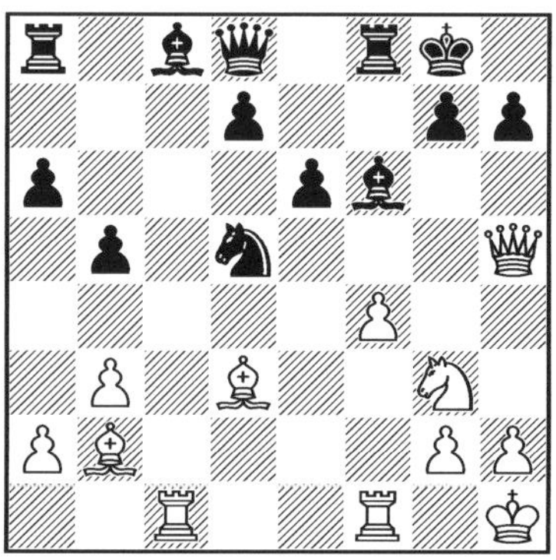

21...g6 22.♗xg6 ♕e7!

Black sees through his opponent's smart plan. After 22...hxg6 23.♕xg6+ ♔h8 white doesn't settle for perpetual check: with 24.♘f5!! ♗xb2 25.♖f3!, he checkmates his opponent.

23.♗xf6 ♘xf6 24.♕f3 ♖b8 25.♗d3 ♗b7 26.♕e2

White's attack is repelled, but he still maintains a positional advantage. Tal slowly outplays the Icelandic grandmaster and goes on the counter-attack.

26...♔h8 27.♖ce1 ♖be8 28.♘f5 ♕b4 29.♕b2 ♖c8 30.♘g3

White has wasted precious time on knight moves, and his opponent has managed to seize the c-file.

30...♕c3 31.♕e2 ♖g8 32.♘e4 ♕d4 33.♘g5 ♖g7 34.♕e3 ♕xe3 35.♖xe3 ♖c3 36.♖h3 b4 37.♔g1

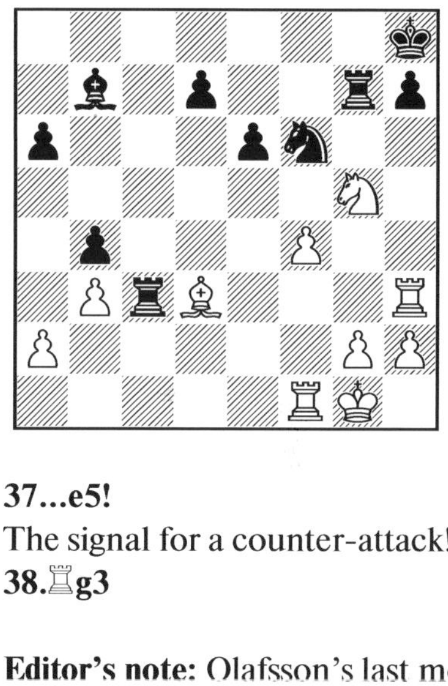

37...e5!

The signal for a counter-attack!

38.♖g3

Editor's note: Olafsson's last move is a blunder. The correct reply was 38.♖h6, and after the subsequent 38...♘g4 39.♖xh7+ ♖xh7 40.♗xh7 ♘e3 41.♖e1 exf4 42.g3 fxg3 43.hxg3, white should draw easily.

38...e4 39.♗c4 d5 40.♗e2 d4 41.♗c4 e3 42.♖d1 ♗d5! 43.♗f1 ♖e7 44.♗e2 d3 45.♗xd3 ♖xd3 46.♖xd3 e2 47.♖ge3 e1=♕+, and **black won**.

The Candidates Tournament win didn't go to Tal's head. The laudatory articles that now and again appeared in the press didn't impress him much. Tal remained the same as he always was. He understood the necessity of hard work and further self-improvement.

He realized clearly that his play was not free of serious drawbacks. It was obvious that in games against Soviet players Tal wasn't always on top of his situation. Didn't his three losses to Keres attest to that? In one of those games, he got carried away and sacrificed two pieces without good reason, the other was won by the Estonian grandmaster in a complicated, maneuvering struggle. The game against Smyslov in round 22 could also have ended badly for Tal, who disregarded the objective requirements of the position. And didn't the games against Fischer (round 27) and Olafsson (round 11) show how much excessive danger Tal voluntarily went for?

Only Fourth Place...

After a short rest, we started preparing for the match against Botvinnik: we read the latest Soviet and foreign chess magazines and opening monographs and, of course, studied the world champion's games.

Tal was very glad to hear the news that an international tournament would be held in Riga. The grandmaster preferred this way of training above anything else.

The tournament didn't bring Tal any laurels. He finished only fourth, behind Spassky, Mikenas and Tolush. Nevertheless, the pre-match competition was beneficial: it was good practice, showing on what we needed to work.

Tal's result in the Riga tournament was predetermined after losing to his main competitor, Boris Spassky. The distance was short, and it soon became clear that Tal wouldn't be able to catch up with the Leningrad grandmaster.

No. 61, Ruy Lopez
B. Spassky – M. Tal
1959, Riga International, round 3

1.e4 e5 2.♘f3 ♘c6 3.♗b5 a6 4.♗a4 ♘f6 5.0-0 ♗e7 6.♖e1 b5 7.♗b3 0-0 8.c3 d6 9.h3 ♘a5 10.♗c2 c5 11.d4 ♕c7 12.♘bd2 ♗d7 13.♘f1 ♖fe8 14.d5 c4 15.g4

Editor's note: This move never found any adherents among strong players. For instance, in the games Landa — P. Nikolic, Germany BL 2004, and Azarov — V. Kovalev, Minsk 2010, white preferred 15.♘g3 and then executed the plan ♘h2 and f2-f4.

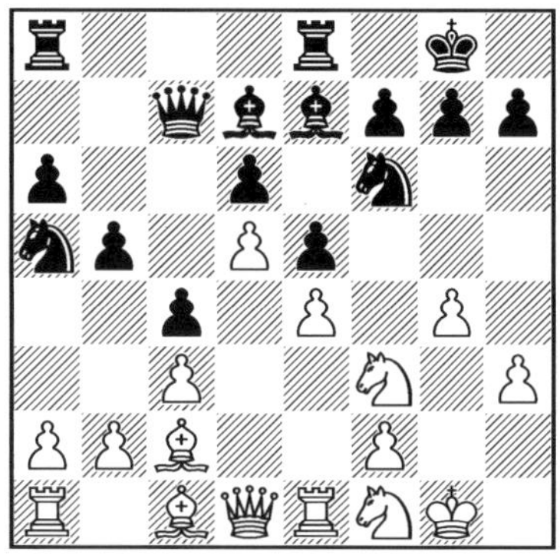

15...h5

This aggressive move is a strategic error. The correct reply was 15...g6.

16.gxh5 ♗xh3 17.♘3h2 ♘h7

Editor's note: It was better to play 17...♘b7, intending ♘c5 at the earliest opportunity. In the actual game, this knight didn't properly enter the battle at all.

18.♘e3 ♗g5 19.♔h1 ♗f4 20.♖g1 ♕d8 21.♕f3

Threatening to start an attack with 22.♘f5.

21...♕h4

Another "active" move. In actuality, black's position is already critical.

22.♘g2 ♗xg2+ 23.♕xg2 ♕xh2+

A forced trade, because after 23...♕f6, white gets a strong attack with 24.♗e3 and the subsequent 25.♕h3 and ♘g4. (**Editor's note:** Instead of 24.♗e3, white had an even stronger move 24.♗xf4! exf4 25.♕h3 with various ideas, for instance, ♘g4, ♘f3, e4-e5, ♖g1-g4 and ♖a1-g1 etc. – analysis shows that in this line white has a decisive advantage.)

24.♕xh2 ♗xh2 25.♔xh2

Spassky has got a noticeable advantage with simple means. The defense is going to be difficult for black.

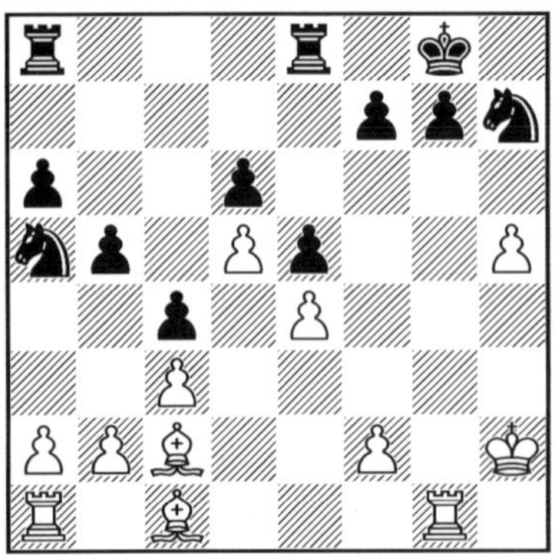

25...♘f6 26.♖g5 ♘h7 27.♖f5 g6 28.♖f3 ♔g7 29.hxg6 fxg6 30.b4! cxb3 31.axb3 ♘b7 32.b4

Fixing the backward pawn a6 in place and taking away the important c5 square from the knight.

32...♖ec8 33.♗d2 ♘f6 34.♗d3 ♖h8+ 35.♔g2 ♘g4 36.♔g3 ♘f6 37.♔g2 ♘g4 38.♖h1 ♖xh1 39.♔xh1

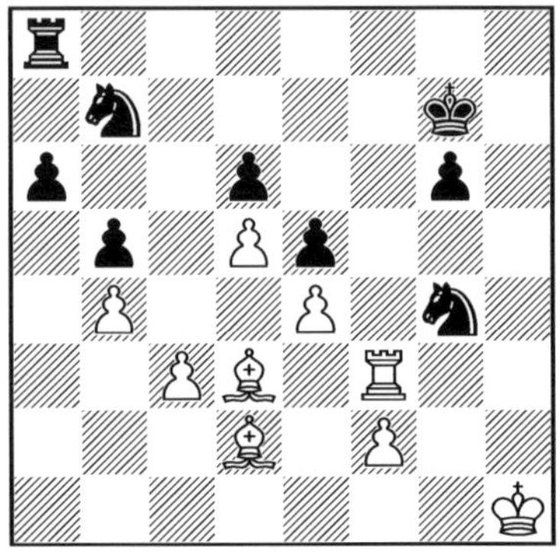

39...a5?

Passive defense does not sit well with Tal, and he tries to activate his queenside pieces. However, the b-pawn is now severely weakened. It was better to transfer the knight from g4 to c7 first.

40.♔g2 a4 41.♖h3 ♘f6 42.♗h6+ ♔f7 43.♖f3 a3 44.♗b1 a2 45.♗xa2 ♖xa2 46.♗g5 ♖c2 47.♖xf6+ ♔e8 48.♖xg6 ♔d7 49.♖g7+ ♔c8 50.♗e3 ♖xc3 51.♗b6! ♖c4 52.♖g8+ ♔d7 53.♖b8 ♘c5 54.bxc5 dxc5, and, without waiting for his opponent's reply, **Tal resigned**.

Vladas Mikenas defeated Tal as well.

Tal's desire to go for complications no matter the cost brought him success in the next game.

No. 62, Modern Benoni
I. Niemela – M. Tal
1959, Riga International, round 7

1.d4 ♘f6 2.c4 c5 3.d5 e6 4.♘c3 exd5 5.cxd5 d6 6.e4 g6 7.f4 ♗g7

8.♘f3 0-0 9.♗e2 ♖e8 10.e5 dxe5 11.fxe5 ♘g4

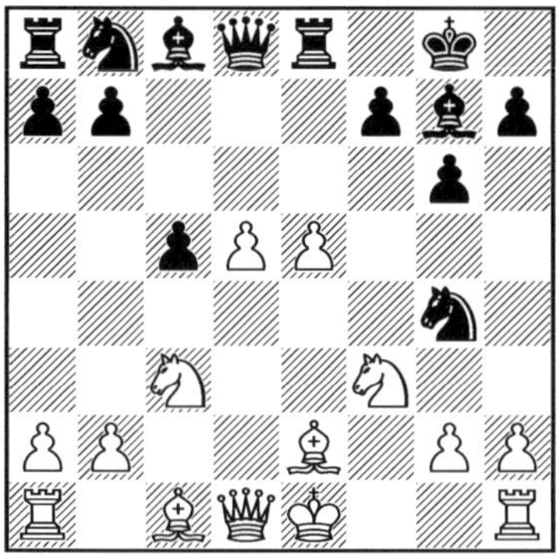

12.e6

A little explored double-edged move, involving a pawn sacrifice. Alekhine recommended 12.0-0 in this position. By parting with the e5 pawn, white retains good attacking chances.

12...fxe6 13.0-0

Editor's note: A bad move. There are two much stronger replies: 13.d6 (the most frequent move) and 13.♗g5 – according to modern theory, chances are roughly equal in both cases (white has fair compensation for the pawn, but no more).

13...exd5 14.♘xd5 ♗e6 15.♗c4 ♘e5

Black provokes his opponent to sacrifice a piece. After 16.♘xe5 ♗xe5, white has no compensation for the pawn.

16.♗g5! ♘xf3+ 17.♕xf3 ♕xg5 18.♖ae1 ♖f8!

Tal placed all his hopes in this move.

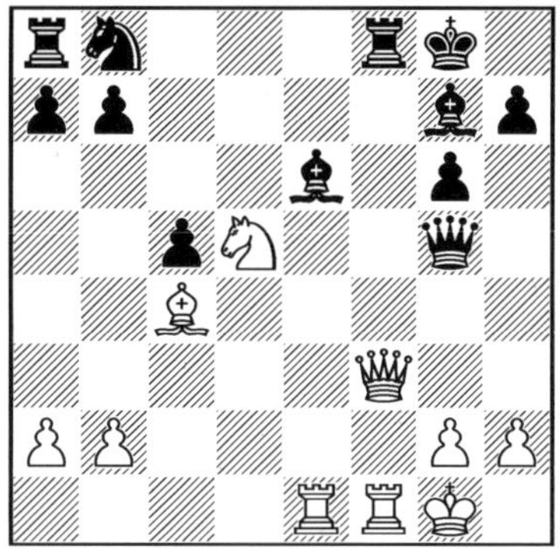

19.♖xe6?

Paul Keres wrote this about the move in the tournament bulletin: "It's hard to master this complicated position even in home analysis. However, one thing is clear: the game move leads to a quick defeat. Perhaps there were two better move for white: firstly, 19.♕xf8+ ♗xf8 20.♖xe6 ♘c6 21.♘c7, and black has to give up another rook; secondly, just play 19.♕e4, and there's no good move to defend the e6 bishop."

Editor's note: Keres' first line doesn't help white: after 19.♕xf8+ ♗xf8 20.♖xe6 ♘c6 21.♘c7, there follows 21...♔g7 22.♘xa8 ♕d8 (threatening 22...♕d4+/22...♕xa8), and black wins (Sassen – Mooij, corr 1974). However, 19.♕e4 is indeed a good move and the only possibility to continue the struggle, even though after the subsequent 19...♘c6 20.♕xe6+ ♔h8 white has no compensation for the pawn.

19...♗d4+!

White missed this Zwischenschach. He expected 19...♖xf3, with a decisive attack after 20.♖e8+. Now the black king can escape to g7.

20.♔h1 ♖xf3 21.♖e8+ ♔g7 22.♖xf3 ♕c1+ 23.♗f1 ♘c6!

Launching a winning counter-attack.

24.♖xa8 ♘e5 25.♖ff8 ♘g4 26.♖f3 ♘f2+ 27.♔g1 ♘e4+ White resigned: after 28.♔h1, black has the elegant 28...♘g3+! (29.hxg3 ♕h6#).

Tal made a fascinating intuitive sacrifice of two minor pieces for a rook and pawn in a game against a Norwegian master.

No. 63
M. Tal – S. Johannessen
1959, Riga International, round 6

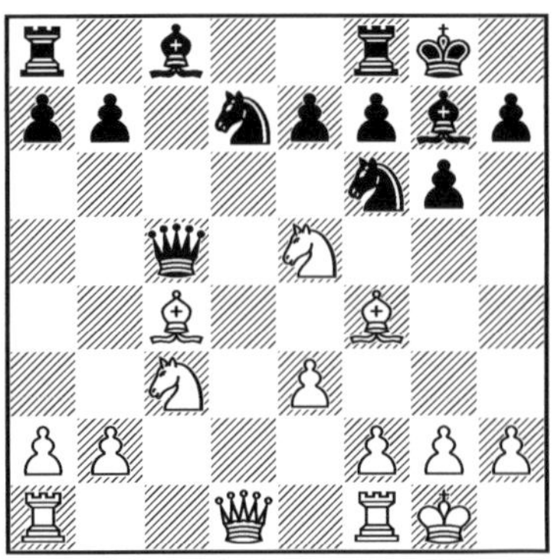

12.♗xf7+!

Like 12...♘xe4 in the game against Averbakh at the 25th Soviet championship, this double-edged move caused much discussion.

"I think that such sacrifices actually don't need any concrete calculations: it's enough to look at the position to see that this sacrifice should be correct" – that's what Tal himself said about the move.

Editor's note: From Koblenz's subsequent notes, it's clear that he wasn't sure that Tal's operation was correct from the analytical point of view (see his note to black's 15th move), so the exclamation mark awarded by him for this move obviously describes only its practical strength. Computer analysis shows that white's move was dubious.

12...♖xf7 13.♘xf7 ♔xf7 14.♕b3+ ♔f8 15.♖ac1

The white pieces have assumed ideal positions, whereas it's hard for black to complete his queenside development.

15...a6?

Preventing the move 16.♘b5. Now, however, black has no time to develop his queenside. Keres recommended 15...♕b6 16.♘b5 ♘e8 here, which Tal intended to meet with 17.♕c4. In this case, it's hard to determine whether white has enough positional compensation for the lacking material. One thing is clear: black would have still faced difficult problems. (**Editor's note:** After the subsequent 17...♘e5 18.♕e2 ♗g4 19.f3 ♗e6 20.b3 ♖d8, black completes his development and gets an advantage: two pieces for a rook and pawn and the bishop pair. As for the game move, it's certainly not good, but awarding a question mark to it was probably too harsh.)

16.♖fd1 ♕a5

Editor's note: This is an error. The correct move was 16...♕b6 — for instance, 17.♕c4 ♕xb2 18.♘d5 ♘xd5 19.♕xd5 ♕b5 20.♕e6 ♕f5 21.♕c4 ♕b5, with threefold repetition.

17.♕c4! (preventing 17...b5)

Editor's note: White had a much stronger reply 17.♘d5! (threatening 18.♘c7/18.♘xe7), and black's position becomes very difficult, for instance, 17...♘xd5 (after *17...b5?*, the simplest is *18.♘c7♖a7 19.♘e6+*) 18.♖xd5 ♕d8 19.♖d2 ♕e8 20.♕d1 ♗f6 21.e4 (threatening 22.e5) 21...♔g7 22.♖c7 ♕f7 23.♖dc2+−.

17...♕f5

Editor's note: Black could resist better with 17...♕c5 18.♕e2 (neither *18.♕e6 ♕b6* nor *18.♕b3 ♕b6* leads to any progress) 18...♕f5 (or 18...♕h5) — the white queen is much less active on e2.

18.h3! ♘e8! 19.♘d5 ♕e6 20.♕b4 b5

Even after 20...♗e5, recommended by Keres in the tournament bulletin, white still maintained a significant advantage with 21.♖c4. (**Editor's note:** Instead of 21.♖c4?!, white has a much stronger reply: 21.♗xe5 ♕xe5 22.f4 ♕e6 23.e4 with an overwhelming position. However, black could have prolonged the resistance with 20...a5! 21.♕b5 b6, not fearing 22.♖c6? due to 22...♗a6!.)

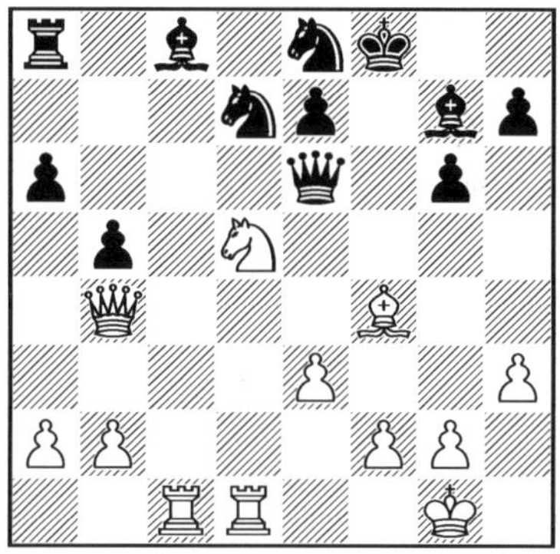

21.♖c6!

Gaining a decisive tempo. Interestingly, white's winning combination follows at the very moment when the Norwegian master seemed to have overcome his troubles.

21...♕f7 22.♘c7 ♘xc7 23.♖xc7 ♕e6 24.♖dc1!

The threat 25.♖xc8+ is unstoppable. After 24...♘e5, there's 25.♕e4, winning.

24...♘b6 25.♖xe7! ♘d5 26.♖xe6+ ♘xb4 27.♗d6+ Black resigned.

The Draw is Made!

We're in Moscow, in Max Euwe's room in the National Hotel; the ex-world champion arrived from Netherlands a few hours ago for the opening ceremony of the Botvinnik-Tal match. The official part is scheduled for the next day, while this evening the draw is made to determine who's going to make the first move in the match.

There's a small crowd around the little round table: world champion Mikhail Botvinnik with his second Grigory Goldberg, Max Euwe, Harry Golombek (the Englishman is one of the arbiters), Lev Abramov (the USSR Chess Federation executive secretary), Mikhail Tal and yours truly – his second.

We're waiting for the match chief arbiter – Swedish grandmaster Gideon Stahlberg, who got delayed somewhere between Stockholm and Moscow. To make the best use of the time, we discuss the match regulations. One of the clauses states: if the tournament hall becomes too noisy, the arbiters are obliged to move the game to another room if one of the players' seconds requests it.

"Do you have any objections?" Botvinnik asked Tal.

"No, why should I?"

The other points are agreed upon just as quickly. Abramov looks at his watch. Stahlberg still hadn't arrived.

Goldberg, who's sitting beside me, tells some story. I'm trying to listen attentively, but understand nothing. In my mind's eye, I involuntarily see episodes of days long past...

May 1935... I'm sitting in a London cafe with Emanuel Lasker, the man who defeated the first world champion, legendary Wilhelm Steinitz, in 1894. I'm talking to the man who deservedly bore the world champion's crown for 27 years and, despite his age of 67, finished third at the Second Moscow International tournament without losing a single game!

The "iron" Lasker is polite and gentle in real life. Before expressing his thoughts, he looks somewhere far away, still holding a cigar in his mouth.

"Many wondered why I forfeited the match against Capablanca after just 14 games," Lasker says. "The official version was that I was defeated by the tropical climate of Havana. But this is not the only reason. I didn't want to die in poverty, like Steinitz, so I demanded appearance fees to play in tournaments, which angered the rich sponsors who organized the tournaments. I was constantly hounded by the press, which was in their pocket."

Lasker fell silent and, exhaling another cloud of smoke, continued:

"With each day, I felt more and more isolated and lonely. I was so fed up that I decided to demonstratively relinquish the world champion's title.

When thousands of spectators flocked to the spacious halls of the Moscow International tournament, my heart was full of joy. I didn't doubt that the talented and hard-working Mikhail Botvinnik would move mountains – it just couldn't be any different!"

...Hastings, an English resort town, January 1935. The traditional Christmas tournament had just finished. Late in the evening, a group of chess players surrounded a short young man in the lobby of a hotel. This is grandmaster Salo Flohr. He's enthusiastically talking about chess life in the USSR, saying that chess has become a part of people's culture, it's played in factories and schools.

When Flohr said that he saw slogans such as "Overtake the capitalist countries on the chess front!" in clubs, his listeners exchanged looks. Many of them smiled ironically. This is a utopia! The West has great players such as Capablanca, Lasker, Euwe, Reshevsky, Fine! And what do they have? They only have Mikhail Botvinnik – a quiet, reserved young man who couldn't show anything remarkable here in Hastings, only sharing 5th–6th place. An argument immediately started, and Flohr exclaimed in exasperation: "Botvinnik will show you all, you'll see!"

The skeptics didn't have to wait for long. Just a few months later, the Soviet grandmaster stunned the entire world by sharing first place with Flohr at the Second Moscow International tournament, ahead of the leading Western grandmasters, including Lasker and Capablanca.

...Moscow, 1948. The Pillar Hall of the House of the Unions, lit by crystal chandeliers. The spectators applaud Mikhail Botvinnik. Far away, on the stage, grandmaster Milan Vidmar, the chief arbiter of the World Championship match tournament, pulls the new world champion into a tight embrace.

As I remember all that, I sense the historical importance of this evening even more sharply. Knowing that tomorrow Misha Tal, a boy from Riga, is going to challenge the renowned leader of the Soviet chess school for the world championship title, makes my heart beat even faster.

And then, the tired, breathless Swedish grandmaster finally arrives. We can proceed with the draw.

The next day, at 4:55 p.m., the arbiters, players and their seconds arrive on stage at the Pushkin Theater, greeted by loud applause. Numerous photographers, both Soviet and foreign, click their camera shutters.

5 p.m. Stahlberg asks the photographers to leave the stage and starts white's clock. The match begins.

No. 64, French Defense
M. Tal – M. Botvinnik
1960, Moscow, World Championship Match, game 1

After thinking for a minute, Tal moves his king's pawn:

1.e4

Botvinnik, also after a minute's thought, moves his king's pawn as well, but only one square forward:

1...e6

Studying Botvinnik's opening repertoire, we of course paid most attention to his signature opening – the French Defense – which he played very successfully with black. We considered the possibility that the world champion would play the first game in a sharp style, to prove to his aggressive opponent that his hopes for success in a combination battle were futile. Eschewing quiet continuations, we concentrated our attention on the line that occurred in the game Gligoric – Petrosian at the Candidates Tournament.

This was precisely the line that occurred in the first game:

2.d4 d5 3.♘c3 ♗b4 4.e5 c5 5.a3 ♗xc3+ 6.bxc3 ♕c7 7.♕g4

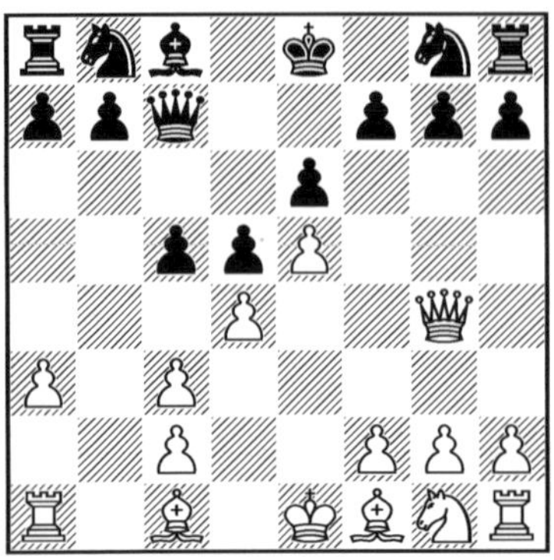

7...f5

Editor's note: The move 7...f6 is now more popular at grandmaster level.

8.♕g3 ♘e7

Editor's note: Modern strong players prefer 8...cxd4 or 8...♘c6 here, while the game move is considered dubious.

9.♕xg7 ♖g8 10.♕xh7 cxd4 11.♔d1

Editor's note: Both actual games and analysis show that 11.♘e2! is more dangerous.

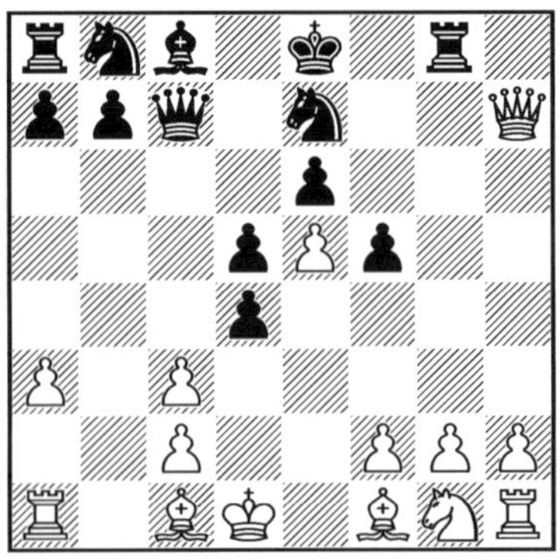

11...♗d7

The world champion uncorks a novelty in the very first game! Petrosian played a much weaker move 11...♘bc6, and after 12.♘f3 ♘xe5 13.♗g5! got a difficult position. The purpose of 11...♗d7 is not just to complete development, but also, if possible, to launch a counter-attack with ♗a4, threatening d4-d3.

12.♕h5+ ♘g6+

Editor's note: A better move here is 12...♔d8!, as black usually played in subsequent games.

13.♘e2 d3 14.cxd3 ♗a4+

It was better to play 14...♘c6 and then castle long.

Editor's note: 1) From the analytical point of view, after 14... ♘c6 15.d4 0-0-0 16.♕f3, white's two extra pawns are more valuable than his opponent's activity. Still, black definitely retains some practical chances. 2) The computer doesn't consider the game move a mistake: it thinks that Koblenz's recommendation 14...♘c6 and Botvinnik's actual move are more or less equally good (but only if after 14...♗a4+, black plays 15... ♘c6, which didn't happen in the game).

15.♔e1 ♕xe5

Editor's note: 15...♘c6 with subsequent long castling gave black far better practical chances; instead of regaining one of two lost pawns, black should have placed his hopes on activity.

16.♗g5! ♘c6 17.d4 ♕c7

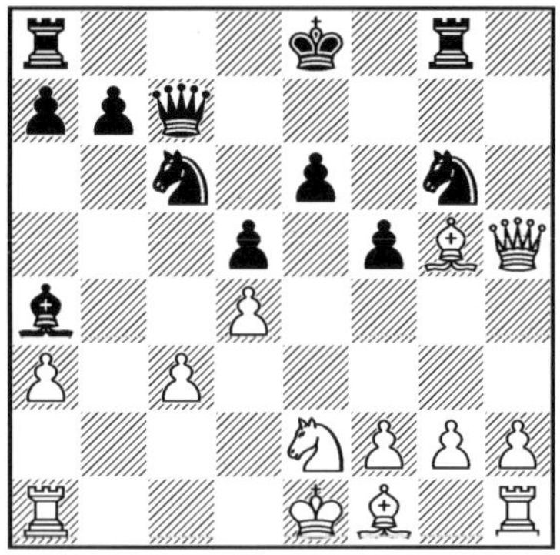

18.h4!

The pawn isn't going to be promoted in the near future. The main purpose of this move is getting the h1 rook into play as soon as possible.

18...e5

Practically the best move.

19.♖h3! ♕f7 20.dxe5 ♘cxe5 21.♖e3 ♔d7 22.♖b1 b6

22...♗c6 was more resilient.

23.♘f4 ♖ae8 24.♖b4 ♗c6

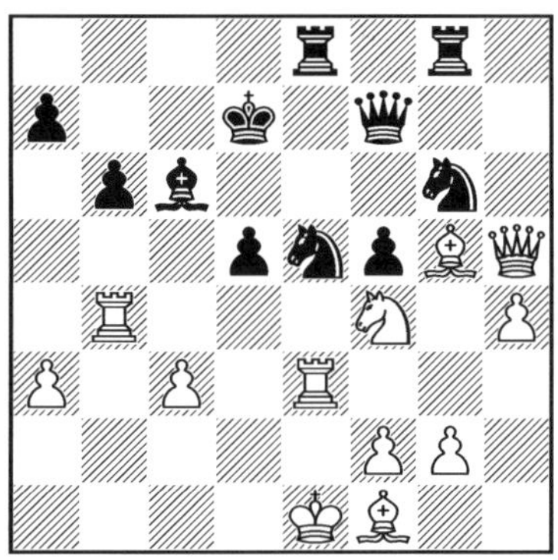

25.♕d1!

Now white's attack cannot be stopped.

25...♘xf4 26.♖xf4 ♘g6 27.♖d4 ♖xe3+ 28.fxe3 ♔c7 29.c4! dxc4

30.♗xc4 ♕g7 31.♗xg8 ♕xg8 32.h5 Black resigned.

Before game 6, Tal asked me, "For how long will I be kept in the stalls?"

This comparison was very apt for the second, fourth and fifth games. All these games were played in a quiet, positional style, and the Riga player had a hard time holding off the attacks of his formidable opponent.

In these games, Tal, as usual, strove for tactical complications, but Botvinnik decided, completely correctly, that trying to compete in line calculations with the young grandmaster, or, to put it simply, playing as his opponent wanted, was not exactly in his interests.

Botvinnik was 25 years older than his opponent. With age, chess "reflexes", especially in positions rife with tactical opportunities, undoubtedly slow down. We also have to consider that the world champion had rarely competed in big tournaments in recent years. The lack of practice also showed most clearly in sharp positions.

This was convincingly proven in the third game, when after **1.e4 c6 2.♘c3 d5 3.♘f3 ♗g4 4.h3 ♗xf3**, Tal made a paradoxical move **5.gxf3!?**.

"You shouldn't play chess like that," Tigran Petrosian said the next day.

The commentators unanimously criticized the move as well.

But should we really have to prove that if a grandmaster plays such a move, it's not because he "doesn't know what's he doing"? He knows the general positional considerations – any first-category player would decide against 5.gxf3 because of them. However, the move 5.gxf3 does have a purely positional foundation: it bolsters white's center and opens the g-file to put pressure along it.

We prepared 5.gxf3 chiefly out of psychological considerations. The resulting position was hard to anticipate beforehand. Tal's calculations paid off: the world champion spent 40 minutes on his first eight moves. In the ensuing battle, Tal needlessly decided not to execute his initial plan, got into a difficult position and had to give up a pawn. Still, Botvinnik ended up in time trouble – precisely at the time when there were great complications on the board. In the end, he had to struggle for a draw.

It became clear to us that, after this game, Botvinnik would avoid lines that led to unclear positions rich with mutual tactical chances.

Only in game 6 did the challenger finally manage to create a double-edged position with great complications on the board.

No. 65
M. Botvinnik – M. Tal
1960, Moscow, World Championship Match, game 6

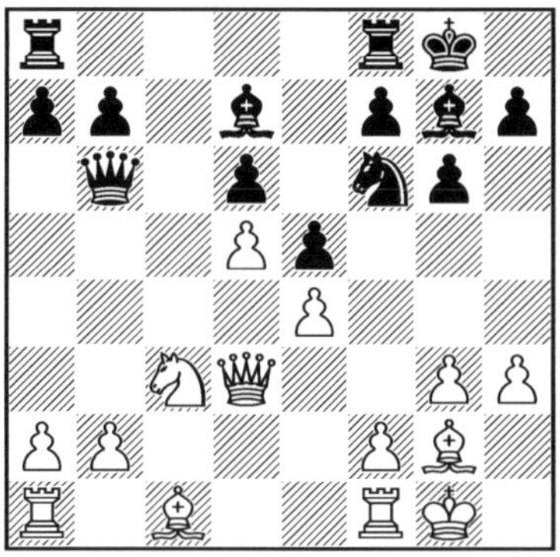

14...♖fc8

Tal wrote about this move: "Black (partly out of psychological considerations) has decided to concentrate his efforts on the queenside and then, when his opponent lets his guard down, play f7-f5. I must admit that I already had the idea of sacrificing a knight on f4, but it was hazy at the time. Black put his king's rook on c8 for two reasons: to keep the a7 pawn protected and to convince white that he wasn't even thinking about the kingside."

15.♖b1 ♘h5 16.♗e3 ♕b4 17.♕e2 ♖c4

Editor's note: From Tal's comment above, it's clear that the psychological aspect played an important role in his plan – as we shall see, black's last move, which is aimed at a very complicated struggle, paid off completely from this point of view. On the other hand, had white found the best (but completely counter-intuitive!) reply a few moves later (see the editor's note after his 19th move), he could have gotten a big advantage precisely because of the black rook's position on c4. Objectively speaking, 17...a6 was stronger (to protect the pawn from possible future attacks), but then, after 18.♖fc1, white would have some space advantage on the queenside and just get a slightly better, quiet position. While had black played 17...f5?!, then, after 18.exf5 ♗xf5 19.♖bc1 ♘f6 20.♘b5, white would clearly have the initiative.

18.♖fc1 ♖ac8

Editor's note: According to the computer, the strongest move here is to return the rook to its previous position, 18...♖cc8, which Tal probably never even considered. On the other hand, the prophylactic 18...a6 (getting the pawn away from the attack) is bad due to 19.a3! ♕b3 20.♗f3, threatening both to capture on h5 or play 21.♕d2, intending to trap the queen with 22.♗d1.

19.♔h2

White's strategic plan is not hard to understand: he's intending to trade queens with 20.a3 ♕b3 21.♕d1! and transition into a better endgame.

Editor's note: Botvinnik likely made his last move to be able to play

♗g2-f3 without worrying about the h3 pawn.

19.♗xa7 would have been met with 19...f5 with good compensation; in many lines, the resource ♕b4-a5 is important, for instance: 20.♗f1 (with the idea 21.♕d2) 20...♕a5 21.♗e3 (after *21.♕e3 ♖b4*, the white bishop on a7 is in big trouble) 21...f4 22.gxf4 exf4 23.♗d2 ♕d8 with dangerous activity for the pawn.

However, the computer first forces black to commit to a queen move with 19.a3!, after which black's position is difficult. After 19...♕b3, it's now good to play 20.♗xa7 (much better than *20.♕d1? ♕xd1+ 21.♖xd1 b5 22.♗xa7 b4 23.axb4 ♖xb4 24.♗e3 f5* with good compensation), getting a healthy extra pawn (20...b6 is not now a threat due to the simple 21.♕c2, while 20...f5 can be met with 21.♕d1 and a clear advantage or, even better, 21.♗f1 with the threat 22.♕d1). However, 19...♕a5 is even worse for black due to 20.♗f1! with a very strong threat 21.♕e1 ♖4c7 22.♖a1!! and 23.b4, with no good defense in sight.

After Tal's reply **19...f5!**, the hall buzzed like a beehive.

20.exf5 ♗xf5 21.♖a1 ♘f4!?

Editor's note: 21...♘f6 is objectively stronger, but with the subsequent 22.g4 ♗d7 23.a3 ♕a5 (after *23...♕b3*, the queen has no good squares and poses no threat) 24.♕d2 (intending ♗g2-f1), white thwarts his opponent's activity and remains slightly better because of his queenside space advantage.

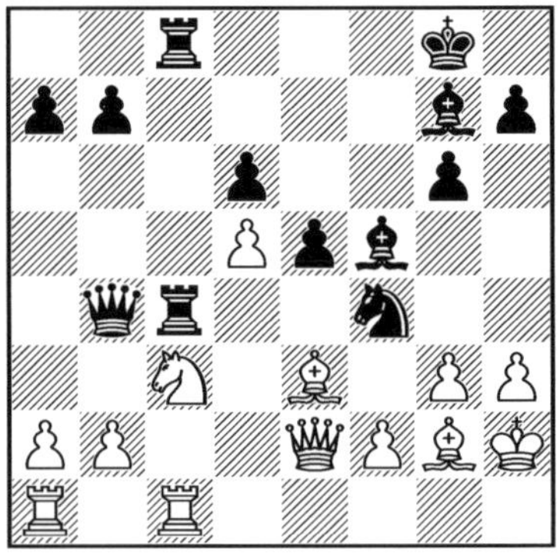

Applause filled the hall.

Botvinnik's second asked the arbiter to move the game to an isolated room.

Stahlberg was trying to quiet the public, while Golombek repeatedly pushed the button that lighted the electric sign "Quiet, please!"

Meanwhile, dramatic events unfolded on the board.

22.gxf4 exf4 23.♗d2

Editor's note: Black's idea was refuted with 23.a3! (but, of course, not *23.♗xa7? ♕a5*) 23...♕b3 *(23...♕a5 24.♗d2+−)* 24.♗xa7. Kasparov discovered that after the subsequent 24...♗e5 25.f3! b6 (up until this point it was Tal's analysis), white won with 26.a4!! with the ideas 27.a4-a5 and 27.♖a3 ♕b4 28.♘a2.

23...♕xb2

23...♗e5 was stronger, but Tal decided against it because of the line

24.f3 ♕xb2 25.♘d1! ♕d4 26.♖xc4 ♖xc4 27.♖c1 ♖xc1 28.♗xc1 ♕xd5 29.♗f1, thinking that the position was equal.

24.♖ab1 f3 25.♖xb2

Botvinnik decided to trade queens while being a piece up, but probably missed Tal's 26th move.

Grandmaster Salomon Flohr showed the following beautiful line several days later: 25.♗xf3! ♗xb1 26.♖xb1 ♕c2 27.♗e4!! ♖xe4

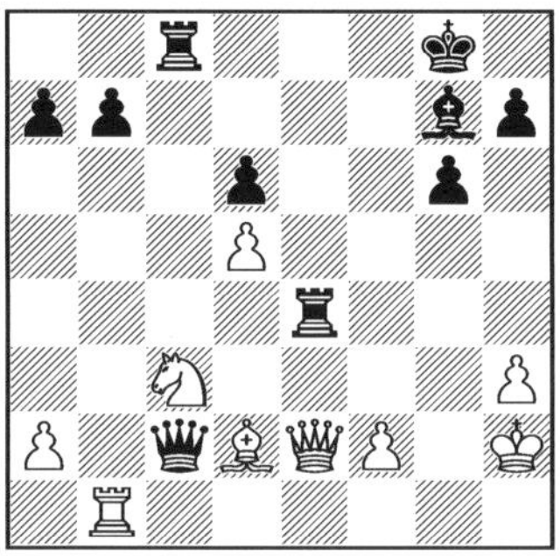

28.♘xe4!!

Now, after both 28...♕xb1 29.♘xd6 ♖f8 30.♕e6+ ♔h8 31.♘f7+ ♖xf7 32.♕xf7 ♕f5 33.♕xf5 gxf5 34.♔g3 ♗e5+ 35.♗f4 and 28...♗e5+ 29.♔g2 ♕xb1 30.♘xd6! ♗xd6 31.♕e6+ ♔g7 32.♕d7+!, white is better in the endgame.

25...fxe2 26.♖b3 ♖d4! 27.♗e1 ♗e5+ 28.♔g1

Here, Goldberg categorically demanded to move the game to another room.

The excitement in the hall had already subsided, so I thought that such a radical measure was not necessary. But the arbiter had already made a decision, and only demonstration boards remained on the stage.

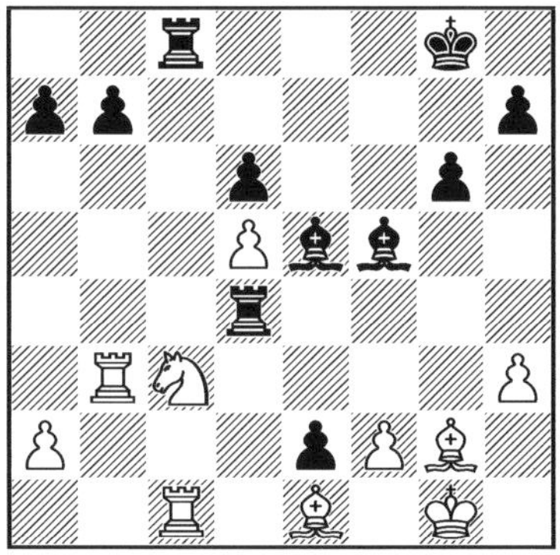

28...♗f4

Here, probably as a result of this sudden change of environment, Tal missed a pretty combination: 28...♖xc3! 29.♖bxc3 ♖d1 30.♖c4 ♗b2, and black wins. However, after this move, white still can't save the game.

29.♘xe2 ♖xc1 30.♘xd4 ♖xe1+ 31.♗f1 ♗e4

With active bishops and an extra pawn, **black won** easily.

This loss affected Botvinnik's play in the next game. The world champion made a mistake in a good position, and the score was 5-2.

Now, having a three-point lead, Tal should have played more quietly, giving Botvinnik the opportunity to sharpen the position himself. However, Tal rejected such considerations right from the outset.

In game 8, Botvinnik gained a substantial advantage, but again got into time trouble and couldn't find the right move.

No. 66
M. Botvinnik – M. Tal
1960, Moscow, World Championship Match, game 8

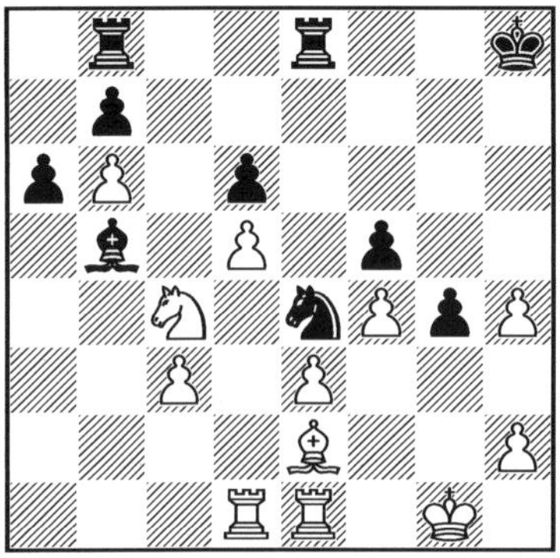

Botvinnik had three minutes left on his clock, while Tal had thirteen. White to move.

34.♖c1

A blunder. After 34.♖d4, white kept his advantage.

34...♖bc8?

That night, during our analysis, we saw that black could have won with 34...♖ec8. Tal had rejected it at the board out of general considerations – the rook could be useful to put pressure on the e-file.

Had Tal won, the score would have become 6-2, and the match would have been essentially over. This thought plagued us for the entire night. The well-known truth – a chess player should embrace his failures – wasn't much consolation in this case.

But let's come back to the game. Events unfolded quickly.

35.♘a5 ♗xe2 36.♖xe2 ♘xc3 37.♖xc3! ♖xc3 38.♘xb7

Here, Tal realized that the position had changed drastically, and I should say that he got confused. He automatically made a bad move, and suffered quickly from the consequences.

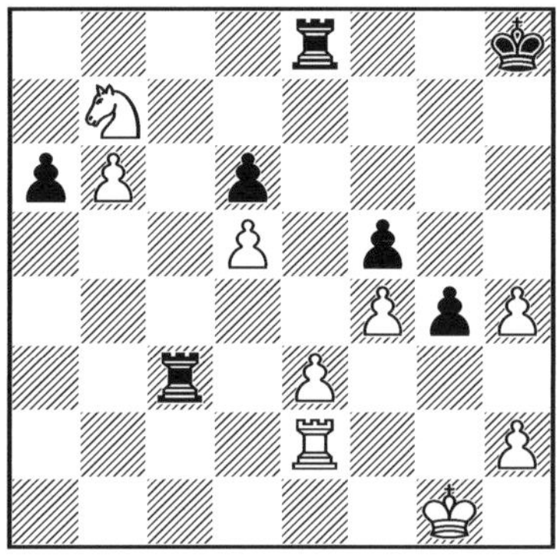

38...♖exe3

Black should have played 38...♖b8 39.♘xd6 ♖d3 40.♘xf5 ♖xd5 41.e4 ♖xf5 42.exf5 ♖xb6, and the game would have ended in a draw. (**Editor's note:** Actually, after the subsequent 43.♔f2 ♖b3 44.♖e3, black loses. But instead of 41...♖xf5, black had 41... ♖b5, after which it's white who has to scramble for a draw. So, instead of capturing on f5 on the previous move, white should play 40.♖c2!, and after 40...♖xb6 41.♘xf5 ♖xd5 42.♖c8+ ♔h7 43.♖c7+, the game ends in perpetual check.)

39.♖xe3 ♖xe3 40.♘xd6 ♖d3 41.♘f7+!

Botvinnik's sealed move. As soon as it was played on the board at the resumption, **black resigned**.

In game 9, Tal, after **1.e4 c6 2.d4 d5 3.♘c3 dxe4 4.♘xe4 ♗f5 5.♘g3 ♗g6 6.♘ge2 ♘f6 7.h4 h6 8.♘f4 ♗h7 9.♗c4 e6 10.0-0 ♗d6**, sacrificed a piece –

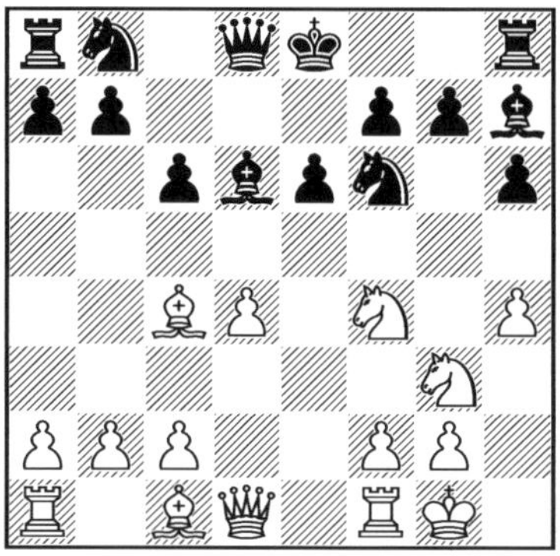

11.♘xe6!?

Tal's own opinion about this sacrifice is quite interesting.

"I can't agree with the numerous experts who criticized my opening choice, in particular, the knight sacrifice on e6. Tellingly, the majority of them don't think that the knight sacrifice was absolutely incorrect. Most commentators agree that this sacrifice creates major difficulties for black. Concerning the psychological side, I think that if a chess player is convinced that his move is correct, he should have no 'buts' and no excuses if he deviates from his initial plan. Before game 9, we did overestimate the knight sacrifice a bit, thinking that black had to go for a difficult defense after the correct continuation, which is not that easy to find. We made a psychological mistake there. The point is not that the player who has a two-point lead (after just one-third of the match played) shouldn't go for sharp lines. This is completely acceptable. Our mistake was underestimating Mikhail Botvinnik's phenomenal analytical power, thinking that he wouldn't expect the sacrifice. But the first moves after the sacrifice, and especially the fact that Botvinnik played rather rapidly, convinced me that my opponent had thoroughly analyzed the position that occurs after the sacrifice."

When, after **11...fxe6 12.♗xe6 ♕c7 13.♖e1 (Editor's note:** An important alternative is 13.♘h5!?, which occurred, for instance, in the game Tal – Vukic, Bugojno 1978) **13...♘bd7 14.♗g8+ ♔f8! 15.♗xh7 ♖xh7 16.♘f5**

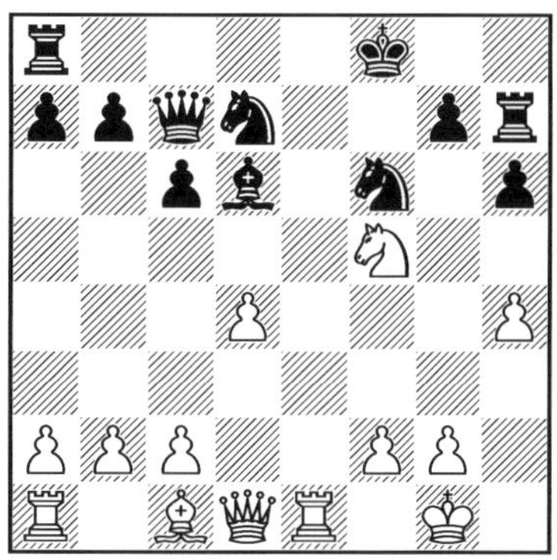

Botvinnik sacrificed a third pawn with **16...g6!**, it was clear to everyone that the world champion's defensive maneuver was prepared beforehand.

White had enough compensation for the piece, but the Riga player failed to convert his chances, and **Botvinnik won** his second game in a row with precise play.

Tal's mood after game 9 was aptly described by the man himself:

"Up until game 8, it was psychologically very hard to play: on the one hand, I had a subconscious feeling that the match was already almost over, but on the other hand, I realized that I still had a long and hard struggle ahead of me against such an unyielding player as Mikhail Botvinnik.

Now, after the match, I think that my losses in games 8 and 9 helped me to get out of that psychological dead end in the best possible way. After the score reached 5-4, the moment of weakness was overcome, and an equal struggle ensued; I believed in myself much more at the moment."

Indeed, Tal played more quietly and confidently in the tenth game, and Botvinnik barely managed to draw.

In game 11, Tal defeated his opponent with his own weapon: giving the world champion no counterchances, he executed an attack in good positional style.

This defeat meant much more for Botvinnik than the simple loss of a point. The world champion had to admit that his opponent was able to outplay him strategically as well!

No. 67, Grunfeld Defense
M. Tal – M. Botvinnik
1960, Moscow, World Championship Match, game 11

1.Nf3 Nf6 2.g3 g6 3.Bg2 Bg7 4.0-0 0-0 5.c4 c6 6.b3 Ne4 7.d4 d5 8.Bb2 Be6

8...a5 was stronger. (**Editor's note:** The strongest players of our time play 8...Bf5 most often.) After the game move, white gets a positional advantage.

9.Nbd2 Nxd2

Editor's note: Black could have gained more chances for counterplay with 9...f5!?, transposing into a line of the Dutch Defense. Another interesting move is 9...Qa5!?, which occurred in Sasikiran – Melkumyan, Bastia 2011.

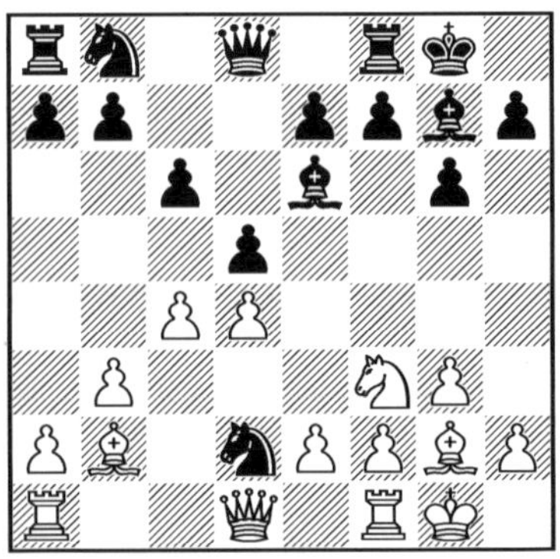

10.Qxd2!

After 10.Nxd2, black had a strong reply 10...c5! After the game move, it's not beneficial for black to win the pawn with 10...dxc4 due to 11.Ng5 cxb3 12.Nxe6 fxe6 13.axb3, and white has enough compensation for the pawn – pressure on both the queenside and the kingside. (**Editor's note:** In the elite grandmaster game Vachier-Lagrave – Aronian, Saint Louis 2014, white, instead of Koblenz's 13.axb3, played a novelty 13.♕e3!?, and after 13...bxa2 14.♕xe6+ ♔h8 15.♕xa2, his compensation was more than enough.)

10...♘a6 (**Editor's note:** According to the MegaDatabase, this move was played only once, in this game) **11.♖ac1 ♕d6 12.♘e5 ♖fd8 13.♖fd1 ♖ac8 14.♕a5**

The queen on this square constrains black's forces. He can't offer a queen trade with 14...♕b4 or 14...♕c7 due to 15.♘xc6!. (**Editor's note:** Actually, both these lines are OK for black: both after 14...♕b4 15.♘xc6 bxc6 16.♕xa6 dxc4 17.♗a3 ♕b6 18.♕xb6 axb6 19.bxc4 ♗xd4 20.♗xe7 ♖d7 and 14...♕c7 15.♘xc6 bxc6 16.♕xa6 dxc4 17.bxc4 c5 18.e3 cxd4 19.♗xd4 ♗xc4 20.♕a4 e5 21.♗f1 exd4 22.♖xc4 ♕b8 23.exd4 ♖xc4 24.♕xc4 ♕d6 25.d5 ♗f8 he has good drawing chances, despite being a pawn down.)

14...dxc4

Editor's note: The best move was probably 14...♗xe5!?, recommended by Tal and favored by the computer – black keeps his center stable, exchanges an important knight and intends to trade the queen as well. Kasparov came to the conclusion that after 15.dxe5 ♕b4 16.♗c3 (up to this point – analysis by Tal) 16...♕xa5 17.♗xa5 b6 18.cxd5 ♗xd5 19.♗h3 ♖a8 20.♗d2, white has only a marginal advantage. Also, in this line, black can play 15...♕c7!? (instead of 15...♕b4). After the game move, black is also only slightly worse, but it's harder to defend in a cramped position when there are still a lot of pieces on the board; in addition, white's pawn center now becomes more dynamic. We should also note that there are some improvements for both sides in the next few moves.

15.♘xc4 ♕c7

Botvinnik attempts to simplify the position with trades.

16.♕e1! ♕b8 17.e4 ♗xc4! 18.♖xc4 ♘c7 19.♗h3 e6 20.♗c1 ♕a8! (**Editor's note:** By defending the c6 pawn, black creates the threat 21...b5) **21.♗g5 ♖e8 22.♕d2 f5! 23.♗h6**

Editor's note: This bishop exchange is not good, because now black manages to successfully regroup his major pieces and equalize. Instead of Tal's move, the computer recommends the following plan: deprive black of the resource ♘b5 with 23.a4, then play ♖e1, put the bishops on f4 and g2 and go for d4-d5 or h2-h4-h5.

23...♗xh6 24.♕xh6 ♖e7 25.♖e1 ♖f8 26.♖c5 ♕d8 27.♖e5

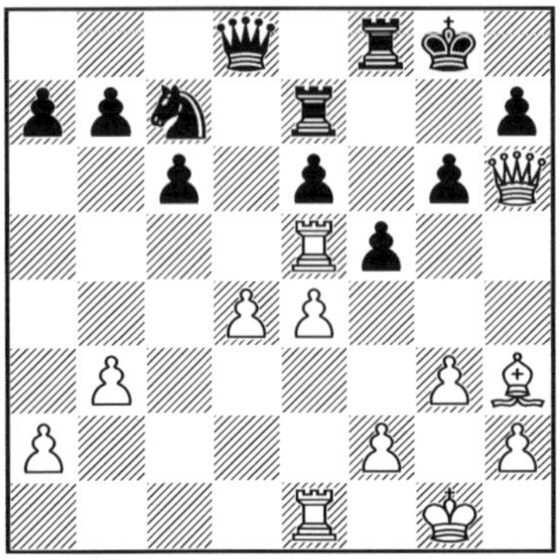

27...♖ef7!

Grabbing the pawn (27...♕xd4) was no good: after 28.exf5 gxf5 29.♗xf5, white retained a minimal advantage. (**Editor's note:** Kasparov showed that in Koblenz's line, black has no difficulties at all: 29...♖ef7 30.♖5e4 ♕f6 31.♕xf6 ♖xf6 32.♗xe6+ ♘xe6 33.♖xe6 ♖xf2 34.♖e7 – Tal erroneously thought that white was still slightly better here – 34...♖xa2 35.♖xb7 ♖d8, with an obvious draw. Also, Kasparov pointed out 30...♕c5!?, after which black is all right as well.) Now white has to think about defending the d4 pawn.

The world champion managed to coolly defend and parry all the threats; however, to fully equalize, he still needs to make some precise moves.

28.♕d2 ♕d6 29.♗f1! ♖d7 30.exf5 ♖xf5 31.♖5e4 ♖f6?

With 31...♖d5!, black could have forced a draw: 32.♗c4 ♖xd4 33.♖xd4 ♕xd4 34.♕xd4 ♖xd4 35.♗xe6+. In the ensuing time trouble, Botvinnik was noticeably nervous.

32.h4! ♔g7 33.h5 gxh5 34.♖h4 ♔g8 35.♗d3 ♖g7

Editor's note: After this move, black is in big trouble. One of the better continuations was 35...♔f8, getting the king to safety. If white plays 36.♖e5, like in the game, then, after 36...♖df7, he has nothing better than 37.♖e2, which, of course, doesn't sit well with his attacking plans.

36.♖e5! ♖ff7

Editor's note: And now, it's too late to double rooks: 36...♖gf7 37.♖exh5 ♖xf2 38.♕g5+ ♔f8 39.♖xh7+–.

37.♕h6

Editor's note: The queen will have to return after a couple of moves. The immediate 37.♖exh5 was stronger.

37...♕e7 38.♖exh5 ♘d5! 39.♕d2! ♘f6 40.♖h6 ♕d6 41.♖f4

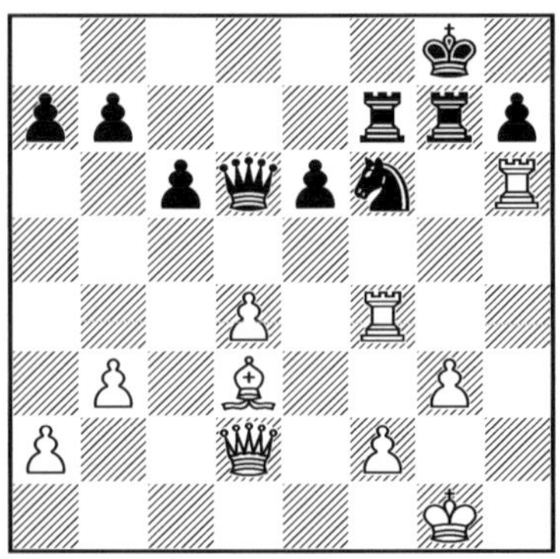

It was time to adjourn the game. After a 40-minute think, Botvinnik sealed the move **41...♕f8.**

Analysis showed that black's position was very difficult. The queen move was the least expected for us. The main continuations we analyzed were 41...♘g4, 41...e5, and 41...♘d7.

After 41...♘g4, there was a strong reply 42.♗xh7+ ♔f8 43.♖xf7+ ♖xf7 44.♖g6 ♖xf2 45.♖g8+ ♔f7 46.♕d3, and black loses one of his pieces.

After 41...e5, we first looked at 42.♖f5. However, we decided against it because of 42...♕xd4, threatening 43...♖xg3+. So we quickly agreed on 42.dxe5 ♕xe5 43.♖f5! ♕a1+ 44.♔g2, and white wins quickly. 41...♘d7 couldn't save black either due to 42.♖xf7 ♔xf7 43.♗xh7 c5 44.♕e2!, and white's attack is unstoppable.

42.♕e3 ♘d5 43.♖xf7 ♕xf7 44.♕e5!

With 44.♕xe6, white could win a pawn; however, after 44...♕xe6 45.♖xe6 ♖g4 46.♗c4 ♔f7, the position was easier for black to defend.

44...♘c7 45.♕c5! ♕f3

A small trade combination follows.

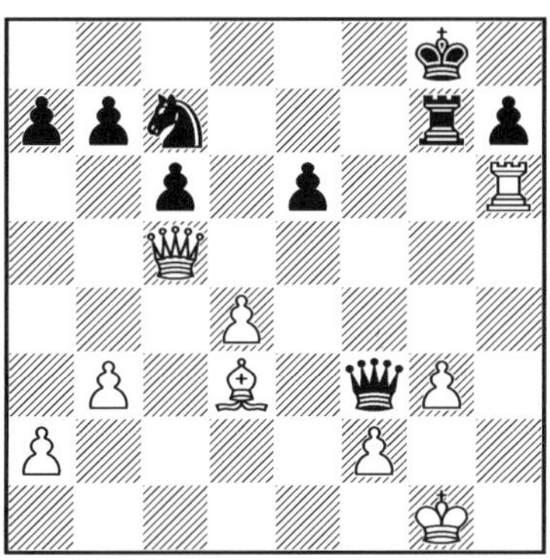

46.♗xh7+! ♖xh7 47.♕g5+ ♔h8 48.♕d8+ ♔g7 49.♖xh7+ ♔xh7 50.♕xc7+ ♔g6 51.♕xb7 ♕e4 52.♕a6!

White is two pawn ups, but to convert his advantage he needs considerable technique. For instance, if white takes the third pawn with 52.♕xa7, black gets a strong passed pawn in the center after 52...♕e1+ 53.♔g2 ♕e4+ 54.♔h2 ♕f3 55.d5. (**Editor's note:** Koblenz means that black will take on d5 with one of his pawns.)

52...♕e1+ 53.♔g2 ♕e4+ 54.♔f1 ♕b1+ 55.♔e2 ♕c2+ 56.♔f3 ♕f5+

If 56...♕c3+ or 56...♕d1+, then 57.♔g2, and white wins an important tempo.

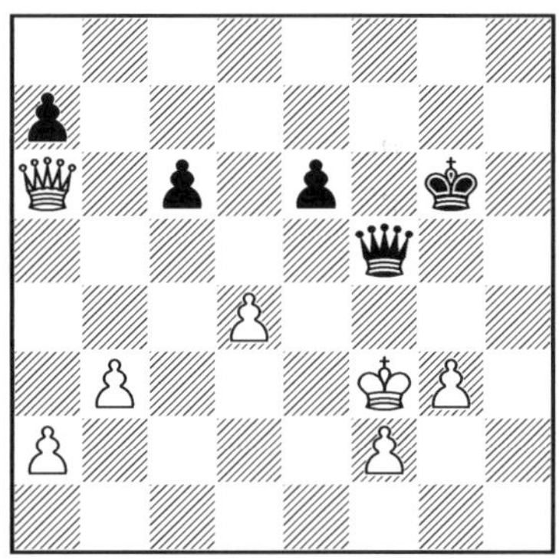

57.♔e3 ♕g5+ 58.♔e2 ♕h5+ 59.♔d2 ♔f6 60.♕xc6 ♕a5+ 61.♕c3 ♕xa2+ 62.♔e3 ♔f7 63.d5! exd5 64.♕c7+ ♔f6 65.♕c6+ ♔e7 66.♕xd5, and **black resigned** several moves later.

This tenacious battle lasted for seven and a half hours.

In game 12, Tal had the initiative as well. However, both players were quite tired and didn't play too precisely. The game ended in a draw on move 72.

Quick bloodless draws upset the spectators, who expect exciting fights in every game. You can understand the spectators, but you should understand the players as well – the match is exhausting and requires total concentration. That's why Tal wanted to make peace quickly in the thirteenth game, even though he played black. He needed to consolidate his success. In addition, the Riga grandmaster felt very tired.

After 50 minutes of play, Tal achieved a draw, but this game upset him a great deal.

Tellingly, Tal left the Pushkin Theater through the back entrance after the game – he didn't want to face the fans...

A month of tenacious struggle, endless analysis of adjourned games that often lasted the whole night – all that was exhausting for both players.

The knowledge that a legion of chess fans is watching the match helped to overcome tiredness. Letters from the whole country flowed in every day. The young grandmaster was greeted by people he knew and people he didn't, but everyone wished him victory. They gave advice, even offered their "proven" opening lines that "guaranteed" success.

"Keep going, Misha, we believe in you!" people of various ages and walks of life wrote.

Mikhail Fetisov, a Don Cossack, sent a touching, encouraging telegram:

"Mikhail, you will win, you have to win! The sons should be stronger than the fathers. If this wasn't so, the world wouldn't make progress!"

The next three games were also drawn, but those weren't "grandmaster draws". Peace was agreed only after all possibilities to fight for a win were exhausted.

Tal turned reserved and reticent. I realized that there was no sense in advising him to "play coolly" and "stabilize the position".

During lunch before game 17, we didn't say a word to each other.

"This time," I thought, "there would be no draw..."

At first, the game was peaceful, and it was hard to predict that it would end so dramatically. When the following position occurred on the board, I was in the press center.

No. 68
M. Tal – M. Botvinnik
1960, Moscow, World Championship Match, game 17

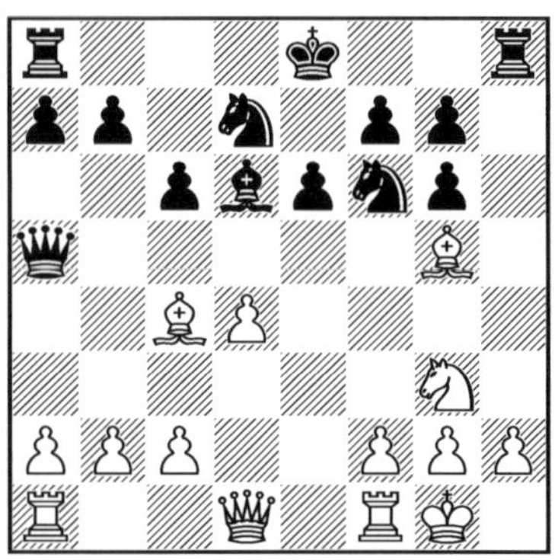

The grandmasters and masters, filling the room as usual, expected 12.♕d2 here and thought that the game would end in a quick draw.

But the clock was ticking, and Tal was still thinking. Finally, he played **12.f4.**

"This looks like suicide!" the oldest Soviet grandmaster, Grigory Levenfish, exclaimed.

"Now it's clear that Tal will lose this game," said someone at the other end of the room.

I quickly came on stage to evaluate the position independently of others' opinions.

If Tal loses, everything starts anew... Yes, white did seriously weaken the center with his last move. Nevertheless, Tal's plan was clear: avoid the queen trade at all costs and increase the pressure.

I often saw Tal go all-out and succeed, but in this game his position was growing increasingly worse. With simple, logical moves, the world champion was improving his position. And Tal tried to sharpen the game at any cost, regardless of material losses.

The battle reached its culmination. Both players were in time trouble. The first to lose his cool was... Botvinnik's second, Grigory Goldberg. He closed his pocket chess set, stood up quickly and left the stage. Sometimes imminent victory makes you even more anxious than impending defeat...

Of course, I was anxious too. Will Tal still keep his fighting spirit, I thought, if the score turns 9-8?

The fate of the game was decided literally in the last seconds. Botvinnik missed a tactical blow – a rook sacrifice. While spectators, seconds and arbiters considered whether the sacrifice was correct, time trouble ended. The match arbiter gave Botvinnik an envelope, so that the world champion would seal his move. But he never sealed a move. Ten minutes later, after Botvinnik convinced himself that his position was hopeless, he resigned. This game decided the fate of the whole match.

There were many discussions about Tal's "strange" twelfth move. In his book about the Botvinnik match, Tal shared his thoughts.

"The unfamiliar quiet match strategy turned out to be more difficult for me than I had imagined. And it suffered a total fiasco in game 17.

It's hard to make yourself play every game with the same desire to win, but it's even harder to move towards the goal with tiny steps. The goal of making seven draws in the remaining eight games seemed incredibly hard for me.

Before the game and during the opening, I was totally sure that I would follow the advice of my experienced coach, the advice that had helped me to keep the pleasant two-point gap. But at a certain time (I think this feeling is familiar to every chess player), I just couldn't help but do what was forbidden. Very, probably excessively risky play completely unexpectedly brought me an important point. I realized that the quiet, waiting strategy wouldn't work for me in the remaining games – I just couldn't keep my nerves in check. I made my moves automatically – sometimes good, sometimes not so good, but playing according to the match score just wasn't working... Such a foolish strategy almost led to a disaster in the next, 18th game. Only Botvinnik's uncertainty in time trouble prevented him from punishing me."

And now, let's look at Tal's concrete considerations for moving the f-pawn.

"Finally, my wandering gaze settled on the move 12.f4. At first, I felt somewhat uncomfortable, because the flaws of this move are quite obvious, but in such a position there are no moves without flaws. The merits of this move are less obvious, but they do exist, even if, if I may say, not strictly in the chess dimension. First of all, this move requires refutation, and this refutation involves a double-edged tactical battle, which, considering M. Botvinnik's playing style in this match, was not desirable for him. Secondly, the weakness of white's position could only be exposed with a break in the center, and after c6-c5 and e6-e5, the white bishops become significantly stronger. And, finally, black would be able to attack the kingside only after castling long, but this would allow white's queenside pawn mass to move forward too. Perhaps black just had to play 12...0-0, but this is not a refutation of 12.f4."

These explanations help to understand Tal's unique creative methods. Objectively, 12.f4 may be a bad move, but against that specific opponent in that specific situation, it provided real chances.

After game 19, where Tal scored his sixth win in a strictly positional style, the world champion's second said, "So, we'll meet in the return match."

To become world champion, Tal needed to score just one point in the last five games. Game 20 was drawn, and Botvinnik came to the 21st game without his customary bottle of vitamin drink – the fate of the match had been already decided. The world champion offered a draw himself on move 17.

The score turned 12.5-8.5. The match was over.

The very next day after winning the title, Tal came to realize that the burden of glory was indeed very heavy. His hotel room was literally "occupied" by his friends and journalists. Even the Riga newsreel film crew were there, with all their bulky equipment.

The closing ceremony and the crowning of the world champion took place on 10th May.

...Mikhail Tal, the Komsomol member and Riga City councilor, takes the stage. FIDE Vice-President Marcel Berman places a gold medal on his chest and crowns him with a laurel wreath.

"On behalf of the International Chess Federation," Marcel Berman says, "I declare Mikhail Tal the world chess champion."

The Soviet anthem plays triumphantly...

Gens Una Sumus

"We are one family". These words from the ancient language of Latin comprise the motto of the International Chess Federation. We're at the 14th Chess Olympiad in Leipzig. People are talking in different languages – German, Russian, English, French, Spanish, Mongolian, many others – but chess players need no translators: the universal language of chess can be understood by everyone.

At the reception organized by the East German government in honor of the chess players, Paul Keres spoke on behalf of the Olympians:

"Despite our opposing interests, there's cordial friendship at the tournament of nations. I think that many should learn how to maintain the spirit of international solidarity here!"

The last words are drowned in applause. The American chess players approach the Soviet team's table and raise their glasses in friendship – friendship between the chess players of all countries, friendship between all nations.

Bobby Fischer offers to tell Tal's future.

"OK. Tell me, Bobby, how will the return match against Botvinnik end?" Tal asks.

Fischer looks intently at the world champion's palm and says, "You don't like to lose!"

"Who does?"

The loud laughter stopped Fischer's palmistry session.

We made a lot of new friends in Leipzig. Chess people from many countries asked the Soviet players for advice, and shared their joys and sorrows with them.

We learned that free Cuba had revived the glorious chess traditions of Capablanca, that chess was becoming widely popular among the people.

"We are proud that our country gave chess to humanity," said the Indian journalist Chandragupta Agrawal in a short interview. "After winning independence, our team is taking part in the team world championship. We are obviously weaker than players from many other countries, but we'll do everything in our power to catch up."

Bombay student Manuel Aaron proved that these weren't empty words. In the match against the Netherlands, he defeated the ex-world champion Max Euwe, while in the Argentina match, he drew with grandmaster Miguel Najdorf.

The English and French chess players had a hard time believing that the Mongolian government had assigned a comfortable three-story building to a chess club.

Concurrently with the Olympiad, Leipzig organized an exhibition entitled "Chess Through the Ages".

It was quite a challenge to view all the exhibits sent by 150 museums and many private collectors from all over the world over such a short period of time.

The Soviet exhibition opened with a stand "Lenin and chess". In the section "Chess is the people's game", foreign chess players could find the answer as to why new chess talents keep coming up every year in the land of socialism. The showcase of Soviet chess literature stunned the foreigners with huge print numbers: 30,000, 50,000, 100,000 copies...

In the same showcase, I saw our *Sahs* magazine, both in Russian and Latvian, as well as books published by the Latvian State Publishing House.

Everyone marveled at the chess pieces made by Russian artisan Shushkanov and inspired by the story of Sadko. These fairytale pieces were earlier awarded a Great Gold medal at the Brussels World Fair. The Central Art Workers' House poster for the David Oistrakh versus Sergei Prokofiev chess match attracted much attention as well.

The average attendance of each round in Leipzig was around 5,000 – it's a record for chess competitions.

The last round couldn't change much in the tournament table. The Soviet team had already won, the US team had finished second, and Yugoslavia had taken third place.

We are accustomed to the success of the USSR national chess team, which always wins gold at the Olympiads. When the event is already won, the days of difficult battles get slowly forgotten. Those who follow the competition only in newspapers may think that the victory of our chess players, who are stronger on average than the foreign masters and grandmasters, was easy, almost a foregone conclusion. But those who witnessed the Olympiad in person know how difficult the decisive games truly were. The results were only settled literally in the last minutes...

The Soviet grandmasters were happy to write a new page in the history book of Soviet sports victories with their Leipzig win.

Mikhail Tal was, without a doubt, the most popular player at the Olympiad (world champions are always the center of attention). In the last round, Tal made sure that there was a sensation – he lost to the English player Johnathan Penrose.

"Now I have enough work for a year," Penrose said after the game with a smile. "I'll be going from town to town and showing my game against the world champion!"

Tal's game against the Hungarian grandmaster Laszlo Szabo was rather interesting.

Szabo, an aggressive, attacking player, got a position to his taste. It seemed that Tal wouldn't be able to withstand the onslaught of the black pieces. But in the close-quarter street fight, Tal suddenly launched a counter-attack and crushed black's position.

No. 69
M. Tal – L. Szabo
1960, Leipzig, 14th Olympiad Final, round 4

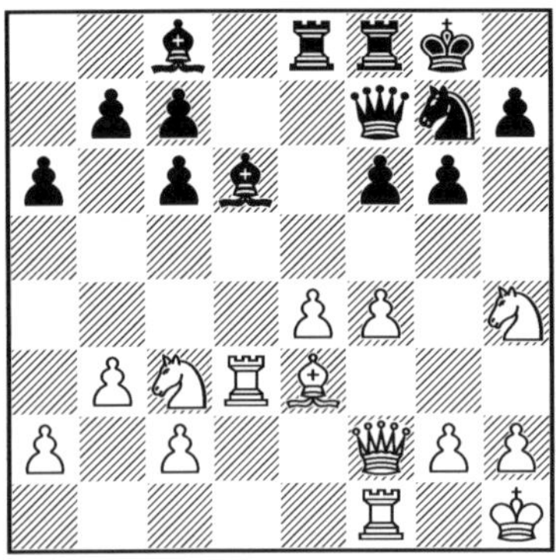

Szabo gets rid of his double pawns and seizes the initiative.

22...b5 23.♗c5 b4 24.♘a4 ♖xe4 25.♗xd6 cxd6 26.♖xd6 ♕e7 (planning to bolster the attack with a pawn sacrifice) **27.♖d2! ♘h5**

Editor's note: 27...♖e8 posed more problems for his opponent, activating the rook and retaining various options for the knight.

28.g3 ♗h3 29.♘g2 ♖e8 30.♘c5

Tal thought for long on each move, while Szabo played quickly and assuredly: he thought that black's attack would suggest itself. The next move was made by the Hungarian grandmaster without much thought either.

30...♖e2

A mistake. The correct move was 30...♗xg2+ 31.♔xg2 ♖e3, with an equal position.

Editor's note: Actually, after the game move the position is equal as well.

31.♖xe2 ♕xe2 32.♔g1 ♗xg2 (white threatened 33.♖e1) **33.♔xg2 ♕g4**

Editor's note: 33...♕b5! was a much stronger move (on this square, the queen protects both the a6 and c6 pawns and completely nullifies the idea ♕d4-c4+) 34.♕d4 ♘g7=.

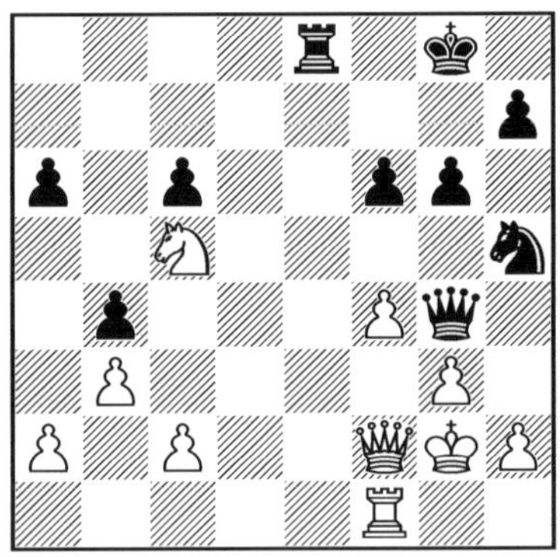

34.♕d4!

White goes on the counter-attack. Now it was Szabo's turn to think for a while.

Editor's note: 34.♕f3 was probably stronger – on the one hand, white is targeting c6, while on the other hand, he offers to transition to an endgame which will be better for him – black's a- and c-pawns are too weak.

34...a5 35.♖f2 ♔f7

Editor's note: This move is a mistake, and black's position is now very hard.

He should have preferred 35...♕f5, improving the queen's position.

36.♘e4 ♔g7

Editor's note: 36...♖e7 still gave black some chances to save the game.

37.♕a7+ ♔g8 38.♘d6 ♖f8 39.♕xa5 ♕e6 40.♕xb4 ♕d5+ (a "death-bed" check!) **41.♔g1**

Szabo sealed his 41st move, but then resigned without resuming the game.

We were sitting in the Astoria hotel restaurant, eating our lunch. Several hours remained until the USSR – Argentina match. Suddenly, the opposing team's leader, Miguel Najdorf, appeared before our table, holding a napkin.

"I'll accept all your sacrifices," he jokingly assured Tal. "You see, I've successfully competed with world champions Capablanca and Alekhine!"

"I'll make a sacrifice for sure. I hope you'll keep your promise," the world champion answered.

In the following game, you shall see if they kept their promises.

No. 70, Sicilian Defense
M. Tal – M. Najdorf
1960, Leipzig, 14th Olympiad Final, round 4

1.e4 c5 2.♘f3 d6 3.d4 cxd4 4.♘xd4 ♘f6 5.♘c3 e6 6.♗e3 a6 7.f4

Editor's note: This move is not popular in modern times. The main line is 7.f3, protecting the e4 pawn and intending ♕d2 and g2-g4.

7....b5 8.♕f3 ♗b7 9.♗d3 ♘bd7 10.0-0

Editor's note: 10.g4 is usually played in this position.

10...♗e7 11.a3 0-0

Black has a somewhat cramped but solid position in this line. It's not easy for white to overcome his defenses.

Editor's note: As a rule, modern strong grandmasters don't castle in this position, instead playing 11...♘c5 (putting pressure on the e4 pawn) or 11...♖c8 (activating the rook, with a positional exchange sacrifice on c3 possible in many lines).

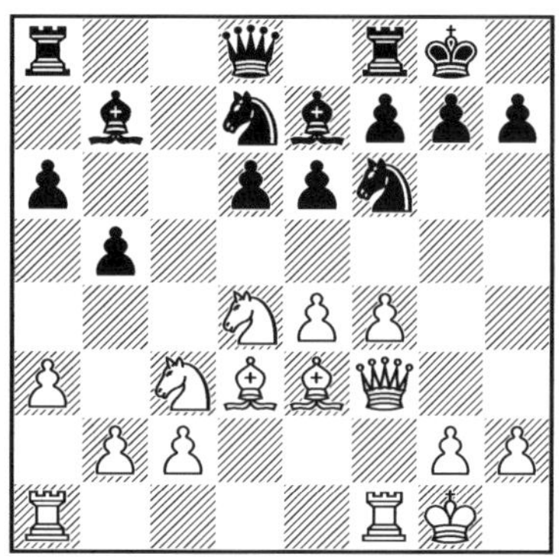

12.♕h3 ♕c7 13.♖ae1 ♘c5 14.♗f2 d5

If black manages to play d6-d5 in the Sicilian, it usually means that all opening difficulties are over. So, after making his 14th move, Najdorf went for a walk around the hall, smiling contentedly.

Editor's note: In this position, 14...d5 is a mistake. One of the possible alternatives is the prophylactic 14...g6, as played in a number of subsequent games.

15.exd5 ♘xd3 16.cxd3 ♗xd5

16...♘xd5 is bad due to 17.♘xe6!

17.♘xd5 exd5 18.♘f5 ♗c5 19.d4 ♗a7 20.♗h4 ♘e4

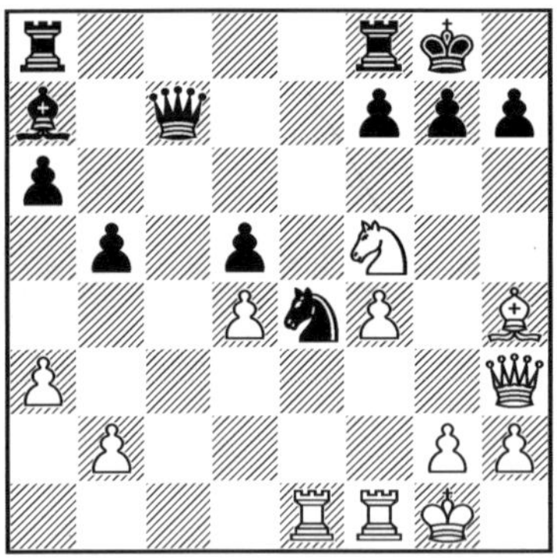

21.♖xe4! dxe4 22.♗f6!

White's attack is now unstoppable. After **22...♕b6** (22...gxf6 23.♕g4+) **23.♗xg7 ♖fe8 24.♗e5 ♕g6 25.♘h6+ ♔f8 26.f5**, **the Argentinian grandmaster resigned**. After 26...♕g5 there's 27.♘xf7! winning, while after 26...♕c6 white plays 27.♕h5 ♖e7 28.♕g5. (**Editor's note:** In the last line, 28.♕g5 doesn't work because of black's reply 28...♖xe5–+. White should play 28.f6 instead, winning immediately.)

Mikhail Botvinnik's play left a very good impression. He didn't suffer from time trouble that had plagued him so much in the match. He managed to achieve that by quick opening play. It seemed like the ex-world champion had set some kind of schedule for spending time. Botvinnik again showed his superior endgame technique and great opening erudition. It was clear that he hadn't lost confidence after his defeat in the match.

Botvinnik's Revenge

And again, like just a year ago, we're in Moscow, in the National Hotel. It's almost ten o'clock. The draw for the return match starts in a few minutes.

Two weeks ago, the medical commission determined that the world champion's health wouldn't allow him to start the match as scheduled, on 15th March. The Council of the USSR Sports Society and Organization Union granted the request of the Latvian Chess Federation to start the match in mid-April.

But something unexpected happened. The world champion said that doctors weren't prophets, and that they couldn't predict how he would feel in a few weeks!

After that, I became completely convinced that Tal totally lacked any self-preservation instinct, and this could eventually lead to serious consequences.

I still tried to convince him to listen to the doctors; however, unlike Tal the world championship challenger, Tal the world champion didn't listen to me. He wouldn't budge.

"You should understand," he assured me, "I've been so anxiously waiting for the chance to play Botvinnik again..."

The draw was held in old style: Stahlberg held a white and a black pawn in his closed fists. The world champion got black.

When grandmaster David Bronstein was asked who would win the return match, he replied, "The one who wins the first game."

And so, on 15th March 1961, Botvinnik and Tal sat at the chess board again. This time, the games were held in the Variety Theater.

Of course, the result of just one game is not important in a marathon competition, but a win in the first round is encouraging, it makes you believe in yourself more.

The opponents make their first moves quickly. The game transposes from a Nimzo-Indian Defense into a line of the Ragozin System.

Botvinnik chooses a rather passive continuation, and Tal seems to be seizing the initiative.

The ex-world champion Max Euwe, who sat beside me, was perplexed. Where is Botvinnik's renowned opening erudition? How did he manage to get a worse position with white?

The Tal fans are obvious to spot in the hall: they are beaming.

"So, it begins. Misha will show him!"

But Misha doesn't "show him". After some poor maneuvering, he gets a worse endgame.

No. 71
M. Botvinnik – M. Tal
1961, Moscow, World Championship Match, game 1

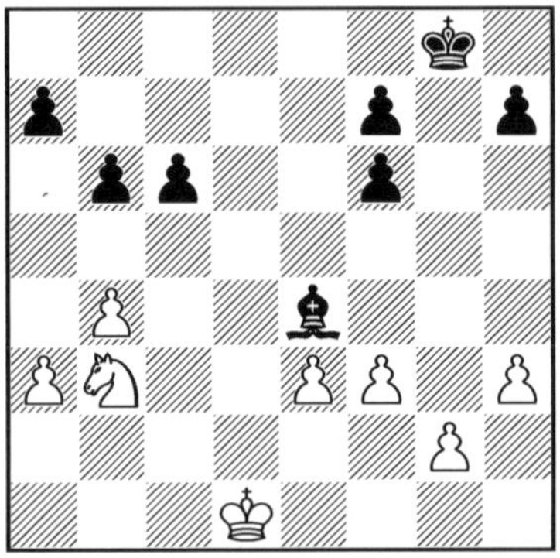

Here, black could still save the game with 30...♗f5! For instance, 31.♘d4 ♗d7, then the black king heads to the center, and white can't convert his small advantage. However, **Tal played 30...♗d5 and quickly lost.**

Editor's note: After Botvinnik's **31.♘d4**, Tal, to prevent the threat 32.e4, was forced to play **31...c5**, and after **32.bxc5 bxc5 33.♘b5**, the white knight's activity, coupled with black's compromised pawn structure, became the decisive factor.

In his career up until then, he was capable of holding even tougher endgames, so this loss was an alarming symptom.

The second game. Botvinnik plays the Caro-Kann.

Before the start of the match, Tal half-joked that if Botvinnik "dared" to play the Caro-Kann, he'd develop his pieces according to the setup that he'd used successfully the previous year (♗c4 and ♘e2) and "checkmate him quickly". However, Botvinnik stopped white's attack with his 9th move and equalized. Still, he made several mistakes in time trouble, and the game was adjourned in a position that looked won for Tal.

The next day, the newspapers reported: "When the game resumed, Botvinnik resigned after a few moves."

So laconic! But Tal had to spend so much energy and work so hard to analyze this won ending! The analysis took almost all night and the morning of the next day. Here's what Mikhail Tal tells us about this analysis.

No. 72
M. Tal – M. Botvinnik
1961, Moscow, World Championship Match, game 2

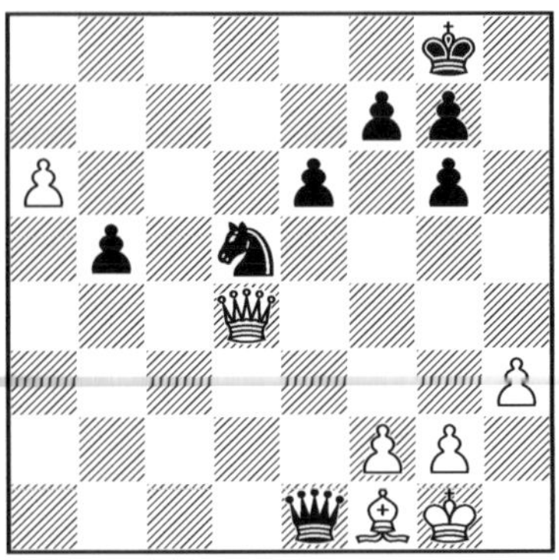

"There was no doubt that black would seal the move **41...♕a5**, because all other moves lost immediately. For instance, 41...♘c3 42.♕d8+ ♔h7 43.♕h4+ ♔g8 44.a7.

After 41...♕a5, white had an important choice. It's easy to see that after 42.♕a7 b4 43.♕b8+ ♔h7 44.a7 ♘c7 white wins a piece, but black's passed pawn was a great hurdle for converting the material advantage. There could follow 45.♕xc7 ♕xc7 46.a8=♕ b3 47.♕a3 ♕c2 48.♕a4 ♕c3 49.♕h4+ ♔g8 50.♕d8+ ♔h7 51.♕d3 ♕b4, and white's win is quite problematic.

Editor's note: The move 48...♕d1 (instead of Tal's 48...♕c3) removes all doubts, for instance, 49.g3 e5 50.♕b5 *(50.♔g2 ♕d5+ 51.♔h2 b2 52.♕c2 ♕d4 53.♗d3 b1=♕ 54.♕xb1 ♕xf2+ 55.♔h1 ♕xg3=)* 50...♕b1 51.♕d3 ♕c2 52.♔g2 e4, and white can't improve his position.

In our search for ways to win, we analyzed the natural move 42.a7 the most. (Interestingly, Botvinnik mostly focused on lines after 42.♕a7.) And so, **42.a7 b4** (the only move that repels the threat 43.♗xb5).

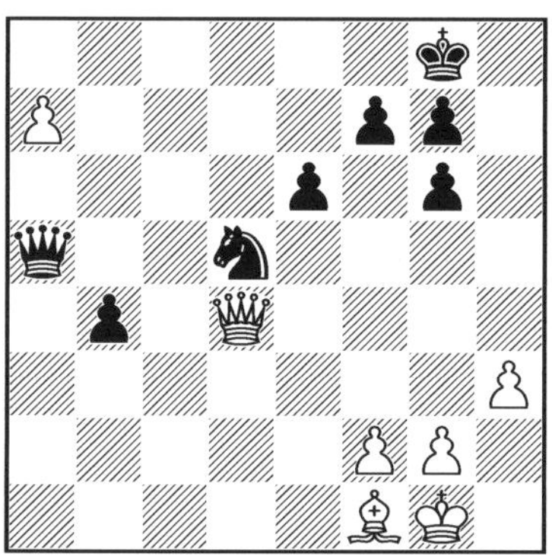

Here's the initial position where white had to search for the winning move. It turns out that it's hard for white to activate his queen. 43.♗b5 attracted our attention: 43...b3 doesn't work due to 44.♕a4. But then it turned out that after 43.♗b5, black had 43...♘c7, and if 44.♗c6, then 44...b3 and it's a draw, as white can't win with 45.♕d8+ ♔h7 46.a8=♕ due to 46...♕e1+.

Alternatively, if instead of 44.♗c6, white plays 44.♕d8+ ♔h7 45.a8=♕, winning a piece, then 45... ♕xa8, and the black pawn can move again.

And so, if white wins a piece while the black pawn hasn't moved beyond b4, then white should win without much technical difficulty.

Editor's note: Tal's last assertion looks questionable and is not confirmed by computer analysis. In a similar vein, below Tal gives the line (after the game move 43.♗c4**)** 43...g5 44.g3 g6 45.♔h2 ♔h7 46.♔g2 ♔g8 47.♗b5 and writes that 47...♘b6 is bad, "because white wins a piece in the most beneficial situation" – without a doubt, he means 48.♕xb6 ♕xb6 49.a8=♕+ here. But, despite several hours of analysis, the computer fails to show a way to win for white after the subsequent 49...♔g7 or 49...♔h7 – and if such positions are indeed impossible to win, then the adjourned position is drawn too!

Coming to this conclusion, we started to analyze the position after the quiet **43.♗c4**, which was the move I played. The moves 43...♔h7 or 43...♔f8 lead to the same position. (**Editor's note:** He means that after 43...♔h7 44.♗xd5 exd5 45.♕h4+ or 43...♔f8 44.♗xd5 exd5 45.♕h4 black is forced to continue 45...♔g8 (in the first case it's the only legal move, while in the second it's the only one that continues resistance), as a result of which both lines lead to the same position analyzed in the next sentence.) After 43...♔h7 44.♗xd5 exd5 45.♕h4, black has only one move – 45...♔g8.

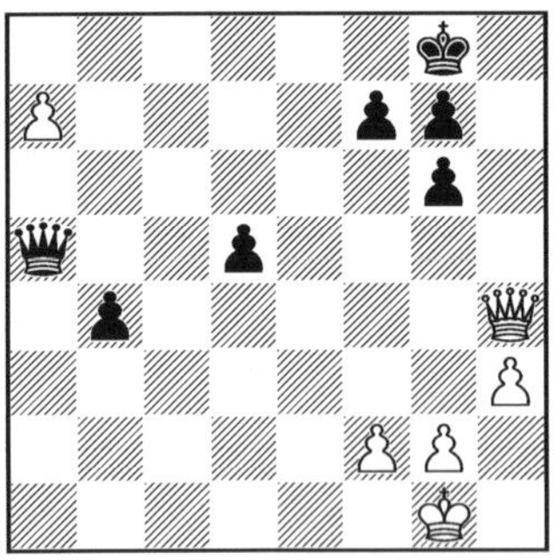

Now, by playing 46.♕e7 ♔h7 47.♕b7 ♕a1+ 48.♔h2 ♕e5+ 49.g3 ♕e2 50.♕xf7 ♕a6 (if 50...♕a2, then 51.h4 b3 52.h5 b2 53.♕xg6+ ♔h8 54.♕e8+ ♔h7 55.a8=♕ ♕xa8 56.♕xa8 b1=♕ 57.♕xd5 with a won endgame for white) 51.♕e7 g5 (white threatened 52.♕h4+ and 53.♕d8+) 52.♕f7!, white wins.

And so, we found a way to exploit the weakening of black's kingside, who now has no remedy against ♕h5+ and ♕e8+, or ♕f8. In the case of 52...♔h6, 53.g4 is winning.

It's clear that king moves won't help black, so now we can analyze the other lines after 43.♗c4.

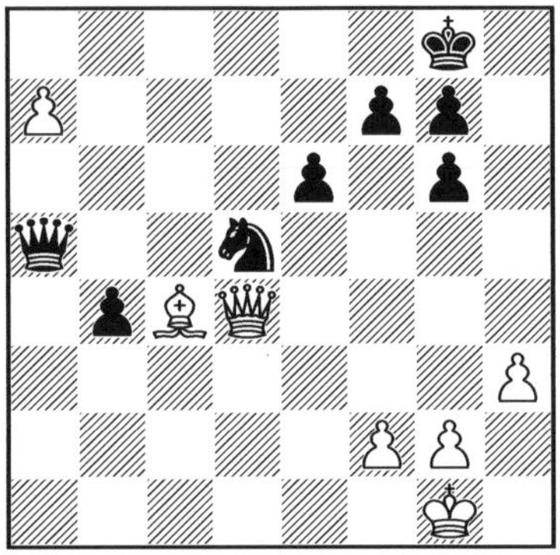

The queen's best position is on a5, so we ignored moves such as 43...♕a3: white wins easily with 44.♗xd5 exd5 45.♕b6 ♔h7 46.♕b8. Therefore, black can only make moves with his knight or pawns.

I. 43...g5. This move takes away the important h4 square from the queen; however, it also weakens the kingside.

Editor's note: Unfortunately, Tal's subsequent analysis contains a number of inaccuracies that lead to erroneous evaluations. It would be impractical to point out all such moments – this would make the text, already heavily saturated with lines, even harder to read. So, we'll show just two critical points:

A) As the reader shall see, Tal gives the line 44.g3 ♔h7 45.h4 gxh4 etc. in his subsequent notes, coming to the conclusion that white should win. But instead of 45... gxh4 (which is a mistake), black saves the game with the study-like 45...g6!! (planning 46...♘b6; the immediate *45...♘b6?* is bad due to *46.hxg5 ♕xa7 47.♕h4+ ♔h8 48.g6! ♕a1+ 49.♔g2 ♕f6 50.♕h7+ ♔f8 51.♗b5!*)

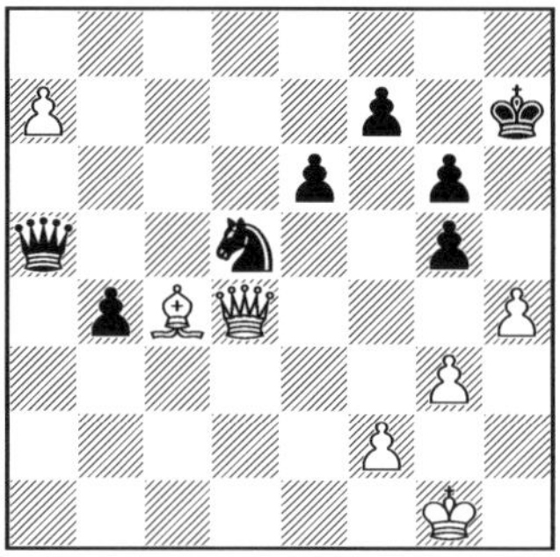

46.hxg5 b3!! (luring the bishop onto a bad square) 47.♗xb3 ♘b6 48.♗xe6 (*48.♕xb6 ♕xb6 49.a8=♕ ♕xb3* – this line shows the point of black's move 46...b3) 48...♕e1+ 49.♔g2 ♕xe6 50.♕xb6 ♕xb6 51.a8=♕ ♕d4, and black holds easily, despite white's extra pawn. The computer's first line 46.♗b3 (instead of 46.hxg5) doesn't win either – after the subsequent 46... ♘b6 47.♕xb6 ♕xb6 48.a8=♕ gxh4 49.gxh4 (or *49.♕h1 ♕d4 50.♕xh4+ ♕xh4 51.gxh4 g5 52.hxg5 ♔g6=*) 49...♕d4, white cannot convert his material advantage.

B) After 44.g3 g6 45.♔h2 ♔h7 46.♔g2

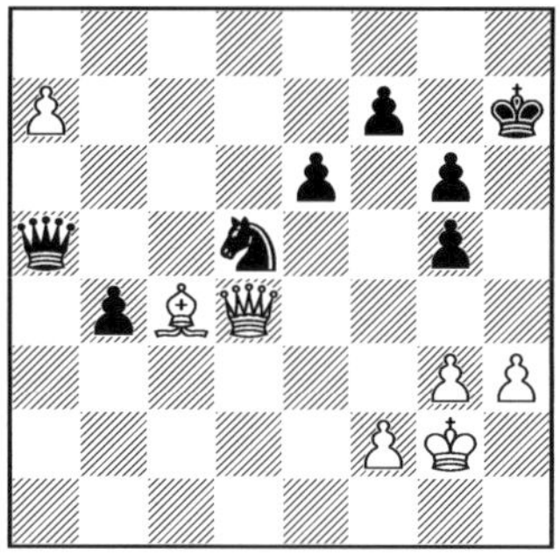

black also immediately achieves a draw with 46...b3!! (instead of 46...♔g8) 47.♗xb3 ♘b6 48.♗xe6 (after *48.♕xb6 ♕xb6*, the bishop is hanging) 48...fxe6 49.♕xb6 ♕xb6 50.a8=♕ ♔g7. So, instead of 45.♔h2, white has a much stronger move 45.♗b5, getting, after 45... ♘b6 46.♕xb6 ♕xb6 47.a8=♕+, an endgame with a piece for two pawns and the black pawn still on b4, which white wanted from the outset. That said, as we pointed out earlier, this endgame might be unwinnable after all!

Now back to Tal:

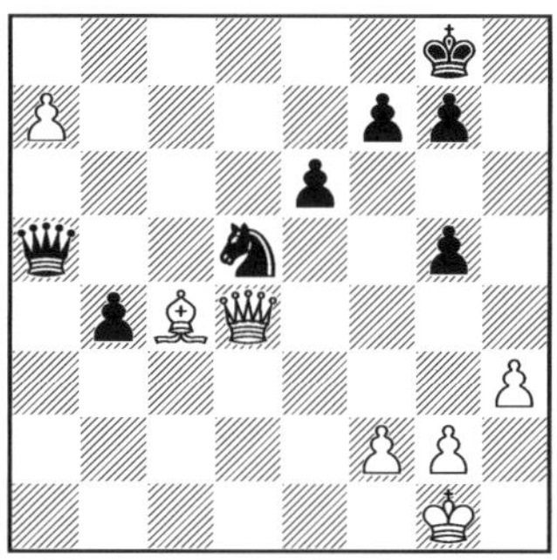

White can just play 44.g3, and black has nothing better than 44... g6 (after 44....♔h7, there's 45.h4

gxh4 46.♕xh4+ ♔g8 47.♗xd5 exd5) 45.♔h2! The idea of this move will soon become clear.

Black should play 45...♔h7 and meet 46.♔g2 with 46...♔g8, after which 47.♗b5! wins.

For instance, 47...b3 48.♕a4; or 47...♘c7 48.♗c6 ♔h7 49.♕f6! (49.♕d7 is weaker because of 49... ♔g7). If now 49...♕xa7, then 50.♕xf7+ with the subsequent ♗e4, and white's attack is unstoppable. 49...♕f5 can't save black either after 50.♕e7.

There's a question why white had to make two king moves. If the black king is on h7, white's plan doesn't work, because after 43...g5 44.g3 g6 45.♔h2 ♔h7 46.♗b5

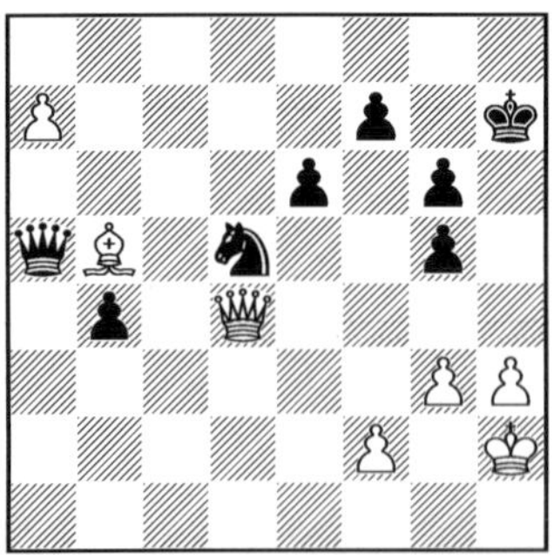

black has the reply 46...b3, and the endgame after 47.♕a4 ♕xa4 48.♗xa4 b2 49.♗c2 ♘c7 is not completely clear (**Editor's note:** Analysis shows that this position is drawn). So, the black king should be on the eighth rank.

And what's the difference between the white king's position on h2 or g2?

Let's return to 43...g5 44.g3 g6 45.♔h2 ♔h7 46.♔g2 ♔g8 47.♗b5 ♔h7 (47...♘b6 is bad because white wins a piece in the most beneficial situation [in the line 48.♕xb6 ♕xb6 49.a8=♕+ see the editor's note three pages earlier]) 48.♗c6 ♘b6. If the white king were instead on h2 now:

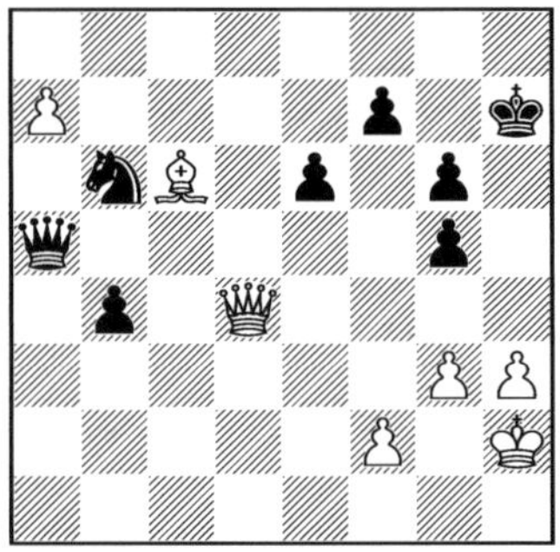

the position would be drawn because of 49.♕xb6 ♕xb6, threatening f2.

If the king is on g2, however:

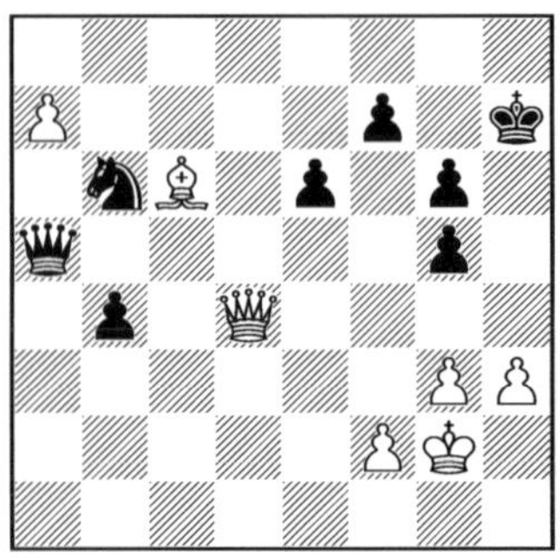

white wins with 49.♕xb6 ♕xb6 50.a8=♕, because black has no time to play 50...b3 due to 51.♕b7. After 51...♕xb7 52.♗xb7 f5 53.♗a6 white's victory is assured.

That's the way to win in the line 43...g5.

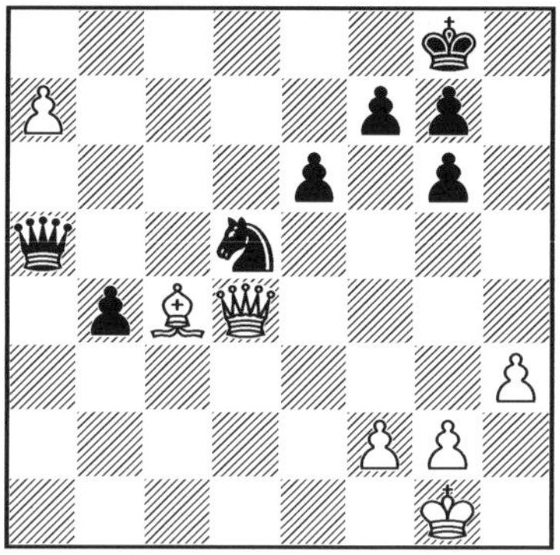

II. **43...f6.**

Botvinnik chose this move. Black wants to bring his king closer to the passed pawn, but he weakens his kingside. White, without wasting time on prophylactic moves, immediately played **44.♗b5.** After **44...b3 45.♕a4 Botvinnik resigned**.

The key idea of the move 44.♗b5 is clearly shown in the main line – 44...♘c7 45.♗d3! f5 (if 45...♔h7, then 46.♕h4+ ♔g8 47.♗xg6) 46.♗c4. Now the white queen controls all the dark squares, and so black's position is hopeless.

Can we say then that the adjourned position couldn't have been saved anyway? It's hard to answer this question. After 43...♘c7 44.♕d8+ ♔h7 45.a8=♕ ♕xa8 46.♕xc7 ♕a1+ 47.♔h2 ♕c1!, black got good counterplay. 47...♕c3 is worse due to 48.♕f4 b3 49.♕h4+ ♔g8 50.♕d8+ ♔h7 51.♕d3.

Had Botvinnik played 43...♘c7, white would have needed to prepare to win the piece with 44.g3 and ♔g2, but black's kingside wouldn't have been compromised. To be honest, we couldn't find a forced win in the last line, but after losing a piece, it would be hard for black to avoid defeat."

Despite this important win, Tal's mood didn't improve. At that time, we received an additional opening card index from Riga, covering more than 5,000 games. Looking through it, we found the game Uusi – Makogonov from the Soviet team championship, where black successfully tried the defense 9...♘d5 (precisely the move Botvinnik played in the second game).

Tal never said a word, but I felt that he was upset. Playing in the Stockholm tournament and a simultaneous display with Czechoslovakian youngsters several months before the return match was of course useful for training, but it couldn't replace deep theoretical preparation.

In the third game, Tal got a good position, but missed his opponent's unexpected move, and Botvinnik gained a substantial positional advantage. The world champion defended valiantly, but he couldn't save the game. That was an impressive Botvinnik victory in a logical, positional style.

In the fourth game, Tal gave his opponent complete freedom in the center and launched a quick pawn onslaught on the queenside.

Grandmaster Boris Spassky said in the press center, "Misha should be punished for such anti-positional play."

International master Lev Aronin disagreed: "Tal is bold, and I like his original plan!"

This was the first game of the return match where Tal got a position to his taste. But this time, Botvinnik played very precisely. With a subtle, deeply considered exchange sacrifice, he repelled the attack and went on the offensive himself. Tal's position noticeably worsened.

In general, Botvinnik didn't suffer from time trouble in the return match, but in this game he did lack time to think and failed to find the strongest move. As a result, Tal managed to salvage the game.

After game 4, Tal thought that Botvinnik's strategic weapon, like in the previous match, wouldn't play a decisive role. However, the very next game showed that these hopes were unfounded. The ex-world champion again imposed a quiet, maneuvering struggle on Tal. The position was approximately equal, but Tal played without inspiration, got into time trouble (he had four minutes left for 16 moves) and ultimately lost a pawn. Still, he managed to avoid defeat in the resumption.

In the sixth game, the young world champion gained a promising position. Then his opponent equalized. In a position where neither player was able to upset the balance without dire consequences for themselves, the grandmasters agreed to a draw.

In the seventh game, Tal deployed the Nimzo-Indian Defense as black. We anticipated that Botvinnik would play the Samisch Attack and prepared a rare line. After nine moves, a well-known theoretical position occurred.

No. 73
M. Botvinnik – M. Tal
1961, Moscow, World Championship Match, game 7

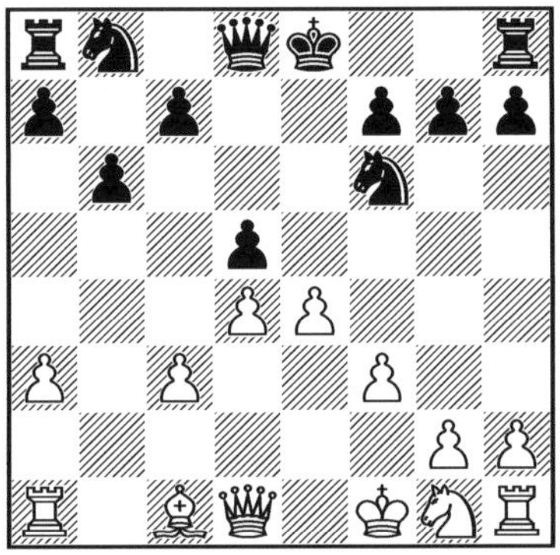

Here, white usually played 10.e5, and after 10...♘g8, continued 11.♘e2 ♕d7 12.♔f2 ♘c6 with the subsequent 0-0-0. Chances are roughly equal in this case. But Botvinnik, after a short think, played **10.♗g5!** After **10...h6**, there followed the stunning **11.♕a4+!**, and **Tal couldn't equalize. He resigned** on move 33.

Late that night, when we analyzed the game, Tal was wondering, "Did Botvinnik anticipate that I'd play this half-forgotten line? It's the first opening 'knockout' in my life!"

Of course, it was unpleasant to see that the line we had specifically prepared for the return match hit us back like a boomerang.

"I saw the true Tal's play again," the ex-world champion Max Euwe wrote to me from Amsterdam after game 8.

No. 74, Caro-Kann Defense
M. Tal – M. Botvinnik
1961, Moscow, World Championship Match, game 8

1.e4 c6 2.d4 d5 3.e5 c5

3...Bf5 is considered the strongest move, but Botvinnik avoids this exhaustively-studied continuation, preferring to interpret the position in the spirit of the French Defense. When he finally risked playing 3...Bf5 in game 10, Tal caught him by surprise with his ultra-original move 4.h4!?

4.dxc5 e6 5.Qg4

Editor's note: In modern practice, white usually plays 5.Be3, 5.a3, or 5.Nf3.

5...Nc6

Editor's note: 5...h5 is good here, for instance, 6.Qg3 h4 7.Qg4 Nh6 8.Bxh6 Rxh6 with unclear play.

6.Nf3 Qc7 7.Bb5 Bd7 8.Bxc6 Qxc6 9.Be3 Nh6

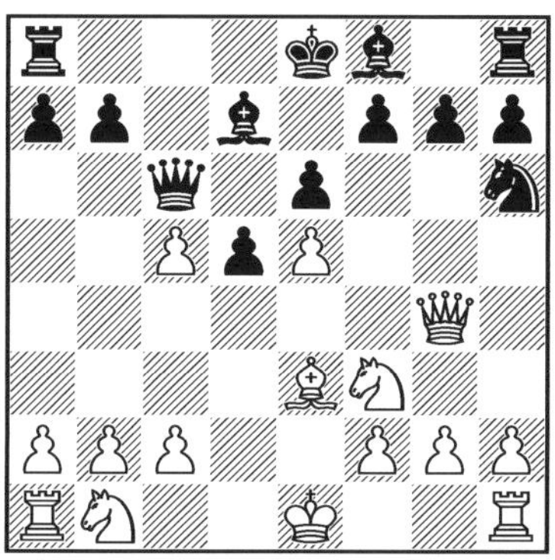

10.Bxh6

Tal went for this trade without hesitation, giving his opponent the "proud" bishop pair. The two bishops usually yield a certain positional advantage. By playing 10.Bxh6, Tal committed to a concrete strategic plan where the white knights play a major role.

10...gxh6 11.Nbd2 Qxc5 12.c4!

It's dangerous to take on c4, because the white knight might get to e4, targeting d6 and f6. White also puts the c-file to good use.

12...0-0-0

Editor's note: 12...dxc4 13.0-0 Bc6 (or in a different order – *12...Bc6 13.0-0 dxc4*) was much more solid, for instance, 14.Ne4 Bxe4 15.Qxe4 Rc8 16.Qxb7 Bg7 17.Rfc1 0-0 18.Qe4 Qd5, with a roughly equal position.

13.0-0 Kb8 14.Rfd1 Qb6

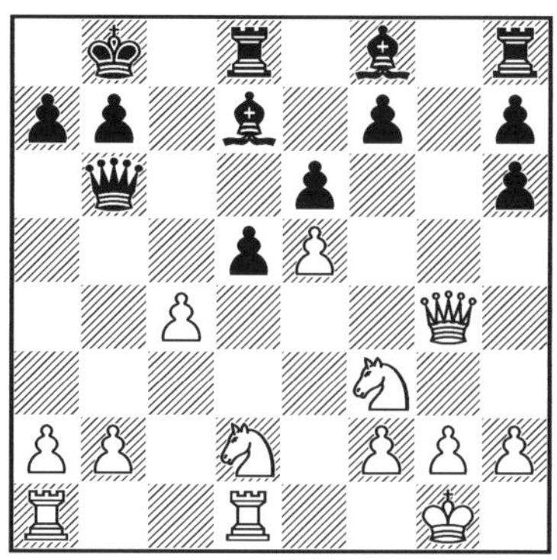

15.Qh4

Controlling the dark squares and attacking the h6 pawn.

15...a5

Black prevents b2-b4, but seriously weakens his queenside. 15...♖g8 or 15...♖c8 were worth considering.

16.♖ac1 ♖g8 17.♘b3! a4

Here, black could have also put up more resistance with 17...♖c8. After the game move, white's attack develops very quickly.

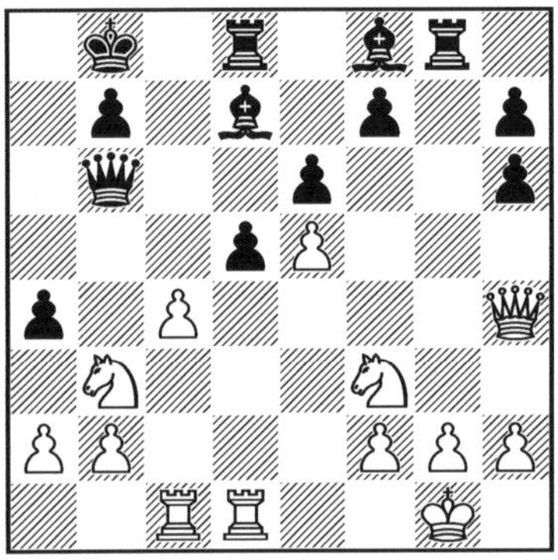

18.c5! ♕c7 19.♘bd4 ♖c8

19...♗xc5 was dangerous due to 20.b4 axb3 21.♘xb3 b6 22.a4!

20.b4 axb3 21.axb3 ♕d8

Even the queen trade doesn't save black from a deadly attack.

22.♕xd8 ♖xd8 23.b4 ♖g4 24.b5 ♖c8 25.c6! ♗e8 26.♖c2 ♗g7 27.♖a1 ♗xe5 28.♘xe5 ♖xd4 29.♘d7+! Black resigned.

After 29...♔c7, there's 30.b6+ ♔d8 31.cxb7, while after 29...♗xd7, white plays 30.cxd7 ♖d8 31.♖c8+! ♖xc8 32.♖a8+.

Botvinnik was still in the lead, but it looked like Tal was slowly recovering his form.

Suddenly, the world champion had to deal with another dangerous opponent – flu. The ninth game didn't take place on schedule – it was only played a week later.

After Botvinnik's first move 1.c4, Tal decided to use a system recommended by Paul Keres, with an aggressive early queen lunge.

Before the match, we decided to avoid excessively sharp lines with black, but this time the world champion wanted to turn things around. Such a strategy wasn't entirely safe, but, on the other hand, it did bring Tal his greatest successes.

Events unfolded in a very unpleasant way for the Riga player. Botvinnik's seventh move showed that even in this rare line he had prepared a novelty. Tal fell victim to a theoretical surprise again!

Leaving the kingside pieces undeveloped, Tal launched a risky queenside attack. The ex-world champion easily repelled it and already had a won position by move 16.

After play resumed, Tal tried to create some complications, but nothing came of that: the score turned 5.5-3.5.

Tal's opening play in the tenth game was quite esoteric. He made his first seven moves with pawns! "Tal probably forgot that he could move pieces in chess as well," grandmaster Tolush joked.

Indeed, Tal's position looked quite strange. "Reckless", "Bad theoretical preparation", I heard from every direction. Only Bronstein said with a smile, "Original idea!"

Tal's strategic plan wasn't as flawed as many commentators thought. This is evidenced, among other things, by the fact that Botvinnik didn't risk repeating the opening in games 14 and 16. Although the strategic plan wasn't erroneous, Tal's two "experimental" moves, ninth and tenth, were. They ruined everything. Those were perhaps Tal's weakest opening moves in the whole match. Botvinnik exploited his opponent's mistakes in quite an instructive way and added another important point to his score.

I must admit that I was surprised when Tal, after a short think, suddenly chose the Slav Defense in game 11. Botvinnik could have gone for the exchange variation that led to a symmetrical position.

It was clear that Tal needed some rest, and he wanted to take a small break. But purposefully playing for a draw is a special skill. Tal lacks that skill, and I hope that the chess world will forgive this flaw of his.

Tal got a difficult position out of the opening and lost again. After the game, Botvinnik told us that he'd analyzed this line 17 years earlier...

By now, Botvinnik had increased his lead to four points. The gap was already big, but Tal still had some hopes – there were 13 games left to play!

In game 12, Botvinnik played the French Defense for the first time in the match. Tal attacked energetically, and his win was quite convincing.

What conclusion could we reach after the first half of the match? How to explain Tal's collapses?

With a deeply thought-out strategy, Botvinnik managed to avoid positions that were rich in mutual tactical opportunities, those positions where Tal's combinational talent could fully manifest itself. Tellingly, in many games, Tal got into adverse strategic situations while still in the opening.

Game 13 was a shining example of Botvinnik's strategic mastery. He didn't allow his opponent to fan the flames of complications.

No. 75, King's Indian Defense
M. Botvinnik – M. Tal
1961, Moscow, World Championship Match, game 13

After **1.d4 ♘f6 2.c4 g6 3.♘c3 ♗g7 4.e4 d6 5.f3 0-0 6.♗e3 e5**, the following position occurred.

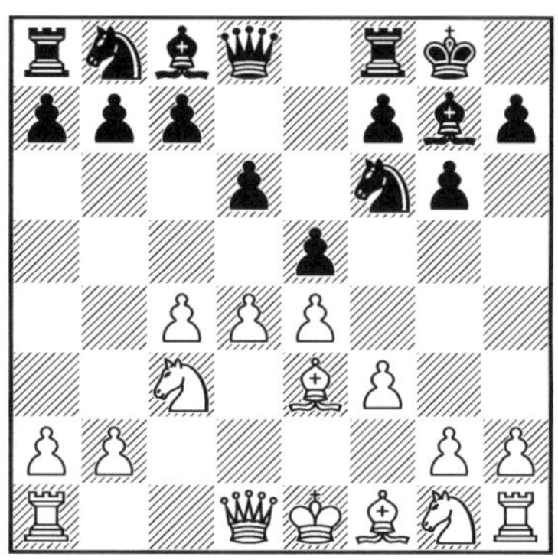

Botvinnik played **7.dxe5**

The queen trade doesn't promise white much, but it's psychologically sound: it's hard for black to organize counterplay. In other circumstances, the capture on e5 would mean a refusal to play for an advantage in the opening, an intention to play for a draw. But each draw got Botvinnik closer to his aim!

7...dxe5 8.♕xd8 ♖xd8 9.♘d5 ♘xd5 10.cxd5

This position had occurred in the game Boleslavsky – Najdorf (Candidates Tournament 1953).

10...c6 11.♗c4 b5

In the aforementioned game, Najdorf played 11...cxd5 12.♗xd5 ♘c6 and achieved a draw relatively easily. But Tal can't be satisfied with such a result, so he tries to complicate the game.

12.♗b3 ♗b7 13.0-0-0 c5

The struggle becomes more complicated, but white now has a strong passed pawn in the center.

Editor's note: In subsequent games, black usually played 13...cxd5, and then, after 14.♗xd5 ♗xd5 15.♖xd5 ♖xd5 16.exd5 ♘d7, black is all right.

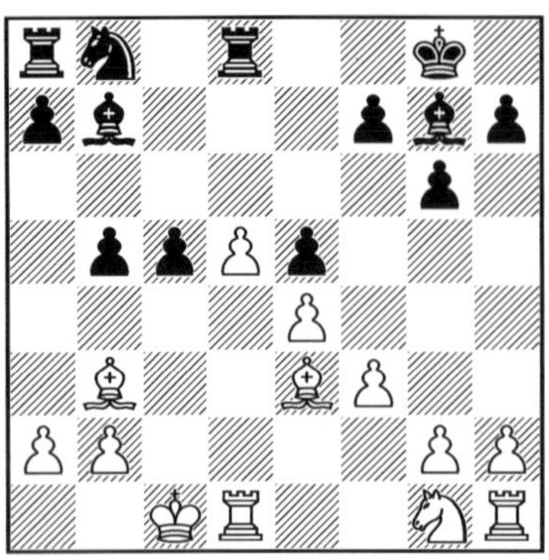

14.♗c2! ♘d7 15.♘e2 ♗f8 16.♘c3 a6

This seemingly logical move almost turns out to be the decisive mistake. It was better to play 16...b4 and then ♘b6.

Editor's note: If white meets 16...b4 with 17.♘a4, then, of course, not 17...♘b6 (this would lose the c5 pawn), but, for instance, 17...c4 with a roughly equal position. After 17.♘b5, black should avoid 17...♘b6 as well (white has an unpleasant reply 18.d6) and play 17...a5 instead, with the idea of a5-a4 and ♖a5.

17.b3! ♖ac8 18.♗d3! ♘b6 19.♗e2! ♖d6

The rook is a bad blockading piece, but the b6 knight needed some protection.

20.♔b2! f5

Black is trying to activate his rook, but he weakens the e5 pawn.

21.♖c1 ♖f6

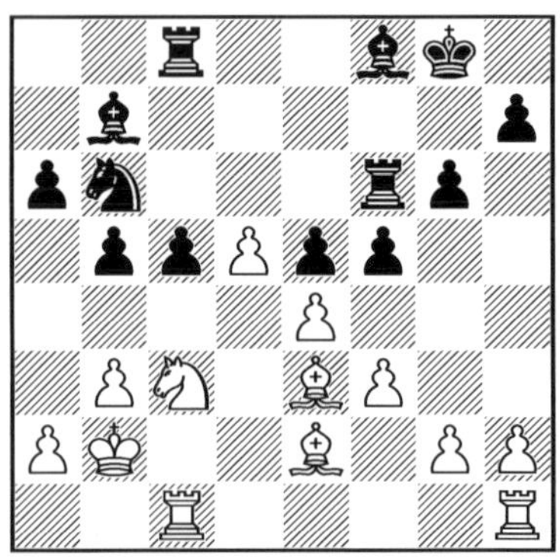

22.a4! bxa4 23.bxa4 a5 24.♔c2 c4 25.♖b1 ♗b4 26.♘a2! ♗c5

27.♗xc5 ♖xc5 28.♘c3 ♗c8 29.♖b2

Editor's note: 29.f4! is much stronger – after the subsequent 29...♘d7 30.fxe5 ♘xe5 31.♖b5 ♖xb5 32.axb5, it's very hard for black to defend.

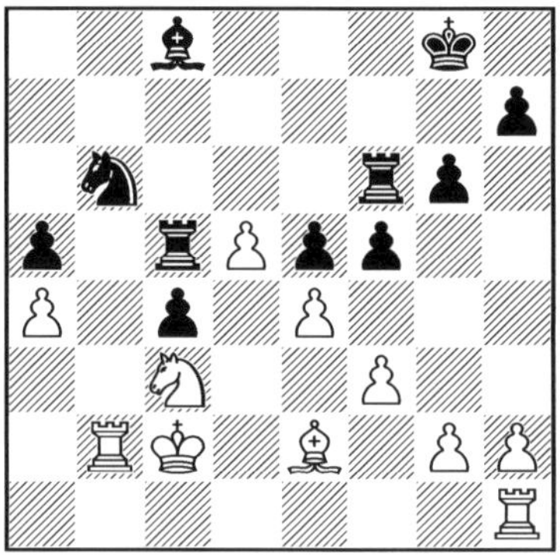

29...♗d7?

After 29...fxe4 30.fxe4!, white would still have needed some effort to win the game. Now, black just falls apart.

30.♖hb1 ♗xa4+ 31.♘xa4 ♘xa4 32.♖b8+ ♔g7 33.♖1b7+ ♖f7 34.d6 ♖xb7 35.♖xb7+ ♔f6 36.♖xh7 ♖c8 37.d7 ♖d8 38.♗xc4 ♘c5 39.♖f7+ ♔g5 40.♗b5 fxe4 41.fxe4 Black resigned.

In game 14, Tal got a dangerous initiative, but Botvinnik managed to hold. The game was drawn.

An unfortunate mistake cost Tal a full point in game 15.

No. 76
M. Botvinnik – M. Tal
1961, Moscow, World Championship Match, game 15

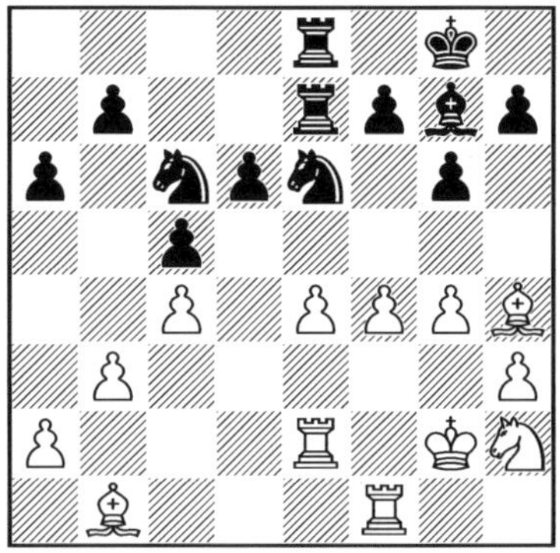

Tal, who had black, played **28...♖d7?**

"I wrote down 28...♖c7 on the score sheet, but mistakenly put the rook on d7," he explained after the game. "When my opponent played 29.g5!, I played 29...h6 automatically, because I was totally sure that my rook was on c7."

There followed **29.g5! h6? 30.gxh6 ♗xh6 31.♘g4**

It turns out that due to the threat ♘f6, black has to part with his bishop: **31...♗g7 32.♘f6+ ♗xf6 33.♗xf6. Botvinnik won on move 63**.

Botvinnik misplayed the opening in game 16, and Tal got good attacking chances.

"It will end in ten moves," the spectators decided.

But Tal played with hesitation, and Botvinnik, who sacrificed a pawn, managed to organize some counterplay. In a complicated major-piece endgame, Botvinnik played very precisely and drew the game on the 90th move, after an eleven-hour battle.

Each draw got Botvinnik closer to the goal, so Tal had to go for complications at any cost. Game 17 is an example of such an all-in approach. Tal turned a completely equal position into a lost one. However, Botvinnik's time trouble helped Misha: the challenger made several mistakes, and Tal managed to win in the resumption.

Tal was always eager to try some unbeaten paths, but now he decided to improvise. In game 18, the world champion made moves that no grandmaster could understand. Even Tal himself couldn't explain them in the post-game analysis. To cap it off, the Riga player also blundered a pawn. The next day, he resigned without resuming the game.

This was Tal's worst game in both matches against Botvinnik.

It seemed incredible that, after such painful defeats, Tal still had the strength to continue the match. After a ten-hour battle, Botvinnik lost the nineteenth game.

In game 20, Tal slowly outplayed his opponent.

No. 77
M. Tal – M. Botvinnik
1961, Moscow, World Championship Match, game 20

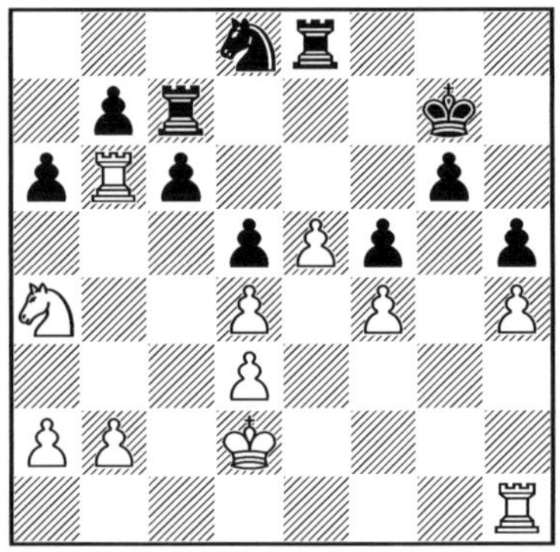

After the game resumed, there followed:

42...♘e6 43.♔e3 ♖d7! 44.b4 ♔f7 45.♘c5?

The waiting move 45.♖c1! would have won the game. If 45...♔e7, then 46.♘c5! ♘xc5 47.bxc5 ♖a8 48.♖g1! ♔f7 49.e6+!, or after 45...♖a8 there was 46.♘c5 ♘xc5 47.♖xc5 with the subsequent 48.a4 and b4-b5.

45...♘xc5 46.bxc5 ♖a8!

We missed this move in our analysis.

Later, Botvinnik made a mistake, and the game was adjourned for a second time.

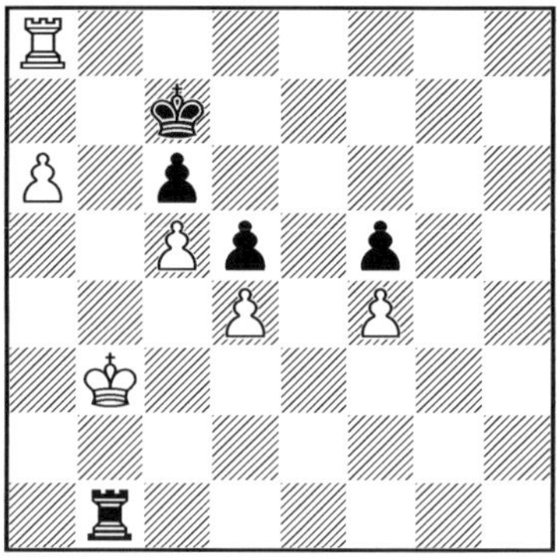

Tal sealed the move **89.♔a2.**

Our plan seemed to lead to a win: 89...♖b5 90.a7 ♖a5+ 91.♔b3 ♔b7 92.♖f8. Here, we automatically continued 92...♖xa7 93.♖f7+ ♔b8 94.♖xf5, and after 94...♖a1, there's 95.♔b4 ♖d1 96.♔a5 and ♔b6, winning. A more complicated, but still won endgame arose after 92...♔xa7.

Editor's note: In the line 92...♖xa7 93.♖f7+, instead of the erroneous 93...♔b8, the correct continuation is 93...♔a6 94.♖xf5 ♔b5, getting enough counterplay, for instance: 95.♖f8 ♖a8 (black can also put the rook on e7, g7, h7 or a1, activating it) 96.♖f7 (capturing on a8 is stalemate) 96...♖a7 97.♖f6 ♖a4 with a draw.

The first moves were made quickly: **89.♔a2 ♖b5 90.a7**

Editor's note: 90.♖f8 won, for instance: 90...♖a5+ 91.♔b3 ♖xa6 92.♖xf5 ♔d7 93.♖f6 ♖a1 94.f5 ♖d1 95.♔c3 ♖c1+ 96.♔d2 ♖f1 97.♖f7+ ♔d8 98.♔c3 ♖b1 99.f6 ♖f1 100.♔b4 ♔e8 101.♖h7 ♖xf6 102.♔a5 ♖f4 103.♔b6 ♖xd4 104.♔xc6 ♖g4 105.♖d7 d4 106.♔c7+−

90...♖a5+ 91.♔b3 ♔b7 92.♖f8 ♖b5+!

The first unexpected move. Tal quickly played **93.♔a4**, not noticing that after **93...♔xa7 94.♖xf5 ♖b1** [which was played] 95.♖f7+ ♔a6! 96.♖c7 ♖b4+! 97.♔xb4, the black king is stalemated.

A draw was now unavoidable. [The game ended in a **draw** after 121 moves.]

Meanwhile, 93.♔c3 still gave white some practical winning chances.

The last ray of hope was extinguished. The score was 12-8. There was no doubt that Botvinnik would score the necessary half-point in one of the next four games.

In game 21, Tal tried to complicate play for one last time, but Botvinnik launched an attack himself and won.

Winning the return match 13-8, Mikhail Botvinnik regained the title of the world's strongest chess player. With his convincing win, he wrote a new, brilliant page in the book of the history of world championships. Regaining the title was a triumph of the will, the result of a well considered training system, deep psychological approach, incredible strategic mastery and precise technique.

Afterword

With his brilliant victories in difficult tournaments, Mikhail Tal proved that he was one of the strongest chess players of our time. He successfully progressed through the numerous qualification stages, overtaking famous grandmasters, and earned the right to face the world champion. He won the ensuing battle convincingly.

Yet just a year passed, and Tal suffered an equally crushing defeat from the seemingly vanquished opponent.

Discussing the reasons for Tal's loss, V. Vasilyev wrote in the *Yunost* magazine:

"As sad as it sounds, Mikhail Tal, who always stood out as a pointedly humble man, who was always reverent towards his grandmaster colleagues, lost his ability to soberly, critically evaluate himself, his own strength and his opponents' strength after winning the world champion's title. Tal's friends worriedly and then anxiously saw that he stopped listening to advice, even if it was given by renowned people of the chess world. The constant victories dulled his sense of danger."

These harsh words correctly describe the reason for the catastrophe that the young world champion suffered in the return match.

Indeed, Tal lost his sense of danger – but wasn't it facilitated by the atmosphere of adoration created around the young world champion, the excessive praise thrown around by his overexcited fans?

"Genius", "crazy boldness", "the ability to play without regard for the logic of the position" – that's only a small part of the things said about Tal!

Didn't all those admiring songs of praise contribute to Tal's feeling of complacency and recklessness?

Losing the return match was a timely, severe life lesson for Tal.

When Tal returned to the hotel after game 21, he sat wearily in a chair. He had a lot to think about, many things became much clearer. The thought that he had deeply disappointed everyone whose care and support he felt at every step weighed heavily on his mind.

The first person who tried to help Tal with friendly advice and restore his self-belief was... Botvinnik! After the last game ended, Botvinnik invited his opponent to dinner. Raising his glass, he said, "Yuri Gagarin flew into space after long, intense training. If Mikhail Tal follows Gagarin's example in this regard, I'm sure he'll reach cosmic heights!"

Several days later, at the closing ceremony, Botvinnik continued his thoughts: "If Tal manages to 'program' himself and prepare for tournaments more carefully, he'll probably be unstoppable."

Many didn't pay much heed to these words. Everyone knew that Botvinnik would remain a tough opponent. Would Tal be able to regain his self-belief and reach the right conclusions from his loss?

Tal put in only a modest performance in the European team championship, sharing third-fourth place, but at the big international tournament in Bled he again shone with brilliant play. The strongest grandmasters of the world took part: Petrosian, Keres, Fischer – the most likely world championship candidates. Tal won the tournament.

This was a brilliant victory made possible by colossal will-power. Most importantly, he overcame himself.

In Bled, Tal displayed the diversity of his talent. He crushed Fridrik Olafsson, Bruno Parma and Ludek Pachman in a sharp attacking style, and made Miguel Najdorf, Borislav Ivkov and Arthur Bisguier resign after a subtle positional, maneuvering struggle.

The victory in Bled showed again that Mikhail Tal, a true chess artist, remains one of the world's strongest grandmasters.

I remember the words of one English journalist who said after Botvinnik's world championship win in 1948: "We respect the new world champion deeply, but we aren't sure that Botvinnik would have become such a brilliant chess player if he lived in another country."

These words are fully applicable to the 1960 world champion as well. No other country provides such a wide array of opportunities for the comprehensive development of human skills and flourishing of great talent as the country that builds communism.

And Mikhail Tal's creative path is a shining example of that.

Riga, 1961

Printed in Great Britain
by Amazon

78596322R00099